NIETZSCHE'S JUSTICE

McGill-Queen's Studies in the History of Ideas
Series Editor: Philip J. Cercone

1 Problems of Cartesianism
Edited by Thomas M. Lennon, John M. Nicholas, and John W. Davis

2 The Development of the Idea of History in Antiquity
Gerald A. Press

3 Claude Buffier and Thomas Reid: Two Common-Sense Philosophers
Louise Marcil-Lacoste

4 Schiller, Hegel, and Marx: State, Society, and the Aesthetic Ideal of Ancient Greece
Philip J. Kain

5 John Case and Aristotelianism in Renaissance England
Charles B. Schmitt

6 Beyond Liberty and Property: The Process of Self-Recognition in Eighteenth-Century Political Thought
J.A.W. Gunn

7 John Toland: His Methods, Manners, and Mind
Stephen H. Daniel

8 Coleridge and the Inspired Word
Anthony John Harding

9 The Jena System, 1804–5: Logic and Metaphysics
G.W.F. Hegel
Translation edited by John W. Burbidge and George di Giovanni
Introduction and notes by H.S. Harris

10 Consent, Coercion, and Limit: The Medieval Origins of Parliamentary Democracy
Arthur P. Monahan

11 Scottish Common Sense in Germany, 1768–1800: A Contribution to the History of Critical Philosophy
Manfred Kuehn

12 Paine and Cobbett: The Transatlantic Connection
David A. Wilson

13 Descartes and the Enlightenment
Peter A. Schouls

14 Greek Scepticism: Anti-Realist Trends in Ancient Thought
Leo Groarke

15 The Irony of Theology and the Nature of Religious Thought
Donald Wiebe

16 Form and Transformation: A Study in the Philosophy of Plotinus
Frederic M. Schroeder

17 From Personal Duties towards Personal Rights: Late Medieval and Early Modern Political Thought, c. 1300–c. 1650
Arthur P. Monahan

18 The Main Philosophical Writings and the Novel *Allwill*
Friedrich Heinrich Jacobi
Translated and edited by George di Giovanni

19 Kierkegaard as Humanist: Discovering My Self
Arnold B. Come

20 Durkheim, Morals, and Modernity
W. Watts Miller

21 The Career of Toleration: John Locke, Jonas Proast, and After
Richard Vernon

22 Dialectic of Love: Platonism in Schiller's Aesthetics
David Pugh

23 History and Memory in Ancient Greece
Gordon Shrimpton

24 Kierkegaard as Theologian: Recovering My Self
Arnold B. Come

25 Enlightenment and Conservatism in Victorian Scotland: The Career of Sir Archibald Alison
Michael Michie

26 The Road to Egdon Heath: The Aesthetics of the Great in Nature
Richard Bevis

27 Jena Romanticism and Its Appropriation of Jakob Böhme: Theosophy – Hagiography – Literature
Paolo Mayer

28 Enlightenment and Community: Lessing, Abbt, Herder, and the Quest for a German Public
Benjamin W. Redekop

29 Jacob Burckhardt and the Crisis of Modernity
John R. Hinde

30 The Distant Relation: Time and Identity in Spanish-American Fiction
Eoin S. Thomson

31 Mr Simson's Knotty Case: Divinity, Politics, and Due Process in Early Eighteenth-Century Scotland
Anne Skoczylas

32 Orthodoxy and Enlightenment: George Campbell in the Eighteenth Century
Jeffrey M. Suderman

33 Contemplation and Incarnation: The Theology of Marie-Dominique Chenu
Christophe F. Potworowski

34 Democratic Legitimacy: Plural Values and Political Power
F.M. Barnard

35 Herder on Nationality, Humanity, and History
F.M. Barnard

36 Labeling People: French Scholars on Society, Race, and Empire, 1815–1849
Martin S. Staum

37 The Subaltern Appeal to Experience: Self-Identity, Late Modernity, and the Politics of Immediacy
Craig Ireland

38 The Invention of Journalism Ethics: The Path to Objectivity and Beyond
Stephen J.A. Ward

39 The Recovery of Wonder: The New Freedom and the Asceticism of Power
Kenneth L. Schmitz

40 Reason and Self-Enactment in History and Politics: Themes and Voices of Modernity
F.M. Barnard

41 The More Moderate Side of Joseph de Maistre: Views on Political Liberty and Political Economy
Cara Camcastle

42 Democratic Society and Human Needs
Jeff Noonan

43 The Circle of Rights Expands: Modern Political Thought after the Reformation, 1521 (Luther) to 1762 (Rousseau)
Arthur P. Monahan

44 The Canadian Founding: John Locke and Parliament
Janet Ajzenstat

45 Finding Freedom: Hegel's Philosophy and the Emancipation of Women
Sara MacDonald

46 When the French Tried to Be British: Party, Opposition, and the Quest for the Civil Disagreement, 1814–1848
J.A.W. Gunn

47 Under Conrad's Eyes: The Novel as Criticism
Michael John DiSanto

48 Media, Memory, and the First World War
David Williams

49 An Aristotelian Account of Induction: Creating Something from Nothing
Louis Groarke

50 Social and Political Bonds: A Mosaic of Contrast and Convergence
F.M. Barnard

51 Archives and the Event of God: The Impact of Michel Foucault on Philosophical Theology
David Galston

52 Between the Queen and the Cabby: Olympe de Gouges's *Rights of Women*
John R. Cole

53 Nature and Nurture in French Social Sciences, 1859–1914 and Beyond
Martin S. Staum

54 Public Passion: Rethinking the Grounds for Political Justice
Rebecca Kingston

55 Rethinking the Political: The Sacred, Aesthetic Politics, and the Collège de Sociologie
Simonetta Falasca-Zamponi

56 Materialist Ethics and Life-Value
Jeff Noonan

NIETZSCHE'S JUSTICE

NATURALISM IN SEARCH OF AN ETHICS

Peter R. Sedgwick

McGill-Queen's University Press
Montreal & Kingston • London • Ithaca

ISBN 978-0-7735-4268-6 (cloth)
ISBN 978-0-7735-4269-3 (paper)
ISBN 978-0-7735-8983-4 (ePDF)
ISBN 978-0-7735-8984-1 (ePUB)

Legal deposit fourth quarter 2013
Bibliothèque nationale du Québec

Printed in Canada on acid-free paper that is 100% ancient forest free (100% post-consumer recycled), processed chlorine free

McGill-Queen's University Press acknowledges the support of the Canada Council for the Arts for our publishing program. We also acknowledge the financial support of the Government of Canada through the Canada Book Fund for our publishing activities.

Library and Archives Canada Cataloguing in Publication

Sedgwick, Peter R., author
Nietzsche's justice: naturalism in search of an ethics / Peter R. Sedgwick.

(McGill-Queen's studies in the history of ideas; 61)
Includes bibliographical references and index.
Issued in print and electronic formats.
ISBN 978-0-7735-4268-6 (bound).–ISBN 978-0-7735-4269-3 (pbk.).–
ISBN 978-0-7735-8983-4 (ePDF).–ISBN 978-0-7735-8984-1 (ePUB)

1. Nietzsche, Friedrich Wilhelm, 1844–1900 – Criticism and interpretation. 2. Justice. 3. Naturalism. 4. Ethics. I. Title. II. Series: McGill-Queen's studies in the history of ideas; 61

B3318.J87S43 2013 172'.2 C2013-904700-X
C2013-904701-8

This book was typeset by Interscript in 10/12 New Baskerville.

For Richard Schacht

Contents

NIETZSCHE'S JUSTICE

Introduction

AMONGST THE VARIOUS DEVELOPMENTS in Nietzsche criticism one of the most striking is the "surge of interest" in the political significance of his thought.[1] There has, in the last thirty years especially, been increasing debate concerning the political and social aspects of Nietzsche's writings and the possible contribution his ideas might make to our understanding of contemporary political matters. As is often the case with things relating to Nietzsche, this debate is marked by various and complex forms of anxiety. Some have responded to it by arguing that Nietzsche's thinking is devoid of any political dimension of significance. On such an account, Nietzsche is held to be a philosopher whose strengths lie elsewhere. He is best regarded as, for want of a better phrase, a "pure philosopher." Such a view urges us to take Nietzsche to be primarily concerned with, and best read in relation to, a range of more or less traditional philosophical questions concerning things like the nature of existence (ontology) or method (epistemology). After all, it has been claimed, whereas he never offers us a theory concerning the nature or legitimacy of the modern state and, because of this, cannot be deemed a "political" or "social" thinker in any meaningful sense, Nietzsche does offer much discussion of methodological issues that he then applies to the task of seeking to articulate a more or less objective analysis of values.[2] This approach to Nietzsche springs from a desire to

1 See Siemens, "Nietzsche's Political Philosophy," 509.

2 See, for example, Leiter, *Nietzsche on Morality*, 296: Nietzsche, it is claimed, "has no political philosophy, in the conventional sense of a theory of the state and its legitimacy." He is, rather, better understood "as a kind of *esoteric immoralist*" who seeks to communicate his ideas concerning the good life to "the select few." Two points regarding this view are worth mentioning here. First, Nietzsche clearly does offer a theory concerning the state, its origins, and the nature of political legitimacy. See, for instance, *On the Genealogy of*

turn him into a methodologist who follows the example of the hard sciences and emulates the spirit of Enlightenment.[3] It also allows for inconvenient elements of the Nietzschean corpus to be set discretely to one side. In this regard, more recent "anti-political" recuperations take their lead from the work of the famous Nietzsche scholar Walter Kaufmann in his mammoth 1950 study *Nietzsche: Philosopher, Psychologist, Antichrist.*[4] Although happy to emphasize the less traditional aspects of Nietzsche's thought (not least his anti-Christianity) Kaufmann's interpretation seeks to cultivate an understanding of him as a figure of Enlightenment ethos whose primary concerns are far removed from the political domain. This may in part be because of the uncomfortable and inaccurate association with Nazism that affixed itself to Nietzsche's name at the time of Kaufmann's writing in the immediate aftermath of the Second World War. Kaufmann's major achievement is to reveal the illusory nature of this association, but the illusion is exposed at the cost of a depoliticized Nietzsche held to be uninterested in society, questions of political power, or the trashy world of everyday struggles that characterize much of human life.

Morality, II, 17 (for some discussion of this see chapter 5). Here, Nietzsche offers an account of the origins of the state: its origins are violent and tyrannical. In other words, the state does not spring from a "contract" between equals, as classical liberal theory would like to suggest. In turn, what we come to call "legitimacy," for Nietzsche, has its origins in the practical world of human life: it springs from our dominant instinct – the urge to follow convention – and emerges as a complex tangle of habits and customs. Second, the contention that Nietzsche seeks a restricted audience (a "select few") to whom he wishes to communicate his notion of "human flourishing" ignores the register of Nietzsche's writings. Whatever he himself might on occasion claim, Nietzsche is no esoteric writer. He can be read with profit by people with little or no formal philosophical training. It is one of the great ironies of Nietzsche's thought that this most anti-democratic of writers should have been read by what must on any accounting be one of the widest and most varied audiences ever afforded to a figure associated with the philosophical tradition. For another variant of the attempt to de-politicize Nietzsche see Brobjer, "The Absence of Political Ideals," 300–18. For a persuasive critical response to Brobjer see Dombowsky, "A Response to Thomas H. Brobjer."

3 One of the most powerful articulations of this approach is offered by Maudmarie Clark in *Nietzsche on Truth and Philosophy*. Clark's contention is that Nietzsche is first and foremost committed to applying the methodological approach of the sciences to the realm of philosophical debate. It is this which makes him an anti-metaphysical thinker who turns against the dominant approach associated with the Kantian postulation of the existence of the noumenon – the realm of things-in-themselves. My interpretation places more emphasis than Clark on history, rather than science. Nietzsche, after all, is no passive adherent to scientific method.

4 See Kaufmann, *Nietzsche.*

Contrary to this view, others have sought in various ways to show how Nietzsche is foremost a political thinker. On this conception, it is possible even to transform the overtly anti-democratic Nietzsche into a figure capable of making a positive contribution to arguments that characterize the modern political milieu. Thus, recent scholarship has explored the ways in which the overtly anti-democratic Nietzsche can contribute even to conceptions of democracy.[5] Some have responded to this enlisting of Nietzsche for democratic purposes critically but not in a manner that simply denies the political register of Nietzsche's thought. Such responses emphasize instead the degree to which this political register cannot be readily translated into an endorsement of modern democratic culture in so far as it poses too radical a challenge to contemporary political preconceptions.[6] Others, in turn, argue that Nietzsche is indeed a political thinker, but that his thought is politically unproductive and even destructive. Pre-eminent amongst these is Jürgen Habermas. For Habermas, Nietzsche is the most destructive critic of bourgeois philosophy. He usurps the pre-eminence of liberal conceptions of legitimacy and supplants them with a philosophy of domination incapable of making a positive contribution to modern political and social debate. Nietzsche's privileging of power, Habermas argues, renders questions of authority contingent and subject to an appalling arbitrariness.[7]

5 See J. Hatab, *A Nietzschean Defense*, and Schrift, "Nietzsche *for* Democracy?" See also Connolly, *Political Theory and Modernity*, and Warren, *Nietzsche and Political Thought.* Warren characterizes Nietzsche as a conservative thinker of aristocratic persuasion, but holds that his account of power offers insights that transcend the limits of his own political views. For an informative critical discussion of these see Don Dombowsky, "A Response to Alan D. Schrift." For another critical account of Nietzsche's relation to democracy see Appel, *Nietzsche contra Democracy*. For Appel, anti-democratic sentiment reaches to the very core of Nietzsche's thought and cannot be separated from it.

6 See Dombowsky's "A Response to Alan D. Schrift." This approach is also developed in a manner critical of Dombowsky by Acampora, "*Demos Agonistes Redux.*" Acampora goes so far as to doubt whether any form of political constitution could bear the stresses placed upon it by what she sees as Nietzsche's incessant demand for social antagonism. However, she does ponder the possibility of a productive role for such an approach, in so far as it might be possible to envisage an agonism that remains situated at the furthest limits of a "democratic polity" (375). For further useful material on the politics of Nietzsche's thought, see Cameron and Dombowsky, *The Political Writings of Friedrich Nietzsche.*

7 See also in connection, Apel, "Regulative Ideas or Truth Happening?" and "The Self-Recuperative Principle," in *From a Transcendental-Semiotic Point of View*, 183–215 and 232–43. Like Habermas, Apel (a fellow member of the second generation of Frankfurt School thinkers) sees in Nietzsche's thought a threat to the validity of the modern conception of critical reason. For Apel, Nietzsche seeks "to call into question absolutely all validity claims of human reason from a genealogical point of view" which "attempts to replace understanding with explaining" (210). This amounts to "an attempt to reduce the normative

Nietzsche's thought suspends any prospect of offering an account of political legitimacy by transforming the progressive historical narrative conventionally taken to ground the modern liberal state into a maelstrom of unrestrained struggles for domination.[8] On such a view, Nietzsche's thought aspires to occupy a position beyond law and reasonableness as it embraces a violence that celebrates and even glorifies injustice and repression.[9] The Habermasean view, in short, is that in so far as Nietzsche is a thinker of power, his thought is oriented toward something inherently unreasonable. Unreasonableness is the epitome of partiality and unfairness, and unfairness the hallmark of injustice. Understood in this way, Nietzsche, in so far as he is a social thinker at all, is a celebrator of gross exploitation.[10] Such a view is echoed by theorist Francis J. Mootz III, who finds in Nietzsche a thinker who offers little comfort for the

---

validity claims of human reason to determining natural factors that make freedom and normative reason to be illusions" that conceal beneath them a hidden world of "material interests" and "will to power" (241). On such an account, historically oriented explanatory modes of meaning are used to neutralize the "self-recuperative" (210) and irreducible element of interpretation inherent in all acts of understanding. On my interpretation, Nietzsche does not seek to perform quite such a radical dissolution of sense. It is, in short, quite possible to offer a genetic account of, say, moral understanding – as Nietzsche does in *On the Genealogy of Morality* – that is nevertheless non-reductive. Just because one has elucidated the historically contingent conditions in virtue of which interpretative norms emerge, and shown thereby the role that these conditions played (and to some extent still play) in the constitution of understanding, it does not follow that one is committed to the view that such understanding is fixed or even entirely characterized for all time by constraints imposed by the conditions from which it emerged. Nietzsche clearly thinks that one can think the limits of these conditions – even if one cannot always escape from them. One can offer an explanation that, even if it relativizes understanding in so far as it locates its origins in contingency, does not simply do away with what understanding has achieved by way of its constituting interpretative norms in the meantime. The legacy of such norms (our presuppositions of value) is, however, now open to critical interrogation.

8 See Habermas, *The Philosophical Discourse of Modernity*.

9 In the words of Richard Rorty, Habermas regards "the line of thought" exemplified by Nietzsche as "a public danger" ("Habermas, Derrida, and Philosophy," in *Truth and Progress*, 311). This view of Nietzsche has been called by Robert B. Pippin a "nearly standard characterization" (see "Nietzsche's Alleged Farewell," in *The Cambridge Companion to Nietzsche*, 252). The view underlying the current interpretation is that Nietzsche contains both much that is deeply insightful and much that ought to disturb us. I no more seek to render Nietzsche a thinker who is passively amenable to our current values than I seek to demonize him.

10 There is, as is so often the case with Nietzsche, justification for this view. Consider, for example, *Beyond Good and Evil*, 259, which holds that the idea of a social order whose members refrain from causing "injury, violence, and exploitation" to one another and which is egalitarian, denies the fundamental principle of life (this principle being life's desire to expand rather than contract). For some discussion of Nietzsche's treatment of "life" see the conclusion to the current volume.

faint-hearted. Mootz, who outlines the benefits of a hermeneutic approach to the quandaries unearthed in recent debates about the nature of law,[11] likewise holds Nietzsche's thought to offer few panaceas. The "Nietzschean challenge" posed to law amounts to reducing it to no more than the play of power relations.[12] Malcolm Bull likewise concentrates on representing Nietzsche as a thinker of power and seeks thereby to unmask a figure incapable of offering anything but a repulsive and regressive political vision. For Bull, Nietzsche uses a strategy of flattering the reader into partaking of a sense of shared participation in an exclusive domain of mastery. Because of this, Nietzsche is a thinker not to be trusted.[13] One of Bull's main points of contention is that this sense of exclusivity feeds Nietzsche's anti-egalitarianism.[14] Egalitarianism, on Bull's account, is Nietzsche's chosen target as the source of European nihilism.[15] In challenging nihilism, Nietzsche sets out an influential anti-egalitarian political agenda that favours a socially regressive return to multiple forms of slavery.

11 See Mootz III, "After Natural Law" 1. Mootz's comment occurs in the context of a discussion of Stephen Smith's *Law's Quandary*. Smith points to the gap between legal theory and practice. Positivistic tendencies have generated a loss of theoretical commitment in the existence of "the Law," yet legal practitioners act in their daily lives as if such a thing exists.

12 In spite of such reservations, however, the burgeoning interest in this aspect of Nietzsche's thought is nevertheless reflected in a number of publications, including a substantial volume co-edited by Mootz. See Mootz III and Goodrich, *Nietzsche and Law*, and Goodrich and Valverde, *Nietzsche and Legal Theory*.

13 Bull, *Anti-Nietzsche*, 31. The issue of trust, Bull notes, is raised by Waite in *Nietzsche's Corps/e*. Waite argues that "The trust Nietzsche most *betrayed* is *ours*: namely our trust that the object of philosophy ... is the creation of concepts that are always new, when in fact Nietzsche's concepts were created to serve surreptitiously ideological interests and agendas that are premodern, *archaic*" (23). Waite thereby urges us to discard our trust in Nietzsche, an attitude fostered by his texts' ability to seduce us into thinking we are amongst the chosen "few" to whom they are addressed (see Bull, 31). One can, of course, read with profit without trusting everything he says or numbering oneself amongst the elite readership he seeks to conjure. As I have argued elsewhere, the more "sinister" Nietzsche, one who does not conform to our presuppositions concerning truth, politics, morality, and the like, and is read with a certain lack of trust, can be of positive value. One need not trust him to value him. Indeed, the kind of objection to Nietzsche that depends upon trust can be raised concerning philosophy generally, as he himself was amongst the first modern thinkers to point out. The insidious nature of philosophy (its levels of often unwitting deception and self-deception) is a central topic in the opening twenty or so sections of *Beyond Good and Evil.*

14 Bull, *Anti-Nietzsche*, 162.

15 See Bull, *Anti-Nietzsche*, chapter 3, for an entertaining, if at times questionable, exploration of Nietzsche and nihilism.

The kinds of tensions noted above are not unique to modern debates about the politics of Nietzsche's thought – or to the domain of academic discussion. The conception of Nietzsche as a politically and culturally engaged figure replete with disturbing undertones versus the image of him as an apolitical thinker primarily concerned with more or less "harmless" traditional questions concerning the nature of existence or questions of method has framed critical and not-so-critical discussion of his writings almost from the outset. In 1895, only six years after Nietzsche's mental collapse, Rudolph Steiner portrayed him as a fighter against his times, seeking to cultivate a conception of personhood that runs counter to the one fostered by dominant modern mass culture.[16] At the same time, some commentators in the world of late Victorian letters saw in Nietzsche an exemplar of the contradictory and sinister *fin-de-siècle* spirit of modernity itself.[17] He was likewise associated with the politics of Social Darwinism[18] and by the second decade of the twentieth century even accused in some quarters of being responsible for starting the First World War.[19] Yet Nietzsche has from the outset also been deemed a "pure thinker" in the sense of being a saint, sage, seer, poet, or prophet.[20] Such a range of contradictory standpoints is perhaps indicative of one thing above all: however one might want to cast him, Nietzsche does not fit neatly into the mould of contemporary political discourse. As Keith Ansell-Pearson has noted, "Nietzsche's political thought ... fails to conform to liberal and democratic sentiments which have prevailed over the last two hundred

16 See Steiner, *Friedrich Nietzsche.*

17 See, for example, Nietzsche's obituary in *The Academy and Literature,* 59 (1 September 1900), 175–6: Nietzsche's "creed ... has been called hideous, ferocious, abominable, insane, but ... he ... is nevertheless a direct, we might almost say a legitimate, product of the age." For an insightful discussion of the age in question see Dowling, *Language and Decadence.*

18 See, for example, Nietzsche's obituary in *The Athenaeum* 3801 by T. Bailey Saunders, 281–2, and Adams, "The Ethics of Tolstoy and Nietzsche."

19 See "Teutonismus" in *The Athenaeum* 4537, 347–8. The tone of this article is reflected in contemporary comments by novelist Joseph Conrad – see Conrad, "The Crime of Partition," *Notes on Life and Letters,* 139–40. See also, Anon., "The Philosophy of Power," 168–72; and H. Milbourne's 1917 article, "The Hammer of Thor," 1–17.

20 Havelock Ellis, for example, held that Nietzsche must be counted as being "one of the greatest spiritual forces ... since Goethe" (this claim is cited in Anon., "Philosophy with a Hammer," 31–2, 31). Another important critic of the time, Holbrook Jackson, wrote of Nietzsche that "a saintlier man never lived" (see his review of Elizabeth Förster-Nietzsche's *The Young Nietzsche,* in the August 1912 edition of *The Bookman,* 215–6, 216); while poet Edward Thomas held Nietzsche to be above all a writer of poetic significance (see Edward Thomas's 1909 review of various Nietzsche literature in *The Bookman,* 140).

years."[21] Does this suspicion of the central tenets of liberalism render Nietzsche a philosophical nomad? Is he a figure destined to occupy an at best uncomfortably marginal role in our understanding of political and social questions?

As we have seen, there are plenty of responses – pro and contra – to the two questions just posed. My own takes its lead from Ansell-Pearson[22] in endorsing the view that Nietzsche must be read politically.[23] For me, Nietzsche is a thinker of social import. Likewise, I see in Nietzsche's works a counter-perspective that resists the hegemony of liberal political discourse, and a resource that invites us to think beyond the limits of liberalism. This does not mean that one must passively endorse what Daniel Conway has deemed to be the dangerously "illiberal" consequences of a Nietzschean approach.[24] But, as Conway notes, this ought not to deter us from contemplating the "founding question of politics" that Nietzsche's thought poses. This is the question of human futurity – of what kind of beings we might or even should become.[25] Nietzsche, in short, can be taken as a thinker who raises the question of the legitimacy of our founding political concepts in a new way by placing them in the context of a notion of selfhood that is fluid, formed, and constantly reforming. The approach developed in this book addresses the conceptions of politics, society, selfhood, and culture in Nietzsche in a way that is also much indebted to the work of Richard Schacht. Schacht is foremost amongst scholars in showing how Nietzsche is, above all, a "naturalistic" thinker. Naturalism, as Schacht puts it, is not to be taken as something that is "little more than a departure from both traditional empiricism and rationalism, and a disposition to interpret all things human in terms of the interactions of one distinctive but natural kind with their environment and each other."[26] It involves, rather, a translation of humankind back into nature by rethinking what "natural" means in terms that acknowledge both the roles biological embodiment (the world of drives) and historically forged social relationships play in

21 Ansell-Pearson, *An Introduction to Nietzsche as Political Thinker*, 2.

22 See Ansell-Pearson, *Nietzsche contra Rousseau.* These texts reveal in exemplary manner the socio-political registers of Nietzsche's thought.

23 Another work worthy of mention here is Mellamphy's *The Three Stigmata of Friedrich Nietzsche.* Mellamphy argues that the political, anti-political, and supra-political aspects of Nietzsche's writings are all essential elements in his work. She then offers an account of a Nietzschean politics of the body that receives its highest expression in Dionysian affirmation. Much of the reading that is offered in this text harmonizes well with this approach.

24 Conway, *Nietzsche and the Political*, 4.

25 Ibid.

26 See Schacht, *Nietzsche*, 54.

fashioning our humanity. Above all, Nietzsche seeks to naturalize our understanding of values. He does not, however, seek to naturalize values in a manner that reduces them to the mere play of drives or social forces.[27] We may spring from a concatenation of natural and historical-cultural origins, but these origins do not explain entirely what we are or might become. It is in this context, Schacht argues, that Nietzsche develops an account of freedom that holds it to emanate from conditions of power and discipline rather than being opposed to them, as traditional conceptions contend.[28] I, too, hold Nietzsche to be a thinker of naturalism in this non-reductive sense. We are amalgams of drives and embodied beings, but we are not simply that. We are also creatures of habit, convention, and custom – social beings fashioned by our unconsciously adhered-to normative allegiances. We are self-interpreters, too (which is not the same thing as saying we are defined by self-consciousness). Naturalism in this sense is never mere worship of the methodologies of the hard sciences, although it is informed by them.[29] I do not, in other words, seek to present a Nietzsche who is merely methodologically naturalistic,[30] any more than a Nietzsche who is simply political.[31] I do

27 Ibid., 399.

28 See ibid., 468, for a discussion of morality as discipline and a precondition of self-overcoming.

29 Eugen Fink argues that Nietzsche's naturalism is often "hyperbole, and intentionally coarse hyperbole at that. In no sense does Nietzsche put man back into nature or give him over to the natural scientists" ("Nietzsche's New Experience of the World," 206). The account offered here, of course, contends that a more subtle naturalism coexists with the rhetoric of Nietzsche's texts – one that is no less resistant to recuperation by "natural scientists."

30 Thus, I do not agree with Robert Legros's claim that "[t]hrough forging a naturalist identity of nature – the idea of a preconventional nature – Nietzsche determines a natural criterion for truth (the concept is adequate to nature), [and] a natural criterion for justice (an attitude faithful to life's nature)" that reflects a metaphysics of life ("The Nietzschean Metaphysics of Life," 133). Although, as I argue in chapter 6, a problematic conception of this kind emerges in one of Nietzsche's final works, *The Antichrist*, this conception is out of character with much that precedes it. Nietzsche does not consistently proffer a simplistic life-metaphysic with pretensions to solve our epistemic, moral, and politico-legal quandaries by naturalistic means. Rather, his primary interest is in rendering problematic the very "naturalness" of such conceptions – there is for him no "natural justice." Justice talk is, for Nietzsche, a consequence of social and historical forces (see the discussion in chapter 3). Indeed, it is hard to conceive how what Legros calls a "preconventional nature" could provide a criterion for anything as wholly conventional as a determinate resolution of what truth or justice might amount to. Nietzsche's conception of what justice amounts to is, I argue, rooted in the inclination to suspend a condemnatory judgemental attitude and celebrates in its place the virtue of mercy (see chapter 5).

31 Leslie Thiele, in one of the most powerful and perceptive readings of Nietzsche proffered in the last twenty five years, argues that for Nietzsche "[t]he greatest struggles are not

not, in short, seek to offer a seamless reading of the development of Nietzsche's ideas.[32] Following Wolfgang Müller-Lauter, I am of the view that Nietzsche is a thinker of contradictions.[33] The various moments of inconsistency that pattern Nietzsche's writings are not to be taken as weaknesses but as a leitmotif of the web of relations that, for Nietzsche, constitutes the path of thinking. One must cut one's own way through this web in the spirit of experiment. In this regard, I am also indebted to the example set by the writings of Theodor Adorno

to be witnessed on the battlefield or in the socio-political arena, but in the rule of the self. The greatest victory is a well-ordered soul" (*Friedrich Nietzsche and the Politics of the Soul*, 65). The well-ordered soul is, for Nietzsche, a kind of political entity: politics, on such a conception, is internalized. My own reading does not so much contradict this view as supplement and amend it. On my account, Nietzsche argues that the self is initially fashioned in virtue of prehistoric conventional structures of normative adherence that characterize the communal-social realm. One can, for Nietzsche, overcome this condition through an act of resistance to the norm. Nietzsche does not therefore see sociality as something that is achieved in the first instance at the cost of individual autonomy (see Thiele, 38). Rather, such things as individuality emerge from their apparent "opposites": the realm of community and society, a world constituted by the iron force of traditional observance ("law"), creates the very conditions that are capable of exceeding it.

32 As Karsten Harries has commented, Nietzsche is often read in a manner that seeks to "translate" him into idioms more amenable to the presuppositions of one philosophical approach or another. Whatever the virtues of such translations, Harries notes, "we should ask ourselves whether such appropriation is not also a defense against a style and a thinking that puts the philosophy guarded by professional philosophers into question" ("The Philosopher at Sea," 23). As the beginning of chapter 5 perhaps suggests, this book stakes no claims to defending philosophy in such a professionalized sense. Indeed, the notion that there is such a thing as "pure philosophy" (an idea that supports at least some of the more dubious professional manifestations of the discipline) is clearly questioned in Nietzsche's writings.

33 See Müller-Lauter, *Friedrich Nietzsche*. Müller-Lauter situates Nietzsche's thought in the context of the "history of modern nihilism" (Preface) and argues that his writings must be approached with the question of their apparent contradictions and inconsistencies foremost in mind. The problem of contradiction is traced by way of engagements with the interpretations of prominent readers of Nietzsche, such as Hans Vaihinger, Georg Simmel, Georg Lukács, and Martin Heidegger. Such interpreters, Müller-Lauter argues, seek to locate a foundation of consistency hidden beneath the surging and contradictory surfaces of Nietzsche's texts and thereby do violence to the "specificity" of contradiction as it plays itself out in Nietzsche's writings (5). Müller-Lauter, in contrast, seeks to do justice to the trajectory of contradiction in Nietzsche arguing, for example, that Nietzsche's conception of power (specifically, will to power) is made manifest in contradiction: power itself has contradiction (resistance) as one of its most refined and pervasive consequences. Contradiction likewise runs through Nietzsche's early thought on history (in the second of the *Untimely Meditations*) in terms of the tension articulated between "scientific-historical thinking" and "the suprahistorical forces of art and religion." In the terms outlined in the current volume, this contradiction is articulated in terms of the tensions between destructive, critical thought, on the one hand, and rejuvenating, oracular myth on the other.

and Max Horkheimer. Their unflinching way with Nietzsche, an approach that is unafraid to appreciate his best and sometimes most disturbing insights, serves as an ideal of engagement that is never easy to emulate.[34]

Nietzsche, well characterized by Terry Eagleton as "an astonishingly radical thinker,"[35] often comes across as an uncanny and uncomfortable blend of modern and anti-modern, radical and reactionary. He foresees the rise of secularism but responds to it in a manner that combines the atheistic with the anti-democratic. He affirms pluralism, but despises liberalism. He rejects the modern nation state as coercive but refuses to offer an alternative, instead appearing to revel in the contingencies of a philosophy of power that spurns notions of natural right and equality. He perceives clearly enough the cruel violence of life and yet we catch him often seemingly affirming it. He despises pity but loves mercy. Nietzsche is like our bad and bruised conscience. His is a painful voice that speaks against us from within ourselves, at once radical and anti-radical, enlightener and counter-enlightener. This uncanny nature comes especially to the fore when one begins to think about his philosophy in the context of questions concerning the nature of law and justice. In this regard, Nietzsche's thinking has received far less attention than it is due. Of recent work in this area, Jens Petersen and Manuel Knoll have offered thought-provoking engagements with Nietzsche's treatment of justice.[36] For them, as for me, Nietzsche's thought performs more than a merely destructive incursion into hitherto sacred territory.

34 See Adorno and Horkheimer, *Dialectic of Enlightenment.* Adorno and Horkheimer's perceptive reading of Nietzsche as an unmasker of the instrumentalism concealed within Enlightenment rationality exemplifies the kind of reading I have in mind.

35 Eagleton, *Trouble with Strangers*, 171.

36 See Knoll, "Nietzsches Begriff der Sozialen Gerechtigkeit." For Knoll, Nietzsche is a thinker who shows a strong commitment to developing a theory of social justice modelled after views outlined by Plato in *The Republic.* See also Petersen, *Nietzsches Genialität der Gerechtigkeit.* For Petersen, the theme of justice is present in Nietzsche's thought as something pervasive yet often invisible with the consequence that it is multi-faceted in its complexity. Nietzsche's approach destabilizes conventional accounts of right: it conjoins questions of legitimacy relating to knowledge to the nature of law, justice, and power. Taking the diverse nature of Nietzsche's thought into account poses the biggest challenge to any interpreter (Petersen criticizes D.W. Yang's book, *Die Problematik des Begriffs der Gerechtigkeit in der Philosophie von Friedrich Nietzsche* (Berlin, 2005) for not taking this complex commitment to the question of justice sufficiently into account). Although he acknowledges that Nietzsche is an anti-systematic thinker, Petersen adopts a quite rigorous methodological approach to the exploration of the Nietzschean thematization of justice that remains acutely sensitive to its ambiguities. My own reading shares much in common

The thesis developed here is simple enough. I hold Nietzsche's treatment of justice to spring from an engagement with themes already charted in his first book, *The Birth of Tragedy. The Birth* is a work of homage to myth that invokes an absolute justice grasped by way of an artistic metaphysics. The young Nietzsche's encounter with Greek tragedy spurs the development of an oracular conception of justice that speaks from beyond the domain of rigid social convention with a power that renders it capable of highlighting and indicting the mediocre and exhausted condition of modernity. In *Human, All Too Human* this metaphysics gives way to naturalism, or what Nietzsche calls "historical philosophy." This gives rise to a radical and original approach to understanding humanity in terms of its law-like nature. Nietzsche holds human identity to be a consequence of the fusion of drives and communal social forces. This fusion happens in such a way that the drives themselves are affected by it. The human being, in short, is above all a creature of embodied culture. The radical reinterpretation initiated by Nietzsche's naturalistic turn initiates a sustained critique of the legitimacy of the notion of punishment. Although *Human, All Too Human* rejects Nietzsche's earlier metaphysics, the development of his thought is not marked by a simple rejection of the terms of *The Birth of Tragedy*'s engagement with modernity. Nor does Nietzsche discard the possibility of redeeming the oracular articulation of justice found in *The Birth.* In fact, in the aftermath of a rejection of traditional accounts of the nature of willing, moral responsibility, and punishment, Nietzsche's mature thought seeks to rejuvenate the conception of an oracular justice in naturalistic terms. This rejuvenation is grounded in a new account of the nature of human freedom, and in a vision of genuine philosophical thought as the creative legislation of values, that embraces an ethic of mercy. The pursuit of this ethic tempts Nietzsche on to the path toward a revaluation of values. Revaluation, too, embraces an oracular element. In *The Antichrist,* however, the oracular invocation of "life" as the source of authority with which to curse the Christian church (a curse that, it is worth noting, is not aimed at the figure of Christ himself but at the institutions that emerge in the wake of

with Petersen's. Thus, the original character of justice is grounded in an exchange principle that ultimately outstrips the realm of law and custom from which it emerges (52ff). Likewise, Petersen appreciates the manner in which Nietzsche articulates this development by way of a critique of the notion of freedom of the will and develops a conception of justice that sublimates its origins in punishment and guilt (105ff). Such a conception turns on the notion of will to power, which is productive of a mode of authority that can be disentangled from the notion of revenge usually associated with conceptions of equivalence and compensation. However, the interpretation offered here traces Nietzsche's concern back to *The Birth of Tragedy* rather than the second of the *Untimely Meditations.*

his untimely death[37]) reveals the limits of Nietzsche's re-evaluative ambitions, compromizing his naturalistic discourse. The integrity of this discourse, I argue, is best served by going beyond revaluation and, ironically perhaps, returning to the ethic of mercy outlined in chapter 5. Such integrity is only possible if one pursues a self-criticism of the kind of naturalistic methodological enterprise associated with the Enlightenment. With this thought one is taken into the problem of Enlightenment as it is articulated by Adorno and Horkheimer in *Dialectic of Enlightenment.*

As can be inferred from the above summary, the present text deploys a largely sequential approach to the discussion of Nietzsche's thought.[38] It begins with the earliest of his published writings, *The Birth of Tragedy*, and the second of the *Untimely Meditations* in order to develop an account of his early metaphysical views (1872; 1874). Chapter 2 then looks at the so-called "middle period" writings (*Human, All Too Human* [1878], *Assorted Opinions and Maxims* [1879], *The Wanderer and His Shadow* [1880], *Daybreak* [1881], and *The Gay Science* [1882]) as a means of elucidating Nietzsche's development of historical naturalism and his account of our law-like nature. Chapter 3 explores these texts further in the context of the account offered in them of justice, community, and power, turning to *Beyond Good and Evil* (1885) toward the end. Chapter 4 seeks to offer an analysis of Nietzsche's views on punishment, and ranges freely from the "middle period" books to the discussions offered in *Beyond Good and Evil*, book 5 of *The Gay Science* (added to the original text in 1887), and *On the Genealogy of Morality* (1887). In chapter 5, I take a slight step back, so to speak, and focus at some length on *Thus Spoke Zarathustra* (1883–85), a work that chronologically precedes those discussed at the end of the previous chapter. Chapter 5 thus offers an account of justice and naturalism grounded in the text of *Zarathustra*,

37 Theologian Jürgen Moltmann concurs with Nietzsche's drawing a distinction between the institution of the Christian church and the teaching of Jesus. Moltmann offers an account of Christ's teaching that effectively positions it within a Nietzschean-style framework of life-affirmation. He comments, "So Nietzsche was right: 'Eternal life is eternal livingness' ... Jesus didn't bring a new religion into the world. He brought new life. He didn't found 'Christianity,' nor did he set up an ecclesial rule over the nations. He brought life into this violent and dying world ... Christ is the divine Yes to life" ("Dialogue or Mission?," in *God for a Secular Society*, 241).

38 For this volume I have elected to concentrate entirely on Nietzsche's published writings rather than his notebooks. I do not dispute that much of value is to be found in the notebooks and have no objection to readings that use them extensively, as some of my other readings of Nietzsche readily demonstrate. However, as the length of this book suggests, there is more than enough material of sufficient quantity and complexity to warrant exclusively treating Nietzsche's engagement with the problem of justice in his published works.

relating this in turn to later material from *Beyond Good and Evil*, the *Genealogy*, book 5 of *The Gay Science*, and *Twilight of the Idols* (1888). The reason for this chronological diversion is simple enough. *Zarathustra* is the work that, according to Nietzsche himself, is his greatest achievement and must be located at the heart of his mature thought.[39] The book is, as Lawrence Lampert notes, "the explosive core of the work of the philosopher who could say 'I am dynamite.'"[40] The so-called "middle period" of Nietzsche's thought ends with the figure of Zarathustra: the first edition of *The Gay Science* concludes with book 4 and the "going under" with which *Thus Spoke Zarathustra* begins (*The Gay Science*, 342[41]). The later writings, too, self-consciously orient themselves around *Zarathustra.* The poem "From High Mountains," which concludes Nietzsche's articulation of a re-vitalized conception of philosophy in *Beyond Good and Evil*, returns the reader to the thought of Zarathustra, who is "the guests of guests." In the *Genealogy* Nietzsche reminds us that we must approach his writings in a manner that involves going back and forth between earlier and later texts. According to the Preface, the sense of what is argued in the *Genealogy* is only truly evident if one has made the effort to explore his earlier writings and bear them in mind (8). As if to hammer the point home, the conclusion of the *Genealogy*'s second essay alludes to Zarathustra as offering the creative paradigm for developing the ideas suggested there (24–5), while the third essay is described by Nietzsche as a "commentary" on the aphorism that is placed at the beginning of it – and this aphorism is prefaced with a quotation from *Zarathustra.* The chronological diversion involved in this discussion is thus, I hope, well justified. Chapter 6 offers a discussion of Nietzsche's very late writings by way of an initial consideration of the 1886 prefaces Nietzsche adds to *Human, All Too Human* and *Daybreak* in order to frame a critical discussion of the attempt at a revaluation of values made in *The Antichrist* (1888), while a conclusion returns us to some of the issues concerning the politics of Nietzsche's thought raised in the present introduction.

39 See, for example, *Ecce Homo*, "Why I Write Such Good Books," 1.

40 Lampert, *Nietzsche's Teaching*, 5.

41 All citations for Nietzsche's texts refer to sections, rather than page numbers.

I

The Divine Justice of Tragedy: Myth, Metaphysics, and Modernity

1. A concern with the nature of law and justice is evident even in Nietzsche's earliest major work, The Birth of Tragedy. *This concern is reflected in the text's deployment of its central concepts, the Apollonian and the Dionysian. The god Apollo is law-like and manifests the order and harmony characteristic of the individuated social realm. Apollonian rules keep lawless nature at bay, concealing it beneath an aesthetic of harmonious proportion. In contrast, Dionysus, the god of intoxication and excess, is associated with lawless nature. Through Dionysian impulses individuated Apollonian order is torn asunder; the normative realm and the rationality associated with it dissolve as ecstatic humankind reasserts its kinship with nature. In Ancient Greek tragedy the horrifying violence of existence is rendered amenable to contemplation through a fusion in which Apollonian elements frame Dionysian terror and suffering, placing it within a divine narrative capable of endowing life with redemptive sense. The Greeks, Nietzsche argues, thus created their gods "from a most profound need." The result is a sufficient and acceptable theodicy. The art of tragedy, as this theodicy's highest form of expression, redeems life.*

Nietzsche engages with questions about the nature of law and justice even in his first book. In order to approach his engagement, however, it is necessary to recall its main arguments about Greek tragic culture and the concepts of the Apollonian and Dionysian. The predominant interpretation of Greek culture was that espoused by figures such as J.J. Winckelmann (1717–1768) and later, Mathew Arnold (1822–1888).[1] This view held the great Greek cultural achievements in the arts and philosophy to be the expression of a calm and enlightened simplicity,

1 Arnold, in 1865, famously described the ancient Greek world as one of "sweetness and light." See *Culture and Anarchy.*

one epitomized by the elegant harmony of design apparent in its sculpture and architecture, but also present in its literature and drama. Against this view, *The Birth of Tragedy* seeks to account for Greek formal simplicity and beauty in terms that are subterranean and sinister. The formal harmony of ancient Greek artistic works, Nietzsche argues, is in fact the sublimated expression of a violence that permeated the ancient Greek cultural experience. In order to explain the nature of such violence, Nietzsche introduces two aesthetic categories: the Apollonian and the Dionysian.

Apollo is the Ancient Greek sun god. He is "the shining one," the god of light and "of all plastic energies" (*The Birth of Tragedy*, 1). Nietzsche argues that the Apollonian aesthetic principle first makes its appearance in Homeric myth and reaches its highest level of expression in Ancient Greek sculpture, with its emphasis on the proportion and harmony of the human form. Scholars like Winckelmann take this Apollonian appearance at face value, interpreting it as encapsulating the reality of the ancient Greek world. As its close association with sculpture suggests, the Apollonian principle is "the principle of individuation": it is the principle that expresses the individual's sense of separateness from others. Individual self-understanding is Apollonian since it rests on this feeling of an unbridgeable isolation and alienation both from others (social differences) and from the realm of nature. Consciousness is threatened by nature because the latter is unruly and no respecter of persons and their socially endowed status. Nature, which is the epitome of the organic, does not value the individual. Rather, nature liquidates the individual, who, in the face of its infinite, lawless force, is helpless and as nothing. As befits something closely associated with the social realm, the Apollonian answer to the chaos of lawless nature is to assert the primacy of rules and laws. These rules thus allow the ancient Greek to throw a veil of illusion over the world as a means of coping with its uncomfortable, inhuman reality. Apollonian sensibilities disguise the threat of individual extinction by creating a conceptual net of beauty and proportion. The Apollonian is an aesthetic that constrains, directing and structuring artistic expression in such a way as to render possible an art of the most individuated and formal kind imaginable, one that, with its assertion of harmony, conceals the threat of individual mortality. An art that is Apollonian is an art characterized by order and the hegemony of the conscious self. Such an art expresses, albeit in a concealed way, the constitutive power social order exerts over all individual thought and experience. It is from this socially generated propensity to create a sense of order and proportion that the iron association between the Apollonian and the "principle of individuation" springs.

In contrast to the dream world of Apollonian representation, the Dionysian aesthetic principle is essentially "nonimagistic." The condition most closely linked with it is one of "intoxication" (*The Birth of Tragedy*, 1). Dionysus is the festive god of the Ancient Greeks. Nietzsche tells us that Dionysian festivals were events of "extravagant sexual licentiousness" in which "the most savage natural instincts were unleashed" (*The Birth of Tragedy*, 2). The figure of Dionysus emerges in the festival as an expression of the ecstasy engendered by abandoning the socially individuated and law-like self in a condition that recalls pre-individuated existence. In Dionysian rapture, "nature which has become alienated, hostile, or subjugated, celebrates once more her reconciliation with her lost son, man." Through this Dionysian reconciliation "everything subjective" vanishes "into complete self-forgetfulness." With this suspension of the principle of individuation, the social barriers separating person from person also evaporate. Dionysian art reflects this, identifying itself with a "primal unity" that signifies the "oneness of man with nature" (*The Birth of Tragedy*, 3). The Dionysian's closest artistic association, it follows, cannot be with conceptually oriented, representational, and individuating sculpture, but rather with the flowing, liquid art of music. If Apollonian art enshrines the representational stability of formal rules of limitation, the Dionysian expresses the immanence of an unrestrained becoming that overflows these boundaries. In this overflowing, the Dionysian sunders imagistic modes of representation and dissolves the very condition of possibility upon which individual self-consciousness rests, returning us to an awareness of the primacy of the de-individuated animality of nature and the body.

Because of its proximity with the Dionysian, the harmonious Apollonian consciousness of the ancient Greek finds itself uncannily mirrored in the disturbed and chaotic Dionysian state. In consequence, the Apollonian Greek's response to the spectacle of the collective release of Dionysian festivity would, Nietzsche argues, have been one of uncomfortable *self-recognition*: "With what astonishment must the Apollinian Greek have beheld him [the Dionysian reveller]! With an astonishment that was all the greater the more it was mingled with the shuddering suspicion that all this was actually not so very alien to him after all, in fact, that it was only his Apollinian consciousness which, like a veil, hid this Dionysian world from his vision" (*The Birth of Tragedy*, 2). Winckelmann, in short, is wrong in thinking of the ancient Greek world as one governed solely by enlightened rational restraint. It is, rather, a realm of repressed violence and inner conflict.

The Birth of Tragedy's central claim is that Attic tragedy restores the repressed, Dionysian aspect of the Apollonian Greek's identity, for it is "an equally Dionysian and Apollinian form of art" (*The Birth of Tragedy*, 1). The Apollonian artist imitates the representational realm of dream concepts, while the Dionysian artist imitates the condition of festive rapture. The tragic artist, however, uses Apollonian symbols to convey the Dionysian truth of nature; in this way the redemptive capabilities of the Apollonian are revealed, for it is the "symbolical analogue of the soothsaying faculty and of the arts generally" and it is these arts "which make life possible and worth living" (*The Birth of Tragedy*, 1). In tragedy, therefore, the Apollonian provides the Dionysian with a language that allows for the latter's retrieval and representation in symbolic, and hence less terrifying, terms. In its earliest manifestations in the works of Aeschylus (525–456 BCE), tragic drama consists of a chorus that interprets the narrative as it unfolds, and a handful of figures whose function is to personify the narrative's central themes. Sophocles develops this model, introducing more characters but preserving the central role of the chorus. According to Nietzsche, it is with the chorus that the Dionysian element in tragedy resides. The chorus is "the symbol of the whole excited Dionysian throng" of non-individuated communal beings that ground social order[2] (*The Birth of Tragedy*, 2). The Dionysian condition engendered by the chorus dissolves the spectator's sense of their own individuality, so that he or she succumbs to the state of self-forgetting necessary to become an active participator within the tragedy and hence fit for the revelation of Dionysian truth.[3]

The Apollonian component of Greek tragedy is the dialogue spoken by the drama's characters (*The Birth of Tragedy*, 9). Nietzsche notes that Sophocles's language is remarkable precisely for its "Apollinian precision and lucidity." This language, however, is a mask: it has the *appearance* of transparency, simplicity, and beauty, but this appearance conceals its genuine significance. The hero's words, for example those of King Oedipus, give the impression that one is gazing straight into the "innermost ground" of his essence. However, if one ignores the conception of the hero that the dialogue generates and looks instead "into the myth that projects itself in these lucid reflections" the initial impression of lucidity is subverted. As the tragic hero's Apollonian language echoes and dies away something occurs that is akin to what happens when one

2 One can think of this in the following way: if the individuated characters in the play are Apollonian, the Dionysian throng that bears witness to their fate is the collective social understanding of the public realm, the impersonal and shared wisdom of the community. Thus, in Sophocles's *King Oedipus* the chorus can be taken to stand for the collective voice of the city of Thebes.

3 Thus, the spectator of *King Oedipus* becomes a citizen of Thebes.

turns one's gaze away from the bright sun after taking a brief glimpse at it. Just as glancing at the sun gives rise to spots in one's vision, so the encounter with the brightness of Sophoclean heroic dialogue allows one a brief glance into the "terrors of nature" as one is engulfed in the darkening effect created by its receding afterglow. It is this after-effect that initiates a reassertion of the mythic power of lawless nature. The tragic hero's language, in other words, functions as a provocation that spurs us to acknowledge the Dionysian terror of existence, yet it allows us to contemplate this terror without ultimately succumbing to it. Thus, as we are driven to the acknowledgement of terror, the Dionysian excitement engendered by the chorus is likewise "transferred ... to that masked figure," the play's tragic hero, who becomes transformed into an instantiated symbol of Dionysus. The audience, now immersed in the play as witnesses, encounter a "Dionysus [who] no longer speaks through forces but as an epic hero" (*The Birth of Tragedy*, 8). The Dionysian power of brute nature is thus given voice as the tragic hero speaks symbolically *through* the language of Apollonian form. As he speaks, the "bright image projections of the Sophoclean hero" reveal the opposite of a representational, "optical phenomenon" dependent upon images (*The Birth of Tragedy*, 9). Apollonian language and concepts, which generally conceal the Dionysian terror of existence are, in tragedy, employed against their ownmost tendency in order to reveal it (*The Birth of Tragedy*, 10).

Tragedy holds the Dionysian and the Apollonian elements together inexorably, since neither can be allowed to gain ultimate purchase over the other if the revelation of Dionysian truth is to be possible. These two aspects are revealed to stand in need of one another to such an extent that neither could be said to be primary. The communication of the nonimagistic reality of the world of nature must take place within the images of language, just as that language must conceal itself at the very moment in which it succeeds in presenting the Dionysian reality from which society and culture originally emerged. In this way Apollonian rational discourse gives voice to the primacy of myth, for it is by way of Apollonian dialogue that the mythical narratives that tragedy dramatizes (i.e. the Prometheus and Oedipus legends) are reaffirmed in their living ability to communicate ultimate truth.

According to Nietzsche, a hidden meaning lurks behind the Greek deities and mythic heroes celebrated by tragedy. This meaning can be made plain enough if one realizes the *great need* from which such cultural creations spring. If one considers the gods of Olympus, one hears "nothing but the accents of an exuberant, triumphant life in which all things, whether good or evil, are deified" (*The Birth of Tragedy*, 3). The Greek gods, Nietzsche tells us, stand *beyond morality* and it is their taking such a stance that *justifies life*. Life is unavoidable suffering, for potential pain accompanies every moment, and even pleasure offers no more than a temporary and illusory respite from the threat of pain. Life is a thing of terror, for life defies all attempts by the living to master it. One's destiny is ultimately out of one's hands. The Olympians, in their heroic and fantastic aspects, mask this violent reality of ancient Greek life, humanizing the inhuman and so making it a fit object of contemplation. The gods keep the terrors and suffering of existence at bay, enclosing them within the bounds of a divine narrative that endows redemptive sense: "It was [hence] in order to be able to live that the Greeks had to create these gods from a most profound need" (*The Birth of Tragedy*, 3). That the ancient Greek gods, Nietzsche tells us, justify the suffering of human life because "they themselves live it" alone makes for a sufficient and acceptable theodicy. In tragedy, this theodicy reaches its ultimate expression as art, "for it is only as an *aesthetic phenomenon* that existence and the world are eternally *justified*" (*The Birth of Tragedy*, 5). With the above brief sketch in mind, it is now possible to turn to a consideration of Nietzsche's treatment of law and justice in *The Birth of Tragedy*. One can divide this treatment into three parts. The first and second concern the tragedies of Sophocles and Aeschylus; the third concerns the emergence of Socratism and the death of tragedy.

2. *Nietzsche's discussion of tragedy concentrates on Oedipus, King of Thebes. The Dionysian spaces between Oedipus's Apollonian speeches open up an abyssal irony. Oedipus, icon of legal authority, is an unknowing agent of injustice. The unsolved murder of Oedipus's predecessor, King Laius, has brought pestilence upon Thebes. Oedipus responds by instigating an investigative process that ultimately reveals he himself is Laius's murderer. Worse still, Laius turns out to be Oedipus's father; Oedipus's wife and queen is his mother; his children are also his siblings. The play reveals Oedipus's hidden identity: the Apollonian monarch and figure of order is at the same time a being of Dionysian chaos and perversion. In this fusion of contradictory elements Oedipus epitomizes the tragic hero, predestined to err and to suffer. His Apollonian poetic language dwells in the realm of law but serves to communicate a yawning Dionysian chasm of religiously inspired horror provoked by the terror of lawless and perverse nature. Oedipus remains heroic and his suffering is thereby revealed as the necessary prelude to Dionysian wisdom concerning the human condition. Tragedy is thus the vehicle of a wisdom that transcends the sphere of moral law by fusing religious and poetic elements. Through it the Oedipal legal knot is unravelled to reveal the hubris of a humanity that seeks mastery over nature.*

Sophocles's plays *King Oedipus, Oedipus at Colonus,* and *Antigone* (written between 442–401 BCE) dramatize various themes from the ancient legend of the fall of the royal house of Thebes.[4] Nietzsche's discussion of Sophocles in *The Birth of Tragedy* centres on Oedipus.[5] In these works, Nietzsche argues, Oedipus's Apollonian speech sits within a plot that engulfs him in dreadful irony, as it is revealed that through his actions he has unknowingly piled injustice upon injustice. *King Oedipus* begins in the midst of traumatic events: the gods have visited punishment on Thebes because the wrong caused by the death of Oedipus's father,

4 The first of these to be written was *Antigone.* The three plays, although related, do not actually form a trilogy, although *Oedipus at Colonus* clearly takes up where *King Oedipus* has left off. For a brief and illuminating discussion of these see E.F. Watling's introduction to his complete translation of these works in the Penguin edition of Sophocles, *The Theban Plays.*

5 The story of *King Oedipus* is well known, but it may be just as well to recall its essentials here. Oedipus is the son of King Laius and Queen Jocasta of Thebes. The parents are allowed no joy in their son, however, for the oracle of Apollo predicts that he will one day kill his father and marry his own mother. The king and queen decide to have the child killed in at attempt to thwart this prophecy. They order a shepherd to take Oedipus and leave him to die on a mountainside, his feet held together by a pin that has been driven into his flesh in order to prevent him from having even the smallest chance of survival. The shepherd, however, cannot bring himself to infanticide, so he instead entrusts the child to another. The person who takes Oedipus happens to be the servant of Polybus, King of Corinth. Polybus in turn adopts him as his only child and heir and gives Oedipus his name (which means "Swollen Foot" – testimony of the scarring caused by the pin inserted through the child's feet). As a young man, Oedipus comes to hear of the prophecy concerning him from a messenger of Apollo. Believing Polybus to be his real father he flees Corinth in an attempt to avoid the prophecy being realized, and ends up approaching Thebes. On the road to Thebes Oedipus encounters a man and is plunged into an argument that culminates in the man's death. Thebes is terrorized by the Sphinx, a creature of dreadful power that torments by posing a riddle that none are able to answer. Oedipus solves the riddle and overcomes the Sphinx. Triumphant, he enters Thebes to find a city lacking a monarch due to its king having been killed on a road by an unknown stranger. Thebes, grateful to Oedipus for vanquishing the Sphinx, makes him its new king. He takes the incumbent queen as his wife. After well over a decade of prosperity under the wise rule of Oedipus, who now has children, pestilence and blight befall the city. Oedipus pledges to uncover the offence to the gods that has brought about such misery. Oedipus's uncle, Creon, discovers from the oracle of Apollo that the cause of the pestilence is the murder of King Laius, whose killer has never been brought to justice. As the play unfolds, evidence (including the scars on his feet) inexorably reveals Oedipus himself to be, as the prophet Tiresias tells him, "the cursed polluter of this land" (*The Theban Plays,* 35), the murderer of his own father, Laius. To compound the misery, it follows that the woman he married is his mother and his children are his siblings. Jocasta kills herself in despair; Oedipus blinds himself. Now robbed of all authority, Oedipus awaits the sentence of exile that he himself proposed for Laius's murderer. Banishment, however, does not happen to Oedipus until he is an old man. Even this does not end his suffering, which only death can overcome.

Laius, has yet to be compensated for. The killer has not been identified. Motivated by a combination of a sense of justice and self-interest,[6] Oedipus initiates an investigation in which he himself is the prosecutor and judge. He declares that if the murderer of Laius should reveal himself willingly then the only punishment that shall be meted out will be banishment.[7] Stage by stage, the investigative process reveals that the proud king and saviour of Thebes, a noble and decent man, is also a patricidal murderer. Worse, Oedipus did more than simply kill Laius; he has also committed incest by marrying his own mother. Oedipus, in other words, is criminal perversion of nature personified. His hidden Dionysian identity returns to destroy him, emerging out of the complex train of events he unwittingly sets in motion as murderer, committer of incest, and monarchical defender of justice. Oedipus must now stand to face the punishment he himself has decreed (which he does willingly). Banishment, however, is slow in coming – as *Oedipus at Colonus* reveals – and it is only as an old man, his children now grown, that Oedipus enters exile in the lands of King Theseus. Even then, the old King is not left in peace, but is tormented by the machinations of his sons, who offer no support but instead plan to use both him and the mysterious power of his mortal remains to further their own ends. As a result, Oedipus conceals himself, dying finally in a secret location accompanied only by the trusted King Theseus. In spite of his dreadful suffering, the dying Oedipus overcomes all bitterness concerning his fate. He is "taken without a pang, without grief or agony – a passing more wonderful than that of any other man."[8]

Sophocles, Nietzsche notes, regards his tragic hero as a noble and wise being predestined for error and anguish. It is what Sophocles achieves in his portrayal of this suffering that matters, for by way of it the spectator of the tragedy gains an insight and wisdom that transcends the sphere of moral law that Oedipus has so plainly transgressed. Oedipus's life engenders

> a magical power of blessing that remains effective even beyond his decease. The noble human being does not sin, the profound poet wants to tell us: though every law [*Gesetz*], every natural order, even the moral world may perish through his actions, his actions also produce a higher magical circle of effects which found a new world

6 The killer, Oedipus decides, might decide to add another king to his list in the shape of Oedipus himself (Ibid., 29).

7 Ibid., 31.

8 Ibid., 121.

> on the ruins of the old one that has been overthrown. This is what the thinker [Sophocles] wants to say to us insofar as he is at the same time a religious thinker. As a poet he first shows us a marvellously tied knot of a trial [*Prozessknoten*], slowly unravelled by the judge [*Richter*], bit by bit, for his own undoing. The genuinely Hellenic delight at this dialectical solution is so great that it introduces a trait of superior cheerfulness into the whole work, everywhere softening the sharp points of the gruesome presuppositions of this process [*Prozess*]. (*The Birth of Tragedy*, 9)

The Dionysian and Apollonian elements of the tragedy are, in other words, reflected in the dramatist's religious and poetic aspects. As a religious thinker, Sophocles affirms the supremacy of the heroic and stoical Oedipus over moral and natural law. As a poet, Sophocles invokes the social realm of legality, making use of the ironic effect achieved by constructing a dramatic scenario in which a trial concludes with the indictment of the trial's initiator and judge. The "cheerfulness" Nietzsche notes here is not the kind of thoughtless happiness that springs from mere comfort and freedom from danger. Rather, it is a forced and ironic cheerfulness that arises from having the suffering, violence, and injustice inherent in the world acted out in front of one's eyes in a combination of religious (Dionysian) and poetic (Apollonian) forms. Judge and accused turn out to be the same person, and opposites collide and disperse as the glittering lucidity of poetic Apollonian language is used to portray events that leave a yawning Dionysian chasm of religiously inspired horror in their wake.

Oedipus's heroic status cannot be compromised by the lawlessness of his deeds. As the religious insight confirms, his suffering is the prelude to the revelation of a deeper Dionysian wisdom concerning the reality of the human condition. Nietzsche argues that the second of Sophocles's plays, *Oedipus at Colonus*, repeats this logic, but with the ironic cheerfulness at the dialectical unfolding of events now raised up into an "infinite transfiguration." The now ancient Oedipus, doomed as ever to suffer, "is confronted by the supraterrestrial cheerfulness that descends from the divine sphere and suggests to us that the hero attains his highest activity, extending far beyond his life, through his purely passive posture, while his conscious deeds and desires, earlier in his life, merely led him into passivity. Thus the intricate legal knot [*Prozessknoten*] of the Oedipus fable that no mortal eye could unravel is gradually disentangled – and the most profound joy overcomes us at this divine counterpart of the dialectic" (*The Birth of Tragedy*, 9). The unravelling of the irreconcilably entwined legal tangle of the Oedipus myth reveals forces superior to us, mocking the hubris of human aspiration. As law undoes itself, reality is made manifest. Myth, in the shape of the primordial Dionysian religious insight, indicates the limitations of human aspiration. The more we strive to master our environment, the more we seek to assert our will, the more we run the risk of paying, as Oedipus does, a dreadful price for our attempt. The Apollonian dialogue of *Oedipus at Colonus* now allows for the ironic Dionysian laughter of the gods who look down upon Oedipus's fate to echo through to the conclusion of his life and beyond as their insight transfers itself to us.

We now appreciate the deep irony of Oedipus's fall from grace on a larger scale. Action, it turns out, is paradoxically a kind of inactivity, since struggle, adherence to the law, and the pursuit of earthly justice ultimately achieves nothing. The passivity that announces one's acceptance of fate, it also turns out, pertains to a resonant power that far surpasses all active striving as Oedipus slides peacefully into Hades. This Dionysian wisdom tells us that we must each of us regard our own life of struggle and suffering with Olympian detachment and irony. Such wisdom reveals the artist's mastery of Apollonian and Dionysian elements to be the spontaneous expression of "healing nature" as our ironic sensibilities protect us. The "abyss" may have been revealed, but in such a way that one can walk away from the spectacle relatively undamaged.

3. Sophoclean tragedy demonstrates the limitation and necessity of the conventions that shape social life. Law and authority are necessary conditions of society, but they are also contingent and powerless in the face of elemental Dionysian nature. The world of reason, law, and ethics is eternally threatened by lawless and monstrous forces. Yet these forces are nevertheless constitutive conditions of cultural life. The Oedipus myth exemplifies this insight: in spite of his social eminence, Dionysian mythic forces compel him to his perverse fate. Tragedy reveals a more profound authority than that of earthly law as, cast down, Oedipus begins to give voice to an unnatural Dionysian wisdom of passivity attained through great suffering. Superficially, one can contrast Sophocles's passive ideal of wisdom with Aeschylus's. The latter's Prometheus *explores heroic striving and the dignity of liberation from the power of the gods. Liberation is sacrilegious: Aeschylus, like Goethe after him, envisions a humanity creating culture out of its own impious efforts. Impiety encapsulates the "Aeschylean demand" that the gods, too, be subject to an all-encompassing "justice" in the form of fate, which can be evaded by neither god nor human. In Aeschylus's work gods and poet are revealed as existing in a state of mutual reliance and equality. Thus, Promethean myth and Oedipal drama are closely connected in that they both overturn the conventions of law and right through the affirmation of sacrilegious striving. In this way, tragedy challenges the Apollonian tendency to impose legislation concerning the relations between humanity and gods. Considered in their own terms, the worlds of human and immortal both have right on their side. However, both suffer from being separated. Tragedy reveals the heroic consequences of attempting a reunification of the human and the divine: any such attempt entails misery as a consequence of its striving to break the iron grip of two conflicting and incompatible domains of right.*

By untangling the "legal knot" of the Oedipus story, Sophocles demonstrates both the limitations *and* the necessity of the formally mediated norms and procedures that shape the world of daily social life. One cannot live without law and authority, but law and authority are contingent to the extent that they cannot ultimately protect the individual from the Dionysian reality that threatens to engulf it. Another way of thinking of this matter would be to say that one is unable solely by way of formal representational concepts, which Nietzsche will ally later in *The Birth of Tragedy* with Socratism and science, to articulate the conditions upon which civilization rests. Rather, as we will see, *The Birth of Tragedy* argues that neither law nor even the kind of authority associated with the modern political state can exist without the sanction vouchsafed by the power of myth. In illustrating this, the tragic genre reveals the delicate and temporary nature of human will, reason, law, justice, and morality, for through it these things stand revealed as eternally open to the threat of destruction at the hands of something that is inhuman, lawless, and monstrous but nevertheless a necessary part of life. Oedipus is an illustration of this because whatever he might choose, however he might seek to resist, whatever social eminence he attains, Dionysian mythic elements compel him to be the abomination he is and thereby drag him down. Oedipus cannot avoid the unnatural destiny nature ploughs for the path of his life.

Oedipus, then, is unwillingly and unknowingly anti-natural – and the tragic drama tells of the bringing to light of this knowledge. Tragedy, as we have already noted, refracts this insight about Oedipus's Dionysian reality by way of its Apollonian language. Oedipus, Nietzsche reminds us, challenges nature. By solving the riddle of the Sphinx, Oedipus forces nature to yield its secrets. Oedipus can do so because he himself embodies something resistant to nature that yet erupts out of it, albeit in distorted form. This is because to resist nature one must always already be a breaker of norms, one must contain within oneself something lawless and inhuman that stands also in an alienated and tangential relation to the social realm. This, too, points up the irony of Oedipus's life: as king he must be the upholder of law, the institutional keeper of sacred order; as a Dionysian dramatic figure (signified by his patricide and incest) Oedipus is a law-breaker unfit for command. "Command no more. Obey. Your rule is ended," Oedipus's successor Creon tells him.[9] A person such as this can no longer command, since he now stands outside the world of norms; he has flouted the law. Oedipus's authority is thus not of a kind fit to be endorsed by the norms of social order and legality. His authority is something of a quite different and disturbing kind: that of an alien voice speaking from the other side of those boundaries we cross only at our peril. This alien state of existence, says Nietzsche, illuminates the meaning of Oedipus's unnatural excess: "It is this insight that I find expressed in that horrible triad of Oedipus' destinies: the same man who solves the riddle of nature – that Sphinx of two species – also must break the most sacred natural orders by murdering his father and marrying his mother. Indeed, the myth seems to whisper to us that wisdom, and particularly Dionysian wisdom, is an unnatural abomination: that he who by means of his knowledge plunges nature into the abyss of destruction must also suffer the dissolution of nature in his own person" (*The Birth of Tragedy*, 9). Knowledge of the Dionysian, in other words, comes at great personal cost.

The dramatic retelling of the Oedipus myth tells us that the kind of wisdom needed to solve the riddle of nature must be such that it draws upon what has become unnatural, dreadful, and perverted. As we stand before nature, we, like Oedipus, do so with the intent of mastering it by way of what we believe to be our autonomous Apollonian reason. We seek to solve nature's hidden riddles with acts of will, employing our rational abilities as if they were independent of the world from which they sprang. When we do so, however, we run the risk of losing our culturally individuated identity. For what we really resort to in our contest with nature is something endowed to us by nature itself – something repressed that must return to us in order to empower us in our struggle, but which can only return as something distorted and unnatural. We are pieces of nature and, for this reason, insofar as we succeed in struggling with nature we must also be able to turn against what is natural in ourselves. The riddle-solver that defeats the Sphinx must also be part Sphinx. The price Oedipus has paid in advance for his victory over the Sphinx is that he is himself Sphinx-like, a kind of distorted monstrosity of mixed species, a freak of nature, something intimately connected with and yet inimical to what is natural. The heroic Oedipus embodies this paradox of nature and anti-nature and acts it out in his destiny. Oedipus is the overturning of the order of things incarnate: as husband to his mother he even

9 Ibid., 68.

subverts the iron grip of temporality, standing symbolically in relation to himself as his own father. This subversion perhaps explains the wise Oedipus's passivity: if even time is out of joint, what can be done that will not have impossible consequences?

For Nietzsche, one can draw an insightful contrast between Oedipus's passivity and the attitude of the tragic-heroic Prometheus presented by Sophocles's predecessor, Aeschylus, the so-called "father of tragedy." The Promethean myth is a narrative of heroic striving, of humanity pitted against the gods, the key element of which is the harnessing of fire, the symbol of the cultural development that transports humankind from barbarism to a rudimentary world of culture.[10] Culture means no longer being entirely in thrall to the gods: "that man should freely dispose of fire without receiving it as a present from heaven … struck these primitive and reflective men as sacrilege, as a robbery of divine nature." Such sacrilege poses "the very first philosophical problem" that drives an insoluble barrier between all cultured humanity and the divine, for by way of it human dignity is attained at the cost of a sacrilegious, rebellious break with the natural order of things; culture and divine nature are rendered heterogeneous realms that cannot be joined together in harmonious unity.[11] The individuation one finds at work in the social realm articulates itself in the relation between the mortal and the divine. Through sacrilege, the mortal and divine become separate spheres, each with its own self-contained normative content, existing in a state of contradiction with the other.

10 Aeschylus (525–456 BCE) deals in *Prometheus Bound* with the aftermath of Prometheus's clash with the king of the gods, Zeus (Apollo's father). Prometheus is one of the titans (the earlier ruling generation of gods) who sides with the victorious Zeus in the Battle of the Gods (the Titanomachy). Subsequently, Zeus commands him to create humanity. He fashions pieces of clay into likenesses of the gods and breathes life and intellect into them. Prometheus then feels sorry for these creatures' lack of comfort in the world, so contrary to Zeus's wishes he gives humanity the gift of fire, a gift that allows it to cook, warm itself, and fashion tools. Zeus responds to Prometheus's act by having him chained up for eternity, each day facing the torture of having his divine and consequently self-regenerating liver eaten out of him by an eagle. This is the point at which the play begins. In the play Prometheus, lamenting his earlier support for Zeus in the Titanomachy, presents himself as the benefactor of humankind. Prometheus claims the credit for giving humanity not only fire, but also civilization (the sciences, writing, and the like), and protecting it from Zeus's wrath.

11 Nietzsche, clearly under the influence of Wagner at this stage in his thinking, contends here that this sacrilege is Aryan and contrasts it with the Semitic conception of original sin. The view that ancient Greek culture was Aryan, or even simply European, is of course questionable. Nietzsche's conception of the Aryan and the Semitic, as is well known, undergoes considerable change between *The Birth of Tragedy* and his later works starting from *Human, All Too Human.*

Nietzsche finds that Goethe's poem "Prometheus" captures Aeschylus's conception supremely. Here, the poet is depicted as fashioning humanity in his own image, creating a world whose characters suffer and celebrate but who are also mortals prepared to defy and struggle with the gods as they strive to master the conditions of their own existence through knowledge.[12] Aeschylus and Goethe, Nietzsche argues, envision an active, self-made humanity forging culture out of its own efforts. Goethe's poem depicts a situation in which "Man, rising to Titanic stature, gains culture by his own efforts and forces the gods to enter into an alliance with him because in his very own wisdom he holds their existence and their limitations in his hands" (*The Birth of Tragedy*, 9). This, however, is hardly the most astonishing feature of Goethe's poem. What it encapsulates even more powerfully for Nietzsche is the impious tone with which the ancient writer Aeschylus not only talks of the gods but with which he *addresses* them. Goethe's Prometheus is impious, a being engaged in rebellion against the gods. This captures perfectly "the profoundly Aeschylean demand for *justice* [*der tiefe aeschyleische Zug nach Gerechtigkeit*]. The immeasurable suffering of the bold 'individual' on the one hand and the divine predicament and intimation of a twilight of the gods on the other, the way the power of these two worlds of suffering compels a reconciliation, a metaphysical union – all this recalls in the strongest possible manner the center and main axiom of the Aeschylean view of the world which envisages Moira enthroned above gods and men as eternal justice [*ewige Gerechtigkeit*]" (*The Birth of Tragedy*, 9). The individual who strives necessarily suffers, for this is the price of impiety. Yet, the gods, too, suffer as a consequence of their separation from and struggle with humankind, for this struggle intimates their dependency, twilight, and passing. In terms of Aeschylus's *Prometheus Bound*, the gods are subject to the demands of an all-encompassing justice no less than humanity: fate (Moira) stands in judgement above all else, and has a power that cannot be evaded even by a god. The separated realms of divine and mortal each suffer, and are thereby forced back together again. Goethe, in making manifest this demand for a metaphysical reconciliation between human and divine, illustrates something "astonishing" about Aeschylus. The ancient tragedian, rightly understood, ought to shock us with his impudent daring, for he does nothing less than put "the Olympian world [of the gods] on the scales of his justice [*Gerechtigkeitswagschalen*]." Aeschylus's play asserts that gods and poet

12 The rebellious defiance of Goethe's "Prometheus" is, as Nietzsche notes, well captured by the concluding lines: "Here I sit, forming men / After my own image, / A race, to be the same as me, / To suffer, to cry, / To revel and to rejoice / And not to respect you, / Like me!"

exist in a state of mutual reliance: the gods need the poet just as much as he needs them. The poet consequently celebrates himself as one who stands alongside the gods, for he is god-like in his artistic ability to create and destroy. Aeschylus is akin to Prometheus, for as an artist he too is a kind of titan: "In himself the Titanic artist found the defiant faith that he had the ability to create men and at least destroy Olympian gods, by means of his superior wisdom which, to be sure, he had to atone for with eternal suffering." The poetic realm thereby stands alongside the divine realm as its equal; the titanic poet challenges the gods for supremacy.

Nietzsche notes that the essence of the Promethean myth, which lies in "the necessity of sacrilege imposed upon the titanically striving individual," is profoundly un-Apollonian. This is because "Apollo wants to grant repose to individual beings precisely by drawing boundaries between them and by again and again calling these to mind as the most sacred laws of the world [*die heiligsten Weltgesetze*], with his demands for self knowledge and measure" (*The Birth of Tragedy*, 9). The Apollonian, in other words, seeks to impose legislation concerning the relations between humanity and gods. From the Apollonian perspective, the law-like social order of the everyday, mortal world has its analogue in the divine kingdom of Olympus; the individual can rest content with his or her place in the mortal order of things, since what is sanctioned on earth receives validation from a parallel world of divine social norms. In contrast, the Promethean and the Dionysian share a common attitude of rebellion, revealed in their striving to transgress limits. Aeschylus's Prometheus is, like Oedipus, an epic hero who speaks as a manifestation of Dionysus: "the Prometheus of Aeschylus is a Dionysian mask." At the same time, Nietzsche adds, the "profound demand for justice" he has already noted in Aeschylus "reveals … his paternal descent from Apollo, the god of individuation and of boundaries of justice [*Gerechtigkeitsgrenzen*]." Aeschylus's Prometheus is, like Sophocles's Oedipus, a figure simultaneously Apollonian and Dionysian. He is a being of duality, moving back and forth between Dionysian striving and the Apollonian demand for order and recognition of just borders and regulations governing the relations between humanity and the gods. The difference between the passivity of Oedipus and the active striving of Prometheus is, it turns out, merely apparent. The presentations of Oedipus and Prometheus share a common fundamental "glory" in their ability to encapsulate the duality of Dionysian and Apollonian elements, for each overcomes the difference that separates immortals from mortals and in doing so dazzles us with its daring. Art, in other words, offers the means whereby we can catch a glimpse of the metaphysical synthesis of two irreconcilable and conflicting spheres.

The meaning that the glory of the shared Oedipal and Promethean duality expresses can be summarized by the following proposition: "'All that exists is just and unjust and equally justified in both [*Alles Vorhandene ist gerecht und ungerecht und in beidem gleich berechtigt*]'" (*The Birth of Tragedy*, 9). In other words, when considered in its own terms, each of the incompatible worlds of human and immortal beings has right on its side. The law and justice of the social realm are legitimate within the confines of that realm, and it is the same with regard to the domain of the gods. Both domains, however, suffer by being separated from one another. Each considered alone is a broken-off fragment, a part yearning for reunification within the whole and, through this yearning, condemned to suffer. In tragedy's representation of the heroic figure, be it Oedipus or Prometheus, one witnesses the most heroic of attempts at such a reunification. However, one also witnesses the consequences of such heroism: the hero "in the attempt to transcend the curse of individuation and to become the *one* world-being ... suffers in his own person the contradiction concealed in things, which means he commits sacrilege and suffers." Seeking to overcome the heterogeneity that separates mortal and divine brings about misery because doing so must involve shattering the iron grip of two contending and incompatible domains of right. Myth as it is engaged with by tragic drama thereby stands revealed as the source of redemptive aesthetic insight, for it shows the painful consequences of playing two different and incompatible games of justice.

4. Greek tragedy ultimately destroys itself through Euripides, who subordinates tragedy to Socratic rationalistic fetishism. Tragic insight is replaced by a slovenly optimism that prefigures lazy, self-contented, modern bourgeois culture, and dangerous Dionysian mysteries are smothered beneath intellectual idleness. Socrates is, however, scandalously original in his invention of the "theoretical man," who uses method to expose hidden "laws of nature." In modernity, this method of rational explanation ultimately recoils into contradictory mythology as science encounters the limits of its possible knowledge. To the extent that it is dominated by abstract reason, modern humanity lacks primordial self-understanding. This malaise can be overcome by a rebirth of myth. Mythological sensibilities are cultivated by reflection on the mutual interdependence of art and people, myth and morality, tragedy and state. The account of tragedy in The Birth of Tragedy *now reveals its political aim to be the legitimization of the modern state and its laws in authentic cultural experience rooted in myth. Myth offers an overarching narrative of identity and so overcomes modern fragmentation. The realms of law and politics, like the arts, benefit from the mythical aura that confers legitimacy upon them. Modernity can learn from the ancient Greek State, which partook of a sense of timelessness capable of inoculating it from the infelicities of daily existence. Myth thereby rescues experience from the ravages of modern secular processes. The ills of modernity, it follows, can be cured by metaphysics. Metaphysical ambition is political ambition – the ambition to ground culture, state, law, and morality in a mythically inspired sense of universal justice.*

The ultimate fate of Greek tragedy is ironic, given its redemptive aspect. It destroys itself (*The Birth of Tragedy*, 11). Nietzsche points an accusing finger at the last of the great tragedians, Euripides.[13] The introduction of the spectator on to the stage was, Nietzsche argues, Euripides's most notable achievement. This inaugurates a revolution in the use of language and behaviour. From Euripides's example, the populace learns how to use language in a subtle and sophisticated manner, it learns how to debate: "Through this revolution in ordinary language he made the New Comedy[14] possible. For henceforth it was no longer a secret how ... everyday life could be represented on the stage. Civic mediocrity, on which Euripides built all his political hopes, was now given a voice ... And so the Aristophanean Euripides prides himself on having portrayed the common, familiar, everyday life and activities of the people, about which all are qualified to pass judgement" (*The Birth of Tragedy*, 11). With Euripides tragedy becomes democratized and degraded. The everyday person immersed in their daily concerns is introduced into the drama, and their desire as spectators to sit in judgement on its contents is validated. The consequence of this is a population that "now philosophized, managed land and goods, and conducted lawsuits with unheard of circumspection" – in short, an increasingly articulate, political, and demanding populace, but one turned inexorably away from the terror of Dionysian reality and incapable of Apollonian elegance. Euripides, then, splits the Dionysian element off from tragedy in an attempt "to reconstruct tragedy purely on the basis of an un-Dionysian art, morality

13 Euripides (c. 480–409 BCE) develops the tragic form in a radical new direction, creating characters of greater inner complexity, developing the use of irony, creating a dramatic language that is more realistic and less heroic. Euripides's radicalism extends even to his portrayal of the gods. Other hitherto marginalized aspects of Greek society are also given voice in the drama. Thus, for example, Euripides gives prominent and powerful roles to women and slave characters. It is Euripides's emphasis on the everyday, his endowing of the market-place culture of Greek society with power and validity that Nietzsche objects to, for this empowers the populace.

14 New Comedy dates from around 320–250 BCE. It is associated most with the playwright Menander (c. 342–291 BCE) and later with the Roman Plautus (c. 254–184 BCE). In it, the heroic has completely vanished and the chorus is demoted to a mere band of musical accompaniment. The characters depicted in New Comedy are based on normal people, and are parodic stereotypes whose function is to provoke humour through their predictable foibles. But no moral knowledge or social criticism can be gained from this process.

and world view" (*The Birth of Tragedy*, 12). However, Euripides, Nietzsche adds, is only a kind of "mask." Through him the voice of Socrates speaks, for the destruction of tragedy comes with the invention of a new conception of law that originated in Socratic rationalism. This is the Socratic "supreme law [*oberstes Gesetz*]," which holds that "'To be beautiful everything must be intelligible'" and which reflects in aesthetic terms "the Socratic dictum, 'Knowledge is virtue.'" Cleaving to this canon of belief, Euripides turns on tragedy and, with the demands of this Socratic principle in mind, measures up all the individual parts. The significance of language, character, dramatic structure, and choral music is revised by a critical, "audacious intelligence" that thinks and speaks in Socratic concepts. The Dionysian-Apollonian opposition of Oedipus and Prometheus is replaced by one that opposes Dionysus to Socrates.

Socrates, with his "one great Cyclops eye" (*The Birth of Tragedy*, 14) is straight away characterized by Nietzsche as someone unfit for the proper appreciation of the tragic. His is a monocular conception of the world. The restricted conceptual-rational domain of the Socratic gaze is one in which the fair lunacy of the tragic artist's enthusiasm can never be permitted to exist. He is a person "denied the pleasure of gazing into Dionysian abysses." Tragedy, for Socrates, does not transport us to the realm of Dionysian insight; instead, it is perceived as something that is really rather unreasonable. The world of tragedy is topsy-turvy: things happen without sensible causal reason, things that ought to follow one another in the sequence of events refuse to do so. A world as garish, multiple, and heterogeneous as this can be nothing but detestable for someone of a prudent and rational disposition. It is an art that cannot tell the truth about existence. Nor is its audience a fit one for the inculcation of this truth, for this audience is not one of philosophers but of deviant artists and poets. The victory of Socratic thought is hence the extirpation of the tragic.

Poetry, that key element of tragedy, cannot however be so easily conquered. Nietzsche notes that Socrates's pupil, Plato, may have destroyed his own poems in order to become a follower – but this did not prevent him from turning to poetry, in the form of the written dialogue, when he needed to propound Socratic maxims. In its flouting of "the strict old law of the unity of linguistic form" platonic dialogue became the "tub" on which a "shipwrecked" ancient poetry was floated and saved, albeit now jammed into the narrow space demanded by Socratic stipulations (*The Birth of Tragedy*, 14).[15] Poetry, the hub of tragic insight, is compelled

15 Nietzsche makes the interesting claim here that in Plato lie the origins of the novel form.

by the thought of Socrates, via Plato, into a subordinate position in relation to a dialectically oriented rationality. In Plato's writings, art is kept under the careful surveillance of philosophical thought by being pegged to the "trunk of dialectic" as forcibly and violently as the infant Oedipus's feet are stapled together by their iron pin. From this standpoint, the only permissible art is the art that serves the interests of rationally perceived truth. Platonic dialogue, Nietzsche argues, can now be recognized for what it is: as a kind of enfeebled drama in which the figure of Socrates takes on the role of a "dialectical hero" who defends himself not through heroic action but by way of drab argument. Tragic sentiment recedes, stifled by "the *optimistic* element in the nature of dialectic." This optimism inevitably strikes at tragic sensibility, overgrowing its "regions" and driving it to an act of self-destruction in the shape of "the death-leap into the bourgeois drama [*bürgerliche Schauspiel*]" (*The Birth of Tragedy*, 14).

It is hard to ignore the social and political resonance of Nietzsche's argument. The Platonic model and the dialogue's hero – Socrates – are both proto-bourgeois. The Platonic aesthetic takes on the form of an optimistic and contented middle-class spectacle, one that acts out the maxim "Virtue is knowledge; one sins only out of ignorance; one who is virtuous is happy." In conformity with middle-class consumer mores, ignorance is held to be the source of all sin, knowledge is the equivalent of virtue, and virtue equates to happiness. These three original forms of bourgeois "optimism" seal the fate of tragedy no less than a lazily self-contented optimism compromises the possibility of a regeneration of modern culture. In such a context the virtuous hero is compelled to be a dialectician. The consequence of this is the dragging down of Aeschylus's "transcendental resolution of justice [*transscendentale Gerechtigkeitslösung*]" into a shallow and impudent "principle of 'poetic justice' with its customary *deus ex machine*" (*The Birth of Tragedy*, 14). The dangerous Dionysian mysteries lurking behind existence are thus subverted by the bland comfort of a morally unproblematic divine intentionality – one that in reality is only an extension of the bourgeois inclination to look for unproblematic conclusions that safely reflect existing moral presuppositions. Socratism distorts the understanding of tragedy, asserting in its stead a hollow self-confidence. Viewed from the Platonic standpoint, the chorus now appears as a contingent feature of the drama rather than as its true cause. Even if in Sophocles, Nietzsche notes, one might detect the seeds of the chorus's destruction, Plato's confident, bourgeois optimism finishes the job, driving "*music* out of tragedy with the scourge of its syllogisms." As a result, "the essence of tragedy" is destroyed.

However much Nietzsche may object to Socrates, he remains a figure of awe. Socrates is scandalously original. He goads with his irony and must be credited with the invention of "the type of the theoretical man." A person of this kind is akin to the artist, for the theoretician, too, derives an endless satisfaction from what lies ready at hand in the world. The theoretical person gains pleasure from uncovering what lies around them, but their happiness, such as it is, does not spring only from that. To be theoretical is to derive satisfaction not merely from exposing things but from discovering hidden "laws of nature [*Naturgesetze*]" by way of method. In the fetishistic cleaving to method lies "the unshakeable faith that thought, using the thread of causality, can penetrate the deepest abysses of being, and that thought is capable not only of knowing being but even of *correcting* it. This sublime metaphysical illusion accompanies science as an instinct and leads science again and again to its limits at which it must turn into *art – which is really the aim of this mechanism*" (*The Birth of Tragedy*, 15). Considered in this light, it turns out that Socratic thought cannot ultimately counter or extirpate myth. Rather, it eventually, and in spite of itself, reaffirms it. When rational explanations fall short, myth emerges again as "the necessary consequence, indeed purpose, of science." It is hard not to notice a commonality here between Nietzsche's argument and the thesis presented in *Dialectic of Enlightenment*.[16] Like Nietzsche, Adorno and Horkheimer argue that there is always a point at which rational enlightenment recoils into the very myth it purports to have overcome. In a similar manner, Nietzsche reveals Socrates as "the mystagogue of science." It is Socrates who first casts the net of a science of universal ambition over the world, he who sows the seeds of its hegemonic ambitions. Science becomes hegemonic in the only way it can: by way of rules dressed up as iron laws, even "actually holding out the prospect of the lawfulness of an entire solar system [*Gesetzlichkeit eines ganzen Sonnensystems*]." Socrates, the archetype of the "theoretical optimist," cleaves to an unshakeable faith in the discoverability of the nature of things, in the contention that reality can be encircled and encapsulated by the laws of conceptual thought. This is the illusion that provokes and inspires the spirit of science. This is also the illusion that brings science to grief. The scientist strives for knowledge, but in the end encounters the boundary limit of this knowledge and from this standpoint looks "into what defies illumination." This, for Nietzsche, is the moment at which tragedy returns. "When they see to their horror how logic coils up at these boundaries and finally bites its own tail – suddenly the new

16 See Horkheimer and Adorno, *Dialectic of Enlightenment.*

form of insight breaks through, *tragic insight* which, merely to be endured, needs art as a protection and remedy."[17]

Nietzsche characterizes his own times as having reached this stage of disillusionment with science. Theory has lost its appeal, leaving the bland legacy of the joyless "Alexandrian man," a being who is fundamentally "a librarian and corrector of proofs" devoid of creative impulse (*The Birth of Tragedy*, 19). The answer to this exhausted state is a return to tragedy by way of "true musical tragedy," which can once again inculcate the truth of myth (*The Birth of Tragedy*, 22).[18] *Myth*, we are reminded, lies at the heart of tragedy (*The Birth of Tragedy*, 25). The ability to respond to the mythic element in tragic drama, Nietzsche argues, is what identifies the presence of genuine aesthetic sensibility. One is endowed with the vestiges of this sensibility, or one responds in the Socratic-critical idiom to the tragic. One greets the mythical narrative of tragedy in the spirit of a suspension of disbelief, or one does not. The difficulty of fostering an attitude of acceptance resides in modern culture's historicism. Such is the denuded nature of contemporary sensibility that dusty scholarly understanding is the most likely means of attaining a grasp of the nature of myth (*The Birth of Tragedy*, 23). Modern society, by implication, stands on the edge of the precipice of a headlong fall into the demise of mythical sensibility and this encapsulates its finitude and fragility, for "without myth every culture loses the healthy natural power of its creativity: only a horizon defined by myth completes and unifies a whole cultural movement." Myth, then, is the indispensible condition of true cultural life. All our powers of fantasy, our Apollonian dream inclinations, are saved from their aimless wanderings only by myth. What Nietzsche here calls "the images of myth" are in effect pedagogical tools, signposts of behaviour that guide the young to maturity by giving them a means of interpreting the "struggles" of life. In order to grow up and turn out well we need to mature in myth. Myth makes sense of the world for us in a way that we do not notice but unconsciously acknowledge through our actions and interpretations of our environment. Myth is

17 Nietzsche here reveals his early adherence to the thought of Kant and Schopenhauer: "The extraordinary courage of *Kant* and *Schopenhauer*" has brought about "the victory over the optimism concealed in the essence of logic – an optimism that is the basis of our culture" (*The Birth of Tragedy*, 18). Such optimism, Nietzsche claims, thought of space, time, and causality as universal and "entirely unconditional laws [*gänzlich unbedingte Gesetze*]." To follow Kant and Schopenhauer and step beyond this naive conception of the universal presages an era where tragic culture is again possible, where wisdom is once again more valued than science.

18 In *The Birth of Tragedy* the path of this return is delineated by the music of Wagner. Like so much else in this work, Nietzsche is to change his mind about this, too.

our great teacher. Myth serves as a means of grounding law. Modern life, it follows, is not so safely removed from myth as its scientific self-image might suggest, but rather stands increasingly and unconsciously threatened by its loss. The need for myth cannot be gainsaid: "Even the state knows no more powerful unwritten laws [*ungeschriebnen Gesetze*]" than the "mythical foundation" that secures its connection with religion (*The Birth of Tragedy*, 23). The modern state rests on primeval mythical representations, and myth now stands revealed as underpinning its legal-juridical structure. It is not written statutes that characterize the essence of modern government, as its liberal-democratic ethos tends to suggest, but rather the unwritten mythical presuppositions that form the "fundament" upon which these laws are inscribed. What is written and codified as law is, in this way, interpretable as an unconscious commentary on an unacknowledged teaching of the mythic principles and signs that ground cultural self-understanding.

Contrast the mythically literate person with the "abstract man, untutored by myth" and one is confronted by a kind of spiritual lawlessness and emptiness: "abstract education; abstract morality [*Sitte*]; abstract law [*Recht*]; the abstract state" (*The Birth of Tragedy*, 23). Such a person is a symptom of a culture that has forsaken its relation to the sacred in favour of bleached Socratic reason. In a culture of this kind, the creative imagination roves unhindered by native myth and consequently lacks the orientation that is endowed by having the sense of a fixed and holy founding place in the order of things. The abstract man lacks a sense of being at home in the world he inhabits. This is a person deprived of a neat fit with their environment; no sense of primordial place grounds their self-understanding. Lacking an inner resource of meaning, the inhabitant of this kind of abstract culture will, Nietzsche notes, seek mythic satisfaction elsewhere, namely by feeding "wretchedly on all other cultures." Modernity is exposed as parasitic. Ours is the era of "unsatisfied modern culture." A derelict and sterile cultural space has emerged out of the triumph of the Socratic project to destroy myth and replace it with the hegemony of the abstract concept. The "all-consuming" contemporary craving for knowledge, "the assembling around one of other cultures ... what does all this point to, if not the loss of myth, the loss of the mythical home, the mythical maternal womb?"[19] The consequence of cleaving to fetishistic and illusory Socratic rationality is that it leaves us in a state of

19 Let us merely note in passing that such a lack could point to the fact of colonial expansion, to the historically decisive European drive to colonize and exploit other cultures, of which the organizing of other cultural domains into convenient dishes for consumption is one telling symptom. One might add that Nietzsche himself, a consumer of Indian

nomadism.[20] Worldly modernity thereby emerges as something destructive and decentred. It is obsessed by a desire for knowledge, wanderlust, an idolizing of the present, and yet unable to think beyond the confines of the spirit of its own times.

For Nietzsche, the possibility of a rebirth of German myth in modernity begins by affirming the fundamental relatedness of what appear to be autonomous spheres. The fact that Greek tragedy and culture died as a consequence of the Socratic tearing apart of the Dionysian-Apollonian duality makes one duty bound to engage in "serious reflection" on the interdependence of art and people, myth and morality, tragedy and state (*The Birth of Tragedy*, 23). With this claim, the spheres of aesthetics and ethnicity, mythology and values, tragedy and political governance are all conjoined. Nietzsche's ruminations on the nature of the Dionysian and Apollonian, on tragic drama, heroism, the tensions between divine and human, nature and culture, are now revealed to serve an explicit political purpose. All these things revolve around the problem of delineating the authentic cultural conditions that can serve to legitimate the authority of the state and its laws by grounding them in an authentic mythical cultural experience. Thinking in terms of myth, as the Greeks of the tragic era did and as Nietzsche urges us to here, means to think in terms of an overarching narrative of identity in relation to which one compulsively relates one's experiences. The act of thinking this relation overcomes the threat of fragmentation posed by the peculiarly bleached individuation that erupts from Socratic rationalism, reincorporating individual experience into a timeless and universal whole that is capable of once again enriching and validating it. The Greeks interpreted all events in terms of mythical narrative: for them everything was related to the eternal and in this way was endowed with mysterious timelessness. The domains of law and politics no less than the arts can partake of the mythical aura that confers legitimacy in this way. The invocation of their relation to myth endows them with meaning. The Greek state, Nietzsche tells

religious and philosophical thought as a result of his youthful love of Schopenhauer, is no less prey to this.

20 Historical thought, too (which is an ironic consequence of Socratic rational absolutism) destroys the mythical grasping of the environment one inhabits. With historical as opposed to mythical consciousness comes the denigration of the tragic works that dwell in the proximity of myth. In conceptualizing itself historically, the secular mind initiates "a break with the unconscious metaphysics of its previous existence, together with all its ethical consequences. Greek art and pre-eminently Greek tragedy delayed above all the destruction of myth. One had to destroy tragedy, too, in order to be able to live away from the soil of home, uninhibited, in the wilderness of thought, custom, and deed" (*The Birth of Tragedy*, 23).

us, dipped itself into this sense of timelessness as a means of unburdening itself from the taint of the infelicities of daily existence. The same principle holds no less for the national-political structures of today: "any people ... is worth only as much as it is able to press upon its experiences the stamp of the eternal" (*The Birth of Tragedy*, 23). Metaphysical ambition is the precondition of political and cultural endurance. To eternalize one's experiences via myth is to retrieve them from the ravages wrought by modern secular processes and ground them in a divine justice. De-secularization, which is the reinvigoration of myth, testifies to the "unconscious inner conviction of the relativity of time" that exposes "the true, that is, metaphysical, meaning of life." Modernity, it follows, can be overcome only by metaphysics. Metaphysical ambition is political ambition, an ambition concerning the interrelation of a culture, state, law, and morality held together by a rejuvenated, mythically inspired awareness of the universal.

The Birth of Tragedy, then, calls upon Dionysian myth to ground Apollonian individuated social life as a cure to modernity's travails. In this way the Apollonian-Dionysian duality is affirmed as a potent social force. The consequence of this affirmation will be a culture of aesthetic sensibility that combines Apollonian grace with Dionysian authenticity. With this, the emptiness of modern existence is swept away, leaving the suffering that necessarily comes from individuated social life justified by a redemptive aesthetic governed by what Nietzsche calls the "eternal law of justice [*Gesetze ewiger Gerechtigkeit*]" (*The Birth of Tragedy*, 25). This law imposes a rigorous, interconnected proportionality that dictates that every Dionysian moment of terror-ridden awareness must be compensated for by a redemptive Apollonian moment of energizing transfiguration. The violent "Dionysian subsoil of the world" upon which Apollonian culture rests can in this way be contained, retained, and even cultivated. In turn, mythical justification is bestowed upon a now authentic culture in payment for its faithful cleaving to Dionysian wisdom. Social order, the state, and the life of the individual are all endowed with an Apollonian aesthetic grandeur that signals the hidden presence of the Dionysian reality that legitimizes them.

5. *Nietzsche's continuing interest in the interrelation between justice, myth, culture and the Alexandrian consciousness of modernity is revealed in the second of the* Untimely Meditations. *History, Nietzsche agues, must be assessed in terms of its value for "life." History is necessary for existence and it can liberate us from the tyranny of past beliefs, but a surfeit is debilitating. Modernity exhibits all the symptoms of the malaise caused by such a surfeit. The creativity made possible by existing in the essentially "unjust" suprahistorical condition that is the source*

from which all just and unjust deeds spring is impossible for it. Thus weighed down, modernity has become self-negating and uncreative. What is needed to counter this is a history infused with art, one capable of criticizing itself and so serving the creative unhistorical forces that are necessary for culture. There are three types of history, "monumental," "antiquarian," and "critical." An analysis of the first two reveals why the third is needed.

Nietzsche's obsession with Apollo and Dionysus does not appear to last long.[21] In the four essays that make up the *Untimely Meditations* – the first of which is published in 1873, one year after *The Birth of Tragedy*, the last in 1876 – the Apollonian is mentioned only once,[22] the Dionysian not at all. However, in "On the uses and disadvantages of history for life" (*Untimely Meditations*, II), Nietzsche returns soon enough to questions concerning the interrelation between justice, culture, myth, and the Alexandrian consciousness of modernity. Indeed, the second of the *Meditations* can in some respects be read as a supplement to the text on tragedy. Just as *The Birth of Tragedy* concludes by affirming the legitimacy of the timeless empowerment of myth-inspired art as a curative for modern cultural and political travails, so the meditation on history develops the same thematic strategy of opposing the timeless creative desire of artistic creativity to the uncreative pathology of modern critical-historical consciousness (*Untimely Meditations*, II, 7). The general shape of the argument of the second meditation is simple enough. The consequences of history oppose those of art. History is a necessary component of "life,"[23] but a surfeit of it is damaging. Where art enhances existence by casting a saving veil of illusion over it, Apollonian-style, history exposes, demythologizes, and thereby destroys. Only a history somehow transformed into a kind of redeeming art would be able to preserve and encourage the creative instincts so necessary to a thriving culture. Modernity has arrived at the point where it suffers from its sense of history in a way that entraps it, forcing it into an attitude of self-abnegation.[24] The historical sense thus presents modernity with the troubled vision of a world

21 Dionysus is to return in Nietzsche's late works, but this return takes place within a radically different framework.

22 See *Untimely Meditations*, II, "On the uses and disadvantages of history for life," 10.

23 Nietzsche does not bother to define this term and nor will I. Suffice it to say that the notion of "life" as it is used in this essay is better regarded as a point of departure for argument than as pertaining to a definite and easily summarized concept.

24 History tells the present historical age of great past eras that were unhistorical and yet achieved more culturally than it can imagine achieving itself, e.g. the Greeks. To be born in the time of modern historical knowledge, in contrast to the unhistorical world of the Greeks, is hence to find oneself trapped in a kind of premature old age.

without future heirs. The only thing to do to overcome this is to expose the historical sense to the sharpness of its own critical edge as a prelude to its transfiguration at the hands of art (*Untimely Meditations*, II, 8).

Nietzsche, oddly perhaps at first glance, arrives at his conclusion by way of an account of the nature of happiness. The striving for happiness allows all forms of living being to cleave to existence.[25] Being happy means being unfettered by past memories, for memories have a nasty habit of interfering with the possibility of contentment (*Untimely Meditations*, II, 1). The person least fettered by memory will thus most likely be the most content; but every judgement such a person makes will necessarily involve him or her committing "injustice [*Ungerechtigkeit*]." To be "unjust" in the sense used here clearly means being unjust to one's environment – it is an epistemic injustice of interpretive violence. Questions of truth and questions of justice are thereby conjoined. Nietzsche (prefiguring ruminations developed in his mature thought) argues that a kind of healthy state of unreflective endorsement of one's beliefs makes life possible and even enhances it. Being seized by an all-consuming passion, for example, shatters the boundaries of conventional life; it overturns norms by drawing one into the "unjust condition [*ungerechteste Zustand*]" of blinkered ingratitude toward the past that made one what one is. This condition is "unhistorical, anti-historical through and through," yet paradoxically it is also "the womb not only of the unjust but of every just deed too [*der Geburtsschooss nicht nur einer ungerechten, sondern vielmehr jeder rechten That*]." Without the injustice accompanying decision, no artist would be able to create, no commander win in battle, no nation attain freedom. Thus, social order – the domain of responsibility, fairness, and justice – rests upon an unarticulated and violent injustice that represses memory and the bite of conscience. Unhistorical action is creative but amoral: a "blindness and injustice in the soul of the doer [*Blindheit und Ungerechtigkeit in der Seele des Handelnden*]" is the precondition of all great historical deeds (*Untimely Meditations*, II, 1). But such injustice is creative. Nietzsche now gives this unjust condition a name: it is the "suprahistorical." History, it follows, is permeated and driven by suprahistorical forces.

Suprahistorical injustice may be a repository of great potential, since it is a precondition of all genuine action,[26] but it is problematic, too. It does violence to the world of experience, suppressing knowledge not

25 This is a view that Nietzsche will come to reject in his mature writings.

26 Clearly, there are many examples of human doing that do not preclude historical states of mind. For Nietzsche, however, such doings are nothing more than the thoughtless articulation of norms. Properly understood, a genuine action (a deed) is something that

amenable to it. History, whatever its dangers, can correct this tendency, for it can function as curative and enhancement to suprahistorical excess (*Untimely Meditations*, II, 2). Nietzsche distinguishes between three types of history, each of which can either enhance life or bring about its degeneration: "monumental," "antiquarian," and "critical." The value of the monumentally conceived past lies in its implication that since greatness was once possible it is possible again. Yet monumental history does unutterable violence to the past, wiping away the myriad differences that distinguish historical periods, and erasing the essential contingency underlying historical development. Monumental history is selective history. It can inspire fanaticism and stupidity and is susceptible to becoming the history of the tyrant, thereby marginalizing the path of genuine creativity that for Nietzsche is at the heart of living culture. Antiquarian history is a kind of curative to monumentalism (*Untimely Meditations*, II, 3). Antiquarian understanding regards itself as the extension of a living tradition. It is instinctively communitarian, imbuing existence with a feeling of justification derived from a sense of belonging. At the same time, the antiquarian mind lacks any sense of the differences of value and proportion necessary if the elements that make up the past are to be done "genuine justice [*wahrhaft gerecht*]" (*Untimely Meditations*, II, 3). The bad consequence of the antiquarian attitude is its cultivation of a stifling reverence that runs counter to the demands of life. These shortcomings tell us why we need critical history.

6. Critical history is a curative for the shortcomings of other historical attitudes. It exposes the contingency at work in past societies and overturns the authority of tradition. When critical history speaks, however, the voice of an objective justice is not really what is heard. What speaks is, rather, life, which judges in a manner that "is always unmerciful, always unjust." Used in this way, critical history does the violent bidding of life, liberating the present from the past through an act of nihilistic judgement. The revelation of the essential contingency of past human existence opens the way to new experiments of living. Life needs to remember no less than it needs, on occasion, to forget. We are beings of second nature, bundles of the accumulated propensities and errors of our ancestors. This second nature makes life possible, but it can also hinder its development and thriving. Critical knowledge thus bespeaks life's requirement that the impedances of second nature need on occasion to be overcome. Such overcoming has a limit, however, since it is impossible to divest ourselves of all prejudices. Hence, what is cultivated is a

---

does not conform to norms but steps beyond them: it is creative and, in the case of the genuine philosopher, legislative. See chapters 3 and 4.

renewed second nature capable of transforming, incorporating, or negating the nature that precedes it.

With Nietzsche's discussion of critical history, we enter the realm of the court of law. It is not always the case, Nietzsche notes, that the suprahistorical blanking out of the past is good for us. Sometimes it is necessary to dissolve those aspects of the past that act as a fetter and impedance to the future. This is achieved by taking what one wishes to overcome and "bringing it before the tribunal [*Gericht*], scrupulously examining it and finally condemning it; every past, however, is worthy to be condemned – for that is the nature of human things: human violence and weakness have always played a mighty role in them" (*Untimely Meditations*, II, 3). Critical history exposes an essential frailty and contingency at work in past events and societies. In effect, it overturns the authority of tradition, for traditions are revealed as accidents that can have no ultimate claim upon us, for even given the same starting point things could have turned out differently.

Critical history thus sits like a judge presiding over a court that has put the entire past in the dock. However, Nietzsche comments, this is not what it might seem. Critical history does not proffer a justice that would seek a fair and objective ruling. When critical history speaks, a "dark, driving power that insatiably thirsts for itself" can be heard. This is the harsh voice of *life* and its ruling "is always unmerciful, always unjust [*immer ungnädig, immer ungerecht*], because it has never proceeded out of a pure well of knowledge; but in most cases the sentence would be the same even if it were pronounced by justice itself. 'For all that exists is *worthy* of perishing. So it would be better if nothing existed.'" Critical history thus does the violent bidding of life, liberating the present from monumental and antiquarian attitudes through nihilistic judgement. Boundary stones can now be toppled, new ways of living experimented with, and new self-understandings cultivated. If it is to create, life needs at times to remember as much as it needs to forget:

> [T]his same life that requires forgetting demands a temporary suspension of this forgetfulness; it wants to be clear as to how unjust [*wie ungerecht*] the existence of anything – a privilege, a caste, a dynasty, for example – is, and how greatly this thing deserves to perish. Then its past is regarded critically, then one takes the knife to its roots, then one cruelly tramples over every kind of piety. It is always a dangerous process ... For since we are the outcome of earlier generations ... of their aberrations, passions and errors, and indeed of their crimes; it is not possible to free oneself wholly from

> this chain … The best we can do is confront our inherited and hereditary nature with our knowledge of it, and through a new, stern discipline combat our inborn heritage and implant in ourselves a new habit, a new instinct, a second nature, so that our first nature withers away. It is … always a dangerous attempt because it is so hard to know the limit to denial of the past and because second natures are usually weaker than first … But here and there a victory is nonetheless achieved, and for the combatants, for those who employ critical history for the sake of life, there is even a noteworthy consolation: that of knowing that this first nature was once a second nature and that every victorious second nature will become a first. (*Untimely Meditations*, II, 3)

It becomes clear from this passage that Nietzsche regards us as creatures defined by our inheritance, creatures of second nature. We are articulations of the accumulated tendencies, sensibilities, and errors of judgement of our forebears. This ensemble of characteristics, while making life possible for us, since we ultimately originated in them, can also obstruct future thriving. Consequently, we are driven by the demands of life to counter what impedes it with critical knowledge. In our critical assassination of the past we stand as representatives of burgeoning life. One should note, however, the peril that critical liberation from the past can engender. We can shatter the past's grip on us through critical history, Nietzsche argues, but by turning on our own origins in this way we question the very conditions that gave rise to our kind. This is a perilous thing to do since such conditions might also be necessary for our continuance. It is for this reason that, ultimately, critical historical understanding makes impossible demands, for we cannot abandon all the prejudices that have gone to making us the kinds of creatures we are. Consequently, the best that can be done is to cultivate a new second nature that supplants and thereby overcomes the nature that precedes it.[27] At the same time, the danger of critical history is that it cultivates a pompous self-importance that does its own specific violence to the past and present and thereby fosters spiritual vacuity.

27 It is hard not to notice in this discussion of history attitudes that will come to have an increasing prominence in Nietzsche's mature philosophy. The human being is already conceived of as the as yet *unfixed* animal, to recall a phrase from *Beyond Good and Evil*. We do not have a determined nature but are second nature through and through. This means that we are first and foremost creatures of culture and cultivation.

7. History weighs down modernity with scientific knowledge: culture is no longer lived but studied. The consequences of this are spiritual vacuity and modern barbarism. Modernity's extensive accumulation of historical knowledge of past traditions and morals looks like cultural wealth. It encourages modern society to envisage itself to be the most self-aware, objective, and just age there has ever been. The essential contingency underlying human fate is thereby ignored and a false sense of justice with regard to the past is cultivated. Genuine justice with regard to the past is antithetical to modern attitudes. Justice cannot be deduced; it overwhelms and is obeyed because its commands are unconditional. An uncompromising "will to justice" makes itself manifest as a desire for truth. Justice is thus the highest virtue. It is also the most susceptible to corruption. In the scholar, for instance, a powerful sense of justice can be placed in service of the professional self-advancement that panders to conformism. The past is denigrated as a mere means, as something in service of the glorification of the unreflective present. Modern history is thus prey to becoming "bad mythology" in so far as it is guided by an uncritical desire to subject the past to bold generalizations. Genuine history, Nietzsche argues, is not a matter of generating "laws" from empirical observation (the pursuit of a false objectivity) but rather the art of interpretation. It must be an extension of "the vigour of the present," not an apparently detached and uninvolved indifference dressed as "objectivity." Genuine history speaks in tones akin to that of an ancient oracular voice. It expresses passionate involvement and has an authenticity revealed by its expressing anew the universally recognized conditions of human existence. Genuine history does not judge past failings; it indicts the present's shortcomings and so exposes the false consciousness of its own times. With this, the divine justice of The Birth of Tragedy *is again affirmed. Greek culture, properly understood, calls us to acknowledge the paucity of the present by serving as a paradigm for what culture can be and how it can be created. The past of Ancient Greece teaches us how to live now by example and so serves as an exemplar for the rejuvenation of tired modernity. With this insight, history, as a conduit conveying the inspiration set by example, can be put to work in the interests of life. The second meditation thereby affirms the metaphysical revelation of truth and justice celebrated in* The Birth of Tragedy. *It is the rejection of this metaphysics and the search for a new conception of justice that most characterizes Nietzsche's mature thought.*

Nietzsche situates his account of critical history in the context of modernity. History has become "the science of universal becoming" (*Untimely Meditations*, II, 4) and we are weighed down by this scientific knowledge. The consequence of this is that we moderns are creatures of hitherto unknown contradictoriness. The content is there but the form is lacking. We are "cultured" internally, but not externally: our culture is not *lived* but *theorized.* Today, Nietzsche notes, "our modern culture is not a living thing ... it is not a real culture at all but only a kind of knowledge of culture." We are becoming ever more inwardly oriented, more "subjective." The view expressed in *The Birth of Tragedy*, which holds modern to mean being a looter of the cultures of other eras, is here reiterated. We cram our world with the artifacts, customs, traditions, and achievements of other ages and societies because "we moderns have nothing whatever of our own" (*Untimely Meditations,* II, 4). An obsession with history testifies to spiritual emptiness. The natural response to the plenitude of stimuli that modern life offers is superficiality, and this is the essence of modern barbarism. Genuine culture, Nietzsche tells us, is a unity of form and content that modernity singularly lacks – a fact exemplified in Germany, where all is conformity to the contemporary economic-industrial demand for efficiency and ease.[28] The modern life is spiritually attenuated and glutted with artefacts borrowed or pilfered from the histories of others. The danger posed by this surfeit lies in the fact that it can be mistaken for wealth. The possession of a vast stock of knowledge concerning past practices and values misleads modernity into thinking "that it possesses the rarest of virtues, justice, to a greater degree than any other age" (*Untimely Meditations,* II, 5). We become inclined to see ourselves as morally superior to the past since we have picked up, used, and incorporated so much of it: as we look back on the past we tend to *look down* on it, too.

The notion that modern humanity is morally superior to the past because it is more just comes from the celebrated "objectivity" that is the hallmark of contemporary critical historical practice. Is it, Nietzsche asks, fair to argue that this "well known 'objectivity'" endows the modern person with "the right to call himself strong, that is to say *just* [*gerecht*], and just in a higher degree than men of other ages?" Can it be the case that this objectivity, such as it is, has its origin in an increased "need and demand for justice [*Gerechtigkeit*]?" (*Untimely Meditations,* II, 6). Certainly, the complacent belief that one is better than others is a dangerous belief. After all, the fortunate person who feels themselves superior to others less fortunate is probably more stupid than not. Such a person has

28 If one takes a walk "through a German city – compared with the distinct national qualities displayed in foreign cities, all the conventions here are negative ones, everything is colourless, worn out, badly copied, negligent, everyone does as he likes but what he likes is never forceful and well considered." This is a world dominated by the rule of haste and a general addiction to comfort and conformity. Nietzsche then interprets the celebrated German national characteristic of "subjectivity" as a symptom of the overwhelming power of external social forces rather than as a sign of "inner" personality (*Untimely Meditations,* II, 4).

an attitude that betrays a lack of understanding of the moral and amoral luck of life. One's good fortune, after all, is a matter of contingency, not God-given destiny. A person who is highly valued because of their sporting prowess, their financial acuity, or their intellectual and communicative skills, does not merely need to be fortunate enough to be born with the propensity for their prowess. They need to be fortunate enough to be born into a place and time where these skills are valued – and valued in a way that is amenable to them, given their other character traits. Such a person also needs to be born into a situation (in fact, really a kind of ensemble of situations consisting of particularities of social class and generalities of theological, secular, and political order) that enables these skills to be developed and exploited. A person's erroneous belief in their superiority over others signals a failure to register the necessary contingency at work in life, and has the consequence of making them continually worse. For Nietzsche, modernity, which is convinced of its moral superiority, is no different from such a deluded individual. The delusion that we moderns command a superior sense of justice will cause us to become ever "more unjust [*ungerechter*]" than we already are. Justice, Nietzsche now asserts, is the most highly valued of virtues, but it is not a virtue associated with a cold, disinterested objectivity: "In truth, no one has a greater claim to our veneration than he who possesses the drive to and strength for justice [*Gerechtigkeit*].[29] For the highest and rarest virtues are united and concealed in justice as in an unfathomable ocean that receives streams and rivers from all sides and takes them into itself. The hand of the just man [*des Gerechten*] who is empowered to judge no longer trembles when it holds the scales; he sets weight upon weight with inexorable disregard for himself, his eye is unclouded as it sees the scales rise and fall, and his voice is neither harsh nor tearful when he pronounces the verdict" (*Untimely Meditations*, II, 6). Nietzsche here offers a rather idealized and sentimentalized image of a legal proceeding in which the judgement moves from a state of venial "doubt" to strict "certainty," where tolerant indulgence is supplanted by an impersonal demand concerning what action is warranted. The rare virtue of generosity gives way to the even rarer demand that one be just. To be a creature of the virtues means to be endowed not merely with the propensity to pursue a virtue, but also with the driving force of discipline sufficient to fulfil the demands that such a pursuit places upon one. The just person is a kind of point of intersection of virtues that, in

29 It is interesting to note here that consistently Nietzsche conceives of even our virtues in terms of the concept of the drive (*Trieb*). This is a notion that becomes increasingly important in his writings.

their coming together, endow him or her with authority. Such a person judges with what comes most closely to an attitude of selflessness, and it is this that makes for the authority of justice. This authority springs from something mysterious and impenetrable, it is an "unfathomable sea" that in its combination of a multiplicity of sources into an uncanny unity defies analysis and inspires a sense of awe.[30] As with Nietzsche's conception of the eternal justice of tragedy, here, too, justice depends upon something that cannot be deduced but is rather simply obeyed due to its capacity to overwhelm.

Such justice, it hardly needs to be added, is necessarily turned even against the one who sits in judgement. Selflessness of this kind is not the same as so-called value-neutral "objectivity," for it entails sacrifice and therefore involvement on the part of the judge. To "hold the scales" and lay weight upon weight in an inexorable manner means to refuse to be swayed in one's deliberations, even by self-interest, for in doing so one must place one's own identity on trial to see if it is equal to the task of seeking justice. The just human being, Nietzsche adds unsurprisingly, is destined for torture as a result of this. To be just is to be confronted by the demands of an "impossible virtue" that comes from being "the most *venerable* exemplar of the species of man." Desiring justice means desiring truth above all things, but not in the form of a detached and "cold, ineffectual knowledge, but as a regulating and punishing judge; truth not as the egoistic possession of the individual, but as the sacred right [*heilige Berechtigung*] to overturn all the boundary-stones of egoistic possessions." The demand for truth thus stakes its claims in terms of *entitlement*. The one who seeks truth seeks a kind of justice whose legitimacy

30 Lawrence Lampert notes that this passage from the second *Untimely Meditation* both invokes the notion of a "solitary few" who are called to the task of fulfilling justice through their deeds and contrasts them with "their look-alikes, *fanatics* whose will to justice is not guided by the strength of judgement that reveals the just to them" (*Nietzsche and Modern Times*, 290). At this point, Lampert argues, the text attains its most profound level of discussion: if all justice rests on a foundation of strength of judgement and the truly just person's identity is only guaranteed by their strength of judgement being guided by truth, by what means does one uncover this truth and thereby "separate Judge from Fanatic?" Lampert additionally comments that here Nietzsche is obviously "speaking of a justice grander than the application of some already present code of just and unjust; he is speaking of the giving of such codes, the bringing of a new good and evil or good and bad, the founding act of the philosophic legislator … The highest exemplars desire truth in order to legislate; truth provides the sacred legitimation of their justice." This quote makes manifest the link between a text that is, Lampert says, "pre-Nietzschean" (291) in so far as it lacks a compelling account of justice and truth and is, instead, content to invoke these notions rather than analyse them, and the mature thinker who embarks upon rethinking philosophy as a legislative enterprise in concrete, naturalistic terms – see the account of this in chapter 5.

springs from redefining the markers that map out the space of a possessive, subjective self-interest. The judge's desire for truth is evidence of an uncompromising "will to justice," and it is this will that grounds its claim to legitimacy. It is only to the extent that the truthful person has the absolute will to be just, Nietzsche argues, that anything can be deemed "great" in the all-pervasive and thoughtless glorification of the striving for truth that is fashionable in contemporary society. The value of wanting truth, in other words, resides in the fact "that it has its root in justice [*das seine Wurzel in der Gerechtigkeit hat*]" (*Untimely Meditations*, II, 6). Truth and justice are therefore conjoined in the second of the *Untimely Meditations* in a manner reminiscent of the Socratic dialectical binding of knowledge, virtue, and justice to one another. Because of its essential link to truth, justice is the most valuable of virtues, of greater worth than magnanimity – but it is also the rarest. It is also the most liable to being corrupted by undesirable forces masquerading under its banner. Justice is consequently always a complex matter, since sorting out the truthful person from the charlatan is never going to be easy.

The "justice drive [*Gerechtigkeitstriebe*]" alone is not sufficient for truthfulness or justice to be realized (*Untimely Meditations*, II, 6). Taken singly, a drive of this kind can lead to distorted narrowness and fanaticism. It needs to be balanced by a sense of judgement. Modern scholarship manifests this danger. When implanted into the "historical virtuoso," the "stern and great sense of justice," which is the kernel of "the so-called drive to truth," does not, it turns out, cultivate the most just and fair-minded of people. To be sure, the historical scholar has a kind of objectivity, Nietzsche agrees. However, this kind of objectivity is akin to the passivity of a "sounding board" that resonates sympathetically with its environment. This person's sense of justice is unappealing because it is merely passive. No moving around of boundary stones, no challenging of the dominant norms of the time, is going to spring from scholars of this kind. At best, they are tolerant of their own times and harshly condemnatory of past societies and cultures. This is the image of scholar as arch conformist. Their aim is to be professionally (and "*profoundly*") successful, and conformity marks the best path to success. The modern historian as presented here takes on the mantle of an easily swayed courtroom judge. This is someone who fails in their duty because they passively reflect popular opinion: "the will to be just is there, as is the pathos attending the office of judge: but all their verdicts are false, for approximately the same reason as the verdicts of ordinary court juries are false" (*Untimely Meditations*, II, 6). Conformity of this kind reinforces popular prejudice by attacking the past, and endorsing thoughtless self-affirmation as people rest content in a firm belief in their unproblematic superiority over all that has been. The historian of this type is revealed as a lackey who serves contemporary fashion and superficial opinion.

Being just when it comes to addressing history involves us overcoming the prejudice that we are superior. It also requires we reject the view that the historian is simply a passive mirror reflecting the past. The view that it is possible for a person to reflect things as they exist in themselves is mere "mythology, and bad mythology at that" (*Untimely Meditations,* II, 6). The past does not snap photographic self-portraits and present them ready-made to the scholar for regurgitation in a book. When one becomes absorbed in something, as any writer does, historical veracity is seldom at stake. The modern historian is really a kind of dramatist who tells a story that weaves the heterogeneous threads of the past together to make a sort of artistic narrative. Any narrative seeks to explain past events in terms of a unified structure, but the meaning proffered by historical narrative is an illusion: a unity is artificially imposed on the parts. The "historical virtuoso" is not very different from the great majority of us in this. We are all driven by a tendency "to think of all things in relation to all others and weave the isolated event into the whole: always with the presupposition that if a unity of plan does not already reside in things it must be implanted into them. Thus man spins his web over the past and subdues it, thus he gives expression to his artistic drive – but not to his drive towards truth or justice. Objectivity and justice have nothing to do with one another [*Objectivität und Gerechtigkeit haben nichts miteinander zu thun*]" (*Untimely Meditations,* II, 6). A history that makes bold generalizations uttered from the standpoint of an apparently disinterested objectivity is a history that cannot teach us to be just with regard to the past. What one learns from history does not come in the form of general maxims that are to count as "laws" generated from empirical analysis, as is the case with the natural sciences. Laws cannot be gleaned from the study of history. The value of history lies in its ability to transform a taken-for-granted, everyday theme in the world of historical experience and make out of it "a comprehensive symbol" that reveals "in the original theme a whole world of profundity, power and beauty." History, understood and practised in this way, is a kind of art of amplification and, like the art of Greek tragedy, its justice and truth content lies in its redemptive power.

What history requires, Nietzsche therefore claims, is an artist's objectivity – capable of combining a sense for the just and the true with the kind of aesthetic sensibility necessary to serve the interests of life. To engage with the past fruitfully one must be creative rather than merely critical. A genuinely fruitful interpretation of the past is an extension of "*the vigour of the present,*" not the detached and uninvolved "ostentatious indifference" that uses the word "objectivity" to conceal impotence.

Practitioners of this kind of sham, Nietzsche contends, ought at least to be on the level. They ought not to try to seek "the appearance of justice [*Schein der Gerechtigkeit*]" by emulating the artistic strength worthy of being called genuine objectivity if they have not been summoned to the terrible "vocation of the just man." The just person, in short, is creative. He or she is endowed with the rare ability to transform the past by bringing it back to life in the present. The real historian is one who represents what is "universally known" in a manner never before encountered: "To sum up, history is written by the experienced and superior man ... When the past speaks it always speaks as an oracle: only if you are an architect of the future and know the present will you understand it" (*Untimely Meditations*, II, 6). The past speaks in oracular tones, like the conduit of the will of a Greek god, by communicating mystery. Only the favoured are granted the oracular right to interpret this mystery. The genuine historian, the legitimate bearer of this right, becomes a conduit through which the universal speaks in the unique idiom of a particular moment from the past. Nietzsche defines the creative historian by their passion, involvement, and success in communicating this universal knowledge. The creative historical voice does not seek to condemn what has been in the name of what is. Rather, like the sternest of judges endowed with an uncompromising will to pursue justice, it sacrifices the narrow self-interest of the present in favour of a wider historical truth. The authentically creative historian-judge does not seek to condemn the past; *he or she indicts the present.* The value of knowledge lies in its potential for stimulating the present to re-examination, in provoking modernity to the realization of its own false consciousness.

We are at this point uncannily returned to the space articulated by *The Birth of Tragedy*, which likewise attempted the creative and recuperative historical celebration of ancient Greek culture that Nietzsche outlines in the second *Meditation. The Birth of Tragedy* revels in its involved attitude to the ancient past, placing the past at the service of creating a redeemed German culture, invoking it in an attempt to sting the present into self-awareness. The final section of the second *Meditation* returns to the Apollonian oracle as if to remind us of *The Birth of Tragedy.* When we look to the Greeks with a creative eye, Nietzsche claims, we are confronted not with a stark and distant inferiority but with a shining cultural paradigm. We encounter an untimely wisdom that relates to the present, for the Greeks "found themselves faced by a danger similar to that which faces us: the danger of being overwhelmed by what was past and foreign, of perishing through 'history'" (*Untimely Meditations*, II, 10). Modern German culture is replete with the dangerous multiplicity of modernity, with its vast array of foreign cultural imports. In the same way, the Greeks faced the threat of being overwhelmed by the cultural influx of the Orient. Their culture was a "chaos" of what is foreign, "their religion truly a battle of the gods of the East." The ancient Greek cure for this was to counter this dangerous multiplicity by exploiting it, using it to fashion cultural unity by way of the organizing power of the Delphic oracle.[31] The oracular power of mystery, leaning back into a suprahistorically imagined past to create its own mythology and moral code, facilitated a pan-Hellenic self-creation and self-discovery. We need, Nietzsche argues, to emulate the Delphic maxim "Know thyself." Greek culture offers us the image of culture as an artistic creation worthy of celebration, "culture as a new and improved *physis*, without inner and outer, without dissimulation and convention, culture as a unanimity of life, thought, appearance and will." The universal and profound wisdom of the Greeks is here held to function as an exemplar for modern life. The organizing power of the Apollonian oracle created a mythic core for Greek cultural self-understanding, one in which the place of humanity in the world is affirmed. Here, at the conclusion of the second meditation, is an example of history being put to work in the interests of futurity. The creatively objective and just historian that Nietzsche seeks, the one who shows the profound truth at work within Greek culture, would be one who relates its relevance to us in the form of a profound mystery that challenges the norms that dominate contemporary culture. This is none other than the Apollonian revelation of Dionysian truth affirmed by *The Birth of Tragedy.*

Nietzsche's concern with justice in the early writings is a concern with the validity of contemporary attitudes and norms. In tragedy, the divine justice of the Greek world of Dionysian myth reveals the limits of the socially mediated world of Apollonian convention and law. Through it the conceptions of law and justice necessary to social life are revealed as forms of contingency easily sundered by the forces of elemental nature. Tragic drama communicates this Dionysian condition of elemental nature in Apollonian terms: it reveals a justice defined by a wisdom whose authenticity springs from its ability to refract and thereby communicate the universal human experience. Grasped in terms of modern historical consciousness, this justice is held by Nietzsche to illuminate the path to a rejuvenated, authentic cultural life. Such illumination is essentially oracular. The world of myth speaks to us as a revelation of

31 The oracle at Delphi dates from around the sixth century BCE. Delphi became the locus of the Ancient Greek world: the "navel of the earth."

the transcending possibilities of the Greek paradigm of greatness. Its voice challenges the conformity epitomized by ancient Apollonian self and modern historically constituted self alike. Dionysian wisdom is excess. Through it the oracular is revealed as a miracle of art and art, in its turn, is shown to be true metaphysics. As we will see, the development of Nietzsche's thought from this point is marked most essentially by a break with this conception of metaphysics that culminates in an attempt to rethink the nature of the oracular in post-metaphysical terms. This break launches him on the path of historical philosophy and naturalism that brings with it a radical re-evaluation of what it means to talk about justice and law, punishment, creativity, and freedom.

2

The Unjust Animal, the Law-Like Animal

1. Human, All Too Human *initiates Nietzsche's turn against the metaphysical ideas of his earlier writings in favour of naturalistic "historical philosophy." Where metaphysics seeks to explain reality in terms of timeless, universal ideas, historical philosophy points to an essential historical contingency underlying all notions of timelessness. Nietzsche's historically informed account of thought, with its blend of history, natural history, and psychology, asserts metaphysics to be a delusion. Historical philosophy seeks to explain human rationality, truth, logic, and the virtues in terms of the prehistoric conditions under which they evolved. On such an account, human identity is not a given but an unconscious achievement rooted in primeval conditions. These conditions imposed demands upon our ancestors, and it is in response to such demands that the rules of thought were forged. Our current nature is an expression of the legacy of evaluative habits endowed to us by our autochthonous forbears. Nietzsche concludes that to be human is above all to be a creature of the passions, i.e. we are embodied beings whose identity is inextricably entangled with our organic drives.*

With the publication of *Human, All Too Human* in 1878, Nietzsche's philosophy enters its so-called "middle period" (one that embraces *Assorted Opinions and Maxims, The Wanderer and His Shadow, Daybreak,* and the first four books of *The Gay Science*). With this Nietzsche turns wholesale against metaphysical notions he has hitherto endorsed. Where *The Birth of Tragedy* cleaves to metaphysics, holding it to be one with art, *Human, All Too Human* divorces art from metaphysics.[1] Where *The Birth* turns to

1 In *Human, All Too Human,* 22, Nietzsche notes that metaphysics is what often bestows much of art's significance upon it. Under metaphysical presuppositions the artwork comes to stand as "an image of the eternally persisting" in contrast to the changeable flux that surrounds it. What, he asks, therefore remains of art in the aftermath of historical philosophy? His answer is that what remains is its legacy. Art has taught us to take pleasure in

myth as a source of redemption from the travails of modern cultural sterility, *Human, All Too Human* rebuffs myth in favour of a demythologizing spirit associated with the Enlightenment.[2] Where the second of the *Untimely Meditations* seeks to explore the dangers that history, the "science of universal becoming,"[3] poses to culture, *Human, All Too Human* points to history as providing the paradigm for philosophical and cultural enquiry. The profound oracular divination of the past that the second meditation invokes when it attempts to counter the "bad mythology" of modern historical attitudes with the empowering metaphysical insight of ancient Greek wisdom is abandoned. Metaphysics, Nietzsche now tells us in *Human, All Too Human,* is pure delusion, even as art. The metaphysician clings to the illusory belief that eternal truths exist "as a sure measure of things," standing out in their invariance from the flux of a world that unceasingly changes (*Human, All Too Human,* 2). Truth, in other words, is conceived by the metaphysician in terms of a reality that remains eternally stable and self-identical. Against this, *Human, All Too Human* extols the virtues of "historical philosophy," an approach to knowledge that holds "everything" to have become (*Human, All Too Human,* 3).[4] On Nietzsche's new view, the illusions of "*eternal facts*" and timeless truths are better read as evidence of an unconscious human egoism whose vanity would like to see its self-image painted on the world in immutable shades. Such vain mythology needs to be replaced by new and "unpretentious" truths that offer concrete insight into the particularities of life.

Metaphysics, Nietzsche argues, seeks to explain reality in terms of the unchanging universality it attributes to specific concepts (truth, reason,

existence and to consider life to be both a piece of nature and always evolving, yet to do so "without being too violently involved in it." Art, in other words, has taught us how to distance ourselves from the world and in this way is a constitutive and abiding element of knowledge: "this teaching has been absorbed into us, and it now re-emerges as an almighty requirement of knowledge. One could give up art, but one would not thereby relinquish the capacity one has learned from it: just as one has given up religion but not the enhancement of feeling and exaltations one has acquired from it. As the plastic arts and music are the measure of the wealth of feelings we have actually gained and obtained through religion, so if art disappeared the intensity and multifariousness of the joy in life it has implanted would still continue to demand satisfaction. *The scientific man is the further evolution of the artistic*" [emphasis added]. Thus, scholarship gains its legacy from the aesthetic.

2 The first edition of *Human, All Too Human* was dedicated to Voltaire.

3 *Untimely Meditations,* II, 4.

4 *Human, All Too Human,* as Müller-Lauter notes, "takes seriously the thesis that … 'the whole of philosophy is henceforth forfeit to history' … He now no longer wants to close his eyes to its knowledge, as had happened in the second *Untimely Meditation*" (*Friedrich Nietzsche,* 31–2).

logic, thought, and selfhood). The problem with this view is that the reality that any concept articulates is historically contingent and therefore limited. Concepts are, by their very nature, not universal but time-bound entities that testify to the conditions under which they arose. By the same token, every metaphysician is a creature of his or her era and cannot escape it. In spite of its pretensions to universality, metaphysics is in fact stubbornly earth-bound. The metaphysical philosopher "sees 'instincts' in man as he now is and assumes these belong to the unalterable facts of mankind and ... provide a key to the understanding of the world in general" (*Human, All Too Human*, 2). This is no more than a delusion rooted in a conceptual fetishism that stubbornly refuses to consider the possibility that the features they denote are not fixed, but are rather historically generated constructions that have come to be and continue to become. Now, for Nietzsche, the metaphysician's speculative and uncritical manner is mere mythology. Even the greatest metaphysician merely articulates unconsciously the falsifying tendencies at work in thought. These tendencies, *Human, All Too Human* seeks to show, constitute the basis of what generally counts as meaningful in the human world. We need, as a curative to this, to pay heed to the lessons of a new kind of history – the unconscious history of human presuppositions. When we look at the past we discover that making "false conclusions was in earlier ages the rule: and the mythologies of all nations, their magic and their superstition, their religious cults, their law are inexhaustible sources of proof of this proposition" (*Human, All Too Human*, 271). The metaphysician's historical ignorance condemns them. However fondly they may think otherwise, the metaphysician cannot elude the bad conceptual habits that characterize this inherited web of primitive belief; instead, he or she unconsciously elaborates the pattern of its weaving.

Nietzsche's notion of "historical philosophy" is a fusion of historical, cultural, psychological, and natural-historical elements. This is a thinking that naturalizes. In other words, Nietzsche's new starting point is the view that humankind has a completely natural explanation – that we emerged from nature and that everything about us needs to be explained within this framework. On this conception, human identity is not to be taken as a given. Who we are is a kind of achievement. This achievement is for Nietzsche largely an unconscious and primeval one rooted in various kinds of contingency. We are who we are because of two kinds of contingency: (i) because of the conditions that our primitive, proto-human ancestors happened to have to deal with in order to survive and (ii) because of *how* they happened to end up dealing with the challenges these conditions posed. Nietzsche claims that primitive humanity responded to the demands of nature by developing and refining certain ways of thinking and doing in order to cope with it. Such practices of thought and action are governed by rules. However, the rules in question, he argues, are not immutable. No eternal ordinances lurk behind the rules of action and thought. Nor are our concepts, and the practices to which they are conjoined, exact copies of the world or of the sense experience to which they purportedly relate. The rules of thinking and doing are, rather, better interpreted as the signs of a developmental process at work. They are testimony concerning the manner in which a certain kind of animal coped with its environment and thereby survived and evolved (*Human, All Too Human,* 18; cf. *The Gay Science,* 110).[5] Evolution here is as much cultural as biological, for human identity is achieved through the mastering and fashioning of biological drives by cultural norms.[6] Above all, our identity is circumscribed by an inexorable contingency. There is no universal purpose to "man." No ordinances, divine or otherwise, inform or dictate the manner in which this animal has developed or what it might become.

For Nietzsche, to be human is to be a creature that has passed from the state of nature to the state of culture. Culture characterizes us in an essential way. At the same time, we remain dominated by that most

5 The degree to which such logical beliefs have their roots in the most primitive conditions ought not, Nietzsche claims, to be underestimated. Thus, logic may well begin with belief, since beliefs are those things in virtue of which judgements are possible about any situation. One's explanation of the possible origins of such beliefs and therefore of logic, however, may go back far further than the metaphysician who believes in their unquestionable status might presuppose. The "primary condition" of all organic entities in relation to their environment concerns the pleasure or pain they encounter by way of it. Primitive beliefs spring from the stimulus of painful and pleasurable sensations in the form of a third sensation that results from the "two preceding single sensations." In between such states of sensation and response, organisms live in a kind of state of non-sensory indifference. In such a state, the world is "devoid of interest" and taken to be likewise unchanging. It is this crude state of a primitive organism's self-identical orientation toward its environment (which Nietzsche says even plants dwell in) that forms the basis for more complex beliefs. "It is from the period of the lower organisms that man has inherited the belief that there are *identical things* … It may even be that the original belief of everything organic was from the very beginning that all the rest of the world is one and unmoving" (*Human, All Too Human,* 18). Thus, the logical notion of identity has its roots in a primitive, reactive tendency, not in any timeless reality set apart from the domain of sensations. One should note from this that having beliefs, as Nietzsche conceives of them here, need not involve entertaining concepts in the sense that conscious thinking beings like us consider ourselves to entertain concepts. A belief is, rather, a matter of an organism's concrete orientation and response to its environment: it concerns how it responds to a stimulus or the lack of a stimulus rather than holding true in any abstract, cognitive sense.

6 For an excellent discussion of this and other aspects of Nietzsche's naturalism in relation to Darwin see Richardson, *Nietzsche's New Darwinism.*

essential feature of all organic life, the drives.[7] We are, in short, creatures of the passions. We have a primitive, passionate ancestry and our inheritance of this is inescapable. Our ancestry erupts continually into the fabric of supposedly "civilized" daily life: "We still draw the conclusions of judgments we consider false, of teachings in which we no longer believe – our feelings make us do it" (*Daybreak*, 99). As this passage suggests and Nietzsche confirms, feelings – *not* thoughts or concepts – constitute the legacy of this primitive inheritance: "thoughts are not hereditary, only feelings" (*Daybreak*, 30). Nietzsche's penchant from the outset of *Human, All Too Human* for making great play of the fact that things originate in their "opposites" springs from his repeated emphasis on this legacy of feelings. Feelings are not "logical," they know nothing of opposites, but the power they possess over us has given rise to the appearance of opposing and incompatible notions in the realm of language, thought, and concept. Thus, for example, the concept of reason presents itself to us as separate and different in kind from unreason, as a concept whose identification with the supposed purity of thought cannot be sullied by anything remotely "unreasonable" or embodied. The reality, Nietzsche argues, is very different. The concept of reason is a development of a primitive conceptual apparatus whose distant roots extend into feelings, not pure, self-identical concepts. Reason is hence no less a matter of the passions than our so-called irrational sensibilities. Historical philosophy thus seek to relate the emergence and transformation of diverse elements of feelings into radically different and even opposing forms (*Human, All Too Human*, 31). We must therefore accept the central role that unreason plays in life: the illogical is rooted in us so firmly – in the structure of our passions, in our language, our reasoning, our religious beliefs – indeed, "in everything that lends value to life" – that it would be impossible to excise it out of human existence without mortal consequences. As Nietzsche will later put it, "an attack on the roots of passion means an attack on the roots of life" (*Twilight of the Idols*, "Morality as Anti-Nature," 1). This insight obliges us to note the extent

7 Müller-Lauter notes in connection with this the influence on Nietzsche's thinking of Wilhelm Roux, "the founder of evolutionary mechanics" (*Friedrich Nietzsche*, 163). Nietzsche acquainted himself with Roux's work, *Der Kampf der Theile im Organismus. Ein Beitrag zur Vervollständigung der mechanischen Zweckmäßigkeitslehre* [*The Struggle of the Parts in the Organism. A Contribution to Complement the Mechanical Theory of Purposefulness*] soon after it was published in 1881. Nietzsche's view that the body is a hierarchy of functions locked together in mutual struggle (e.g. *Daybreak*, 119) is clearly in sympathy with the ideas he would have subsequently found in Roux. That said, Nietzsche nevertheless goes well beyond the mechanistic conception (see in connection the discussion offered by Müller-Lauter on 179ff).

to which illogic is an essential ingredient for healthy life: "Even the most rational man from time to time needs to recover nature, that is to say *his illogical original relationship with all things*" in order to carry on living (*Human, All Too Human*, 31). Human life, in other words, rests upon an irrational condition from which it cannot escape. Pure thought can never save us, for we are constituted in such a manner that we must, at some time or another, embrace our "original" passionate nature.

2. *Our concepts are not pictures or representations of the world but instrumental mechanisms that answer to the demands of life. Because of this, there is no neutral "representation" of reality available to us. All concepts are always already evaluations. In consequence, all judgements are, strictly speaking, acts of injustice against the world because they are selectively evaluative. Being human means, amongst other things, being aware of the epistemic injustice that one's own habits of judgement inexorably commit one to. Nietzsche's conception of epistemic injustice does not, however, invoke a noumenal realm of things-in-themselves against which the violence of thought discharges itself; such violence is rather something perpetrated against the multiplicity of life that each of us is aware of since each of us embodies it. We are, it follows, bundles of contradictions.*

From the outset, *Human, All Too Human* urges a radical reassessment of what it means to be human and of that most cherished of human attributes, rational thought. Human conceptual habits (of which the use of reason is but one) emerged as practical coping mechanisms. They were not designed to reflect the world as it really is, but emerged as practical responses to the need to coordinate action in relation to environment in order to survive. Such coordination requires judgement, but the judgement in question is of a sort that involves vague approximation rather than meticulous and accurate reflection. Judgement depends upon presuppositions, and presuppositions are evaluations prompted by feelings. Nietzsche thereby deliberately blurs together questions about what we know and what we value. He thus collapses the distinction between supposedly cognitively pondered facts and felt values. The evaluative feeling, he contends, is a feature of all acts of thought. Even to posit the existence of "things" is to have already engaged in evaluating one's environment by presupposing it to consist of entities that have determinate properties amenable to being subordinated to one's concepts. To live, on this account, is to act in some way; and acting in any way at all means evaluating according to criteria that have no basis in an ultimate and rational order of things. Such criteria relate only to needs (that is, the needs one has in virtue of being a member of one's species). The consequence of this is that we are inheritors of presuppositions and all guilty of committing a kind of violent injustice as soon as we think and thereby judge. Lack of justice typifies us: "All judgements as to the value of life have evolved illogically and are therefore unjust [*ungerecht*]" (*Human, All Too Human*, 32). Our crude, partial, and premature assessments distort and falsify what they seek to grasp in the very act of reaching out to the world. The notion of epistemic injustice that Nietzsche outlines in the earlier meditation on history is in this way extended into a domain that history itself constitutes inescapably: the domain of human identity. We are creatures compelled into adopting evaluative attitudes by our primitive emotional-conceptual inheritance. This means that when we evaluate we do so in a manner that commits violence, for our inheritance is concerned with our animal needs, not with doing justice to what we encounter.

One needs to grasp the precise nature of the violence of this epistemic injustice as Nietzsche conceives it. The injustice we perform is not one that involves an act of injury to some hidden, noumenal realm lurking behind what we experience. It cannot be denied, Nietzsche notes, that such a world *could* be there (*Human, All Too Human*, 9). However, a noumenal realm of this kind would be valueless and without meaning to us, since what characterizes us most decisively is our engaged, embodied nature. As soon as one exposes the passions that give metaphysical beliefs their peculiar appeal (i.e. the feelings of the estimable, frightful, and delightful) such beliefs become worthless. Hence even if the noumenon could be grasped, it would, at best, "be a thing with negative qualities,"[8] and consequently knowledge of it would be the most useless one could possibly have, for nothing could be inferred from it. The epistemic injustice that clouds human thought, therefore, does not concern how things "really are" independently of our ability to experience them. Nietzsche would not claim such injustice if he thought it did, for it would make no sense to do so. Rather, the injustice considered here concerns the fact that all experience occurs within a world of becoming (*Human, All Too Human*, 2), and a world that becomes is one of *multiple* surfaces whose diversity cannot be exhausted by any single feeling or by concepts articulated into a standpoint on the basis of that feeling.

All things, Nietzsche comments at the beginning of *Daybreak*, can demand that we do "justice [*Gerechtigkeit*]" to them (*Daybreak*, 4). Such a comment concerns a world that is never wholly out of our reach in the sense in which a noumenal world of things-in-themselves would have to

8 In other words, it is akin to Kant's conception of it in the *Critique of Pure Reason*.

be. What is multiple can always be felt differently and because of this can be considered from another standpoint that reveals an initial perspective's partiality and injustice. Indeed, we ourselves exemplify this multiplicity. To be human, Nietzsche notes, means to be able to see differently. No one person ever encapsulates merely one perspective. We are each of us a plurality of feelings and, therefore, standpoints on the world. This is why we are able to note the contingent status of our judgemental habits even as we cannot abandon them: "We are from the very beginning illogical and thus unjust [*ungerechte*] beings *and can recognize this*: this is one of the greatest and most irresolvable discords of existence" (*Human, All Too Human*, 32). To be human, in other words, is to be prey to the vicissitudes of concepts that, in spite of their apparent clarity and exactness, are vague and generalizing, and yet at the same time to sense this violence even as one commits it. We encounter the injustice of our various evaluative dispositions because they exist in a state of tension, because they, and consequently we, are always more than one inclination. Conceptual thought, as an articulation of feelings and therefore valuations, seeks to reduce non-conceptual multiplicities down to a conceptual specificity that they do not pertain to as a matter of experience – including our experience of ourselves. This is its injustice. Thus, when Nietzsche claims that language and logic, for example, rest "on presuppositions with which nothing in the real world corresponds" (*Human, All Too Human*, 11), he does not mean that there is a real world that does not correspond to our logical judgements. What does not correspond to such judgements is the world of becoming that, as it is limitless in its unfolding of different planes, cannot be said strictly to "correspond" with anything thinkable at all. Fortunately, Nietzsche adds, it is far too late in the history of the development of human rationality for such errors to be corrected, for without them we would not be able to think at all. Our illogical nature thus reveals itself to us at the cost of our being its living contradiction. We think in terms of identity, but since we can think otherwise and invoke other identities, we become aware of our own partiality.

3. The scepticism historical philosophy generates extends to the domain of our moral preconceptions: existence threatens the loss of value and absurdity. Nietzsche proffers the image of cultivating a knowing rather than a moral humanity as a remedy to this threat. The therapeutic practice of historical-psychological observation provides a paradigm case of this form of knowledge. Here is a form of enquiry that is free from metaphysics and capable of resisting nihilistic thought. Here, also, is the path of enquiry that leads into a re-evaluation of the concept of human nature. Such a re-evaluation turns on a critical analysis of the concept of law and the related spheres of custom and tradition. These spheres, for Nietzsche, are articulations of our measuring, exchanging, and esteeming nature.

Nietzsche realizes soon enough that the trajectory of thought he has embarked upon threatens a loss of faith in the value of humanity itself. If all our most deeply ingrained conceptual habits rest on feelings and error, it follows that "Every belief in the value and dignity of life [likewise] rests on false thinking" (*Human, All Too Human*, 33). If the source of our sense of justice, human dignity, and worth is epistemic injustice, its exposure as error compromises what we have become accustomed to value most deeply about ourselves. Humanity, stripped of the pomp of its conceptual surety, comes increasingly to look like a sophisticated but ultimately deluded and grotesque beast. The average person, Nietzsche comments, takes the world to be an extension of his or her own ego. People "*believe* in the value of existence," but only because they are for the most part unable (or in rarer cases disinclined) to step outside their own standpoint. Our kind is as a rule a passive and unreflective mass of socialized creatures ignorantly taking for granted the inheritance of an illusory and ready-made domain of value-feelings and crassly celebrating this ready-made world as if human dignity was unproblematically bestowed by way of it. The insight of historical philosophy into human existence thereby offers a first glimpse of the revelation of an appalling and inconclusive arbitrariness. The past is a necessary and constitutive feature of human life, but its contingency wreaks havoc upon the being it has fashioned. We cannot step outside of history, for it has made us and continues to exert the force of ancient inheritance upon us.

The problem is that living with the above revelation does not mean merely being sceptical about what we know. It initiates scepticism about what we value. The defining, tragic-absurd insight of *Human, All Too Human* is that there are no necessary "oughts," only contingent "musts." We must think, but we do so in partial ways, for the necessity concerning how we must think goes no deeper than the demand that, being the sort of creatures we are, we must be what we are. These narrow perspectives contain no more moral veracity than they do objective knowledge about the world of things. Thus, Nietzsche notes, "morality, insofar as it was an 'ought,' has just been annihilated by our mode of thinking, as has religion" (*Human, All Too Human*, 34). The conventional understanding and valuing of morality has ceased to compel. If it turns out that humanity's "inclination and aversion and … very unjust assessments [*sehr ungerechten Messungen*] are … the essential determinants of pleasure and pain" then the cost of this insight is profound disillusionment. All human life will be revealed as being immured so "deeply in untruth; [that] the individual cannot draw it up out of this well without thereby growing profoundly disillusioned about his own past." Scepticism might be the only option, were genuine scepticism really possible: maybe "one ought not to judge at all; if only it were possible to *live* without evaluating, without having aversions and partialities!" (*Human, All Too Human,* 32) Can the sense for truth, for doing justice to what one encounters in experience, a sense which itself has sprung from contingency and error, be fruitfully brought to bear in such a context? Or is it the case that all that remains possible is a last gasp, "a philosophy of destruction" (*Human, All Too Human,* 34) for which there remains only the dubious pleasure of smashing up the hollow idols that used to count as worthy truths and moral guides?

Human, All Too Human does in fact offer a tentative and pragmatic answer to this painful question. Inevitably, our most ambitious flights of fancy in the realm of metaphysical and moral thought are going to plunge back to earth with a bump. We simply have to cope with this trauma. Our best bet is to be as sceptical as we can (*Human, All Too Human,* 21), but we can become so with a certain degree of comfort. We can treat our "all too human" aspirations as if they were ailments in need of medication. "Psychological observation" (*Human, All Too Human,* 35) is the medication Nietzsche prescribes for our disease. We cannot hope to overcome entirely the ills that beset thought and judgement, but we can learn to cope with our inabilities by gaining insight from them. What looks like it might be a limitation can, it turns out, be an invitation. Psychological reflection is therapeutic. It is a means of coping with trauma, for it allows one to pick experiences from the most thorn-ridden and unpleasant passages of one's life and mould pithy, redemptive aphoristic insights out of them. It is also resistant to the threat posed by the strain of metaphysical sickness to which we are prone, for an explanation of the motivations for beliefs "which is free of mythology" is, Nietzsche points out, "a purely psychological explanation" (*Human, All Too Human,* 132). In other words, the route away from metaphysics that avoids nihilism requires a historical philosophy that is psychological.[9] The illusory universal panacea of metaphysics must be replaced by salves and ointments, by more modest treatments designed to treat specific ailments so that one can get by on a day-to-day basis.

9 One should note here that psychology in this sense is essentially political psychology in so far as "the overcoming of modern (European) nihilism is … primarily a political predicament" (Mellamphy, *The Three Stigmata of Friedrich Nietzsche,* 76).

The psychological enquiry that Nietzsche envisages is not a new invention,[10] nor is it a mere passive mirroring of the hard sciences.[11] What characterizes Nietzsche's psychology most starkly, as one might guess from what has already been said, is its stance with regard to morality. If one is serious about the pursuit of knowledge, Nietzsche argues, one needs to construct a "genuine psychology," that is, a psychology of the sort resistant to our most deeply held moral preconceptions, one that bespeaks "unbelief in the metaphysical significance of morality" (*Assorted Opinions and Maxims*, 33). It is on the basis of this contention that Nietzsche's post-metaphysical thought begins to address the question of the significance of law. Nietzsche develops an account of law that turns on the contention that one must make sense of it by looking at it in natural-historical and psychological terms. Any consideration of law necessitates looking back beyond the sphere of theoretically defined modern-day discourse concerning the nature of legality to the primitive, prehistoric conditions that underpin law's emergence. The illumination of law thus requires one to consider the related spheres of morality, religion, custom, and tradition, for these are on Nietzsche's account inextricably entwined with one another. Nietzsche approaches these spheres by emphasizing one of the most striking primeval characteristics of humanity, one that fashioned it, and consequently us, decisively: its esteeming nature.

4. Humans are measuring animals. Practices linked to this constitute our esteeming nature. Our ancestors were from the outset doers rather than thinkers. We are creatures of custom and the drives and, as such, are best characterized in terms of embodiment. Morality is an extrapolation of this embodied nature. Nietzsche's

10 The works of seventeenth century writer La Rochefoucauld furnish a good example of the kind of experimentalist hypothesizing Nietzsche has in mind when he talks of psychology. La Rochefoucauld (1613–1680) was famous for his *Memoirs* and *Sentences and Maxims*, which Nietzsche read in the early 1870s. Nietzsche's comments in *Daybreak* (103) reveal the extent of his sympathies and the different emphasis of his own approach. Where La Rochefoucauld regards morality as a mere disguise for ulterior motives, Nietzsche argues that morality, conventionally understood, is also better understood as metaphysics – a view that does not preclude the other.

11 Although Nietzsche's view in this most "positivistic" of his works thus cleaves to science as an exemplar of enquiry, it is clear that he by no means considers the methods of the sciences to be the sole paradigm of the kind of project that *Human, All Too Human* initiates. Nietzsche's conception of science (or better perhaps, of scholarly enquiry) is one that embraces it in a spirit of "*gaya scienza*," i.e. as a joyful pursuit (which means engaged, involved, and committed) rather than as a value-objective one. His later, more acid comments about the sciences (see, for example, *Beyond Good and Evil*, 14, 22, 211) ought not, it follows, to come as a shock.

account begins with habits, which are the source of the power of custom. Habits are thoughtless, species-defining forms of unthinking action. The latter are taken up and fashioned by communal forces; they thereby become customs. Custom is hence the fashioning of drives into second nature. Customs are characterized by Nietzsche in terms of primeval measuring propensities. The adherence to custom marks out the emergence of humanity as a law-like animal.

As I have argued elsewhere,[12] for Nietzsche being human does not mean being the measure of all things. It means being the *measurer* of all things. On his view, the ability to measure is not some coincidental feature of our kind, something that we could choose to have or not. It is, rather, constitutive of us. We are compulsive evaluators: we are the estimating and esteeming animal. We live and act on the basis of evaluative feelings. Our estimating and esteeming existence is a matter of what we do, of the practices we find ourselves in simply by virtue of being creatures of culture and of the drives. This condition of embodiment is constitutive of our identity. We do not exist simply because we think and have reason, as Descartes held, for our reason is an achievement of embodiment (that is why reason has a history). On the other hand, nor are we like little, empty cabinets of consciousness waiting for events to intrude into the passive space of our minds and create image-concepts like little copies of experience, as empiricism maintained.[13] We carry our historical inheritance of psychological and cultural-moral feelings with us as a condition of having any experiences at all. Human life in all its aspects is driven by evaluation: "As soon as we see a new image, we immediately construct it with the aid of all our previous experiences, *depending on the degree* of our honesty and justice. All experiences are moral experiences, even in the realm of sense perception" (*The Gay Science,* 114). According to such a view, nothing is simply given to us as a brute experiential "fact." What counts as "given" and "factual" always stands as a sign of an evaluation, of a feeling. Facts are a kind of interpretation.[14]

Our moral propensities are part of the interpretive tangle of measuring cultural practices and propulsive habits and drives that endow us with identity. Indeed, moral evaluation is inseparable from them. It may even be the case, Nietzsche notes, that "all the morality of mankind has its origin [*Ursprung*] in the tremendous inner excitement which seized on primeval men when they discovered measure and measuring, scales and weighing (the word '*Mensch*' ['human'], indeed, means the

12 See Sedgwick, *Nietzsche's Economy.*

13 For some discussion of these issues see Sedgwick, *Descartes to Derrida.*

14 This, one should add, does not make them any less real for Nietzsche.

'measurer' ['*den Messenden*'], he desired to name himself after his greatest discovery!)" (*The Wanderer and His Shadow*, 21). Morality, which is normally numbered amongst the most significant of human achievements, springs from our ancestors having stumbled on the notion of measurement. In an act of unconscious self-baptism they hit upon a truth about themselves. Given that humanity is foremost an evaluator and valuator, it is practices of weighing, counting, and the like that characterize it most powerfully in its evolution from the primeval past. That our ancestors unconsciously developed such practices and adhered to them had as its unintended consequence a re-fashioning of their primitive identity. All that has come to be rich with significance in the human universe, Nietzsche implies in section 21 of *The Wanderer and His Shadow*, gained its initial impetus from this first unconscious embrace of measurement.

An estimator is someone endowed with feelings that drive them to distinguish between what is more and what is less, what is bigger and what is smaller, to separate like from unlike, to assert relations of equivalence, etc. Measurement, it follows, is coterminous with exchange, for through it something always stands to something else in a relation of value that holds it equal, greater, or smaller. Exchange, in turn, forms the groundwork that enables webs of purposes. One estimates the number, extent, or weight of things only because something may, and indeed ultimately *must*, be yielded in exchange for them. The nomadic plunderer no less than the sedentary cultivator of the environment presupposes a return in exchange for the investment of their efforts. "Labour," which can also be war, is only labour when it is undertaken on the basis of an exchange for food, shelter, and raiment. Exchanging, measuring, labouring, and the like are hence among the most basic conditions out of which human life develops. They are incorporated from the outset into the fabric of social norms from which primitive custom is weaved, endowing the crudest communal orders with the potential to develop habitual structures fit to solidify into customs. They give rise to the structures of authority and command that are called "tradition."

Nietzsche's conception starts with habit. Habit is a necessary condition of the primitive social creature's transformation into an animal of custom and tradition. The fact that habit is pleasurable to us, Nietzsche notes, is a sure sign of its social utility (*Human, All Too Human*, 97). Habit is thoughtless presumption. The one who successfully pursues their habits does so in an untroubled state. Consider the confusion that arises when habitual expectations are frustrated. The car refuses to start or the key snaps in the lock and one is jolted out of trouble-free thoughtlessness. This confusion reveals why habits are powerful: their power resides in their being unconscious conditions of action. They allow for the smooth progress easily confused with spontaneity. Their pleasure is the pleasure of ease, the sense of comfort that accompanies the unproblematic feeling of being at home in the world. Our significant habits are collective species habits, the unthinking webs of presuppositions that ground the emergence of conceptual thought in human communities. Habit is likewise a source of the power of customs. The latter transform mere habits by organizing them into structures of wider social significance. "Custom," Nietzsche comments, "is the union of the pleasant and the useful" (*Human, All Too Human*, 97). Here lies the source of its social utility. Communities are webs of shared habits solidified into customs. Their strictures compel each individual member to adopt the same modes of acting, the same rituals of performance. Such strictures stamp the primitive beginnings of identity on those who collectively follow the rule and thereby become observers of customs. Customs cater to communal needs (*Assorted Opinions and Maxims*, 89) and the practices of exchanging, weighing, and measuring serve these needs. Such practices have a social utility that indicates they emerge as intrinsic to customs, which fix in place the raw material of habitual observance making it amenable to ritualization and finally commanding authority in the form of tradition. Thus, custom, which is none other than the patterning of measuring habits, of ritual observance and formalized exchange, makes possible the regulated, law-like realm of communal social life. Here lie the beginnings of culture and civilization. Here, along with them, lie the origins of law and justice.

5. *The account of custom intimated in* Human, All Too Human *is formalized by Nietzsche in* Daybreak *as "the morality of custom" – the primeval condition under which the human animal was decisively fashioned with regard to its dominant evaluative propensities and conceptual abilities. The notion of morality of custom reveals morality itself to be nothing more than the adherence to what is customary. Such adherence is the precondition of the formation of human culture, which is characterized by Nietzsche in terms of the power of the normative authority of law and tradition. One acts on custom without a thought. Following custom, in other words, is unthinkingly following the law. What most characterizes adherence to custom is action, the observance of more or less fixed patterns of ritual. The prehistoric origins of such patterns are necessarily repressed. Their authority springs from the apparently mysterious nature that this repression endows. The power and authority of primitive law, in other words, is preserved by the aura of myth. As myth recedes, so does the authority of law and tradition.*

In *Daybreak* the insight into the communal preconditions of social life is given a name. Nietzsche baptises the concatenation of norms that makes possible the emergence of culture the "morality of custom" (*Daybreak*, 9). The morality of custom stretches back in time to the era before historical documentation was possible, to the "*actual and decisive eras of history which determined the character of mankind*" (*Daybreak*, 18). Here is the domain that is first identified in *Human, All Too Human* as being the irrational, illogical sphere out of which were articulated all our most valued abilities. To act according to the dictates of the morality of custom is to adhere unthinkingly to traditional modes of behaving and estimating. Morality, Nietzsche tells us, is in reality nothing more than this; it is simply "obedience to customs." If one removes tradition, one thereby deletes morality (although not necessarily what it has achieved). It follows from this that to be "moral" is to be one who cleaves to custom, who *obeys the law*, that is, the rules of the community, the commanding authority of its tradition. Civilization, it follows, is a domain of rules. Such rules are customary. That is, they are like the rules one adheres to when playing a game: they cannot be deduced from reality and they are not objects of thought when playing the game, yet they function as decisive conditions without which there is no game. One simply moves the chess piece, calls "foul," rolls, bowls, or throws the ball in the manner deemed fit for the practice. Games are articulations of our propensity for customs, reenforcing customary power by supplementing it with celebratory and festive pleasure, the excitement of competition, feelings of belonging, and a sense of investment. Without customs, says Nietzsche, there is no civilization, no culture, and no humanity as we understand it, for all manifestations of civilization rest on the weighty sentence that declares "any custom" to be preferable to none at all (*Daybreak*, 16). To become a creature of civilization, in other words, requires a leap across a boundary that, once made, separates a life of mere drives and habits (the realm of nature) from one of drives and habits organized and shaped by ordinances (the realm of culture). Through the formative power of primitive custom a rudimentary proto-humanity was moulded into the kind of being that foreshadows what we feel familiar with when we look in a mirror. Look at prehistoric humanity, says Nietzsche, and you will see yourself, but as a negative image: in the prehistoric world of custom violence was the norm, and cruelty, deceitfulness, and irrationality were celebrated. The realm of the morality of custom is the realm of discipline, the irrational breeding ground of the habits out of which, in turn, our rational conceptual abilities received their later elaboration.

With the morality of custom comes the invention of social authority, in the form of tradition. One is obedient to custom because it stretches back behind one and reaches forward in front of one. Ultimately, long obedience gives rise to a being that obeys simply because it is commanded – that *wants* to be commanded. Just like the soldier who will not think to question the orders of his or her superior, the being subject to tradition obeys *because* he or she stands in thrall to the commanding power of tradition. The obedient communal being sees in tradition something to fear. The authority of tradition is supernatural and mythological – it is the realm of the gods. As the realm of iron law, Nietzsche comments, custom and tradition are a tyranny that even now one can hear echoing down through modern sensibilities. Doubt unsettles. The feeling of displeasure that accompanies scepticism and relativism (thinking against the norm) is a symptom of our inheritance of the prehistoric ancestor's yoke (*Human, All Too Human*, 631). This disquiet comes from the ancient power of the tyranny of custom and tradition, and reflects the profound role they played in human development. We have a natural tendency to give way to the power of authority – the convictions one is *supposed to have* exert a powerful influence because they are the norm, i.e. simply because one is supposed to adhere to them in order to be oneself.

Initially, the tyranny of custom was one that lacked both repressive tyrants and innocent victims. In the prehistoric setting custom ruled over nothing more than the brute conditions of animality from which human identity was painfully harvested by the long drawn-out self-battering that customary observance demanded of our proto-human forbears.[15] As the notion of the observance of the morality of custom implies, it is what is adhered to and acted upon – and not conscious thought – that always come first for Nietzsche. In matters of legality, morality, and religion, he tells us in *The Wanderer and His Shadow* (77) what matters are those features frequently dismissed because they are the most external and evident, namely custom, gesture, ceremony, not what is often taken as primary, not the "inner" meaning that accompanies an act of observance. This external element alone has the potential for "*durability*." Ritual is *enacted*. It is a matter of the body and its habituation. The body comes first and the ritualized pattern of its actions endures even as their "meaning" changes. The body is a *habitus*: the locus of a bundling together, harmonization, regulation, and regularization of an individual's behaviour in conformity with generally observed norms of behaviour. To this relatively stable medium, Nietzsche says, "a *new soul* is always being added." In other words, the meaning of a ritual or custom (which we often

15 For the most detailed account of this, see *On the Genealogy of Morality*, II.

take to be primary) is always amenable to reinterpretation. What stay consistent are the form of the ritual and the realm of value feelings out of which ritual emerges, not the meanings one might attach to them. The morality of custom is habit legislated and sanctified. All subsequent meaningfulness rests on an extrapolation of this legislation and sanctification.

Since ritual precedes all possible meaning, the significance of law as it emerged in tandem with primitive, customary exchanging and measuring humanity is something that can never be taken to concern the possible meanings attributed to it at any one moment. What most decisively characterizes the origins of law is, rather, the persistence of ritual and unthinking adherence to norms – the "solid" ritualistic sphere of doing what is customary *because it is customary*, the obedience to authority *because it is authority*. Anyone looking for a rational articulation of the historical basis for law is likely to be disappointed. The authorization of power is as tautological as it is contingent. In the prehistoric social order, law does not receive its first formulation in the shape of reasoned statements about the meaning of questions of right and entitlement, but as unthinking deed, as thoughtless adherence to interrelated networks of customary observance. To be habitual, to estimate and exchange, to observe custom and bow down before tradition, to conform: to feel and to do these things, not to theorize them, is, for Nietzsche, the first intimation of the human. Through observing and adhering to customs with law-like regularity the primitive individual is endowed with a sense of identity. Who they are corresponds to a role within the communal body. Customs and traditions are thus preconditions of creatures like us having self-understanding, for it is only in virtue of them that the individual is slowly endowed with the beginnings of a sense of their place in the world.

To be "subject to the law" means to act in such-and-such a way, and thereby, in the long run, to become able to understand oneself in terms of one's adherence or lack thereof to the norms of one's social order. "Law," one should note here, is in its origins a matter that revolves around the dynamic of the "inner" realm of human communal existence. It concerns, in this regard, almost exclusively the regulation of relations between individual members of a community – the fact that all adhere to the law. At the same time, its emergence is also conjoined with what lies outside the communal body, with a realm not subject to the dictates of custom. Law has, in this regard, an intimate connection with the development of religion, for the latter springs from the human need to master the "external" realm of nature. If we look back to the era when religion was most powerful, Nietzsche argues, "we discover a fundamental conviction which we no longer share" concerning our relationship with nature (*Human, All Too Human*, 111). Modern humanity, fashioned by Newtonian physics and the spirit of Enlightenment, has a tendency to see nature as an iron realm of rigid causality and law. The ancient human, in contrast, did not understand nature in terms of "*natural* causality," for the primitive was a being who knew nothing of "natural laws [*Naturgesetzen*]." Our ancient religious forbears saw nature as the opposite of themselves, as lawlessness itself, as a magical flaunting and overturning of the regular and predictable norms of conduct that epitomized the communal and socialized human individual: "The whole of nature is in the conception of [primitive] religious men a sum of actions by conscious and volitional beings, a tremendous complex of *arbitrariness* ... [For them] it is we who are more or less secure and calculable; man is the *rule*, nature is *irregularity* – this proposition contains the fundamental belief which dominates rude, religiously productive primitive cultures" (ibid.). In undeveloped, "raw" cultures (a notion that for Nietzsche, in a perhaps typically racist nineteenth-century vein, includes "present-day savages"), law – the structure of norms and customs that constitute the social fabric – determines subjectivity in a decisive manner. The individual, as we have noted, is bound to this powerful institutional structure so closely that he or she is not even aware of it. Law and tradition have a near mechanistically symbiotic relationship to the self, motivating the individual's actions through an invisible normative force that operates "with the regularity of a pendulum." The organized religious cult arises because of the conflict between this ordered, inner social world and the disorderly, external chaos of nature. Nature is a realm of terrible and unknown powers that threaten the community, the domain of a freedom unthinkable within the constraints of an identity governed by the straightjacket of communal norms; it slices into the human world, Dionysian-style, threatening to overturn it. The response is to try to control nature, to subjugate "the domain of freedom" through acts of incantation and ritual that project the structure of meaning that animates and orders the social realm on to this unstructured, unruly domain. Primitive humanity confronts nature and seeks to master its chaos by casting spells in its direction. Religion is in this way revealed in its origins as being little more than an organized cult devoted to the control of nature, a proto-science that unwittingly projects normatively generated law-like propensities on to a rebellious world that can in reality know nothing of ordinances or statutes. The unconscious religious aim is to impose upon nature "*a regularity and rule of law* [*eine Gesetzlichkeit*, i.e. a legality] *which it does not at first possess*" (ibid.). In this way, the emergence of law precedes distinctions, such as we make, between so-called "physical laws" and merely "law-like behaviour" (social norms). To be law-like means to first encounter and interpret the natural realm in terms of socially generated dictates that fashion and regulate primitive selves. "Law," as Nietzsche understands it, is not derived from the passive observing of regular nature. It is, rather, a human articulation, an expression of socially mediated feelings that can also subsequently be directed toward environmental demands and threats with a view to their negation.

The same principle applies to the primitive attitude toward other human beings, to those who do not conform to what is customary and lawful. One seeks to subdue others, too, by way of incantation and sorcery. Religion, in other words, emerges as the articulation of a primeval desire to control not only the nature that lies beyond the communal body, but also the nature that erupts through the web of the social veneer from time to time. The lawless person, the alien and outsider, the one who observes other laws and does things differently, he or she whose power is a threat and who for this reason represents a danger to communal security and identity, also provokes the cultic-religious response of seeking control through ritualistic invocation. Thus, the emergence of religion, Nietzsche argues, is connected with not only the law-like attempt to regulate nature but also other human beings. A weaker tribal grouping, for example, resorts to wizardry (a proto-priestly form) to "dictate laws [*Gesetze*] to the *Stronger*" so as to secure some kind of control over it (ibid.). The origins of the holy, of the veneration of law and tradition, now stand revealed in the interaction between social and environmental forces. The religious cult has a mundanely un-metaphysical source in law-like practices. It is like a firmed-up "word text": its "fluid" elements, i.e. the meanings and concepts associated with it, are reinterpreted continually and are consequently unstable in comparison with the relatively "solid" ritualistic observance of customs (the ritual of incantations) that frames them (*The Wanderer and His Shadow*, 77). History undercuts metaphysics.

As the above account implies, religion, law, and morality are not grounded in any revelation of the supernatural, but in concrete conditions that govern the life and continuance of communal beings governed by the law of custom and tradition. What matters most in this regard is the ancient, and because of this venerable, nature of the legal and moral realms: "To be moral, to act in accordance with custom, to be ethical, means to practise obedience towards a law or tradition established from old" (*Human, All Too Human*, 96). The notion of "evil" gains its meaning from the same logic: it is simply that which does not accord with custom, tradition, and law. "Good" likewise derives the selfless connotations that have accrued to it in the same manner. Moral value judgements spring from the observance of social norms ("laws") that have become endowed with the mysterious, antiquarian, authoritarian quality of the sacred. The question as to how a specific tradition arises does not matter here, Nietzsche adds. All traditions and laws are, initially at least, targeted on preserving "a *community*, a people." If one grasps this essential utility one has grasped what matters about the origins of our law, religion, and morality: all are rooted in the need for survival. A necessarily un-historically inclined humanity has simply allowed awareness of these origins to slip away, since the greater the distance from the sources of its tradition, the more these sources are forgotten and venerated. The power of authority is thus above all an aura. Once the aura is dispersed by historical awareness it is demythologized. The more we demythologize, the more mundane things hitherto endowed with otherworldly significance appear to be to us, which is why "Stone is more stony than it was formerly" (*Human, All Too Human*, 218). In other words, the sacred sheen that arises from veiled origins is obliterated by historical revealing: the religious building viewed as an historical object is rendered mere dead stone rather than something inhabited and animated by the aura of the dwelling god, the sacred ordinance shown to be mere words of desperate incantation.

6. Custom for Nietzsche characterizes our species in an essential way. It is the origin of culture, which in turn is the constitutive condition of subjectivity and selfhood. To be human is to be a creature of culture, i.e. a being of drives and norms. The normative social realm is the source of our law-like nature. It is also the source of human injustice and error, since the habits of thought cultivated by this realm are rooted in the demand for survival, not in any requirement for veracity. Yet, because these errors give rise to faith in truth, the desire for truth takes root in human identity and can be turned against that identity itself. The realm of law-like custom thus creates an animal that can, within certain limits, go beyond its confines. We are revealed in the light of this as paradoxical beings: desirers of truth and justice who are immured in untruth and injustice. Metaphysics may not be easily avoided, but an ethics of scepticism is possible. Such an ethics seeks to evaluate human judgement on the basis of the criterion of "life." For Nietzsche, the terrain of such judgements includes the conceptual field underpinning our notions of law and justice.

The general propensity our species has toward custom and tradition defines us in a decisive sense (*Daybreak*, 19). This propensity gives rise to culture, the realm of the law-like animal, and with it selfhood. Culture, on Nietzsche's view, generates subjectivity by harnessing the drives and situating them in various normative arrangements, the differences of arrangement giving rise to different cultural forms and different manifestations of subjectivity (i.e. of the kind of selfhood that is valued). The human being is not therefore in essence a smooth space of calm self-consciousness surrounding a unified will, but a tide of competing inclinations that have been selected, suppressed, cultivated, fashioned, honed, and regulated and thus unified into something synthetic and law-like by cultural forces. Being human, it follows, involves being a frequently conflicting and uncomfortable blend of culture and body: one is a bundle of anti-social drives and regularized behaviour. Such regulation suppresses the multiplicity of environmental conditions that culture must negotiate in order to survive giving rise to the conceptual illusions of unity, identity, permanence, and the like. Out of this condition of compulsion and error the realms of legality, justice, and the state are forged. We judge on the basis of inherited feelings that have no grounding in an ultimate reality or truth. To judge "is the same thing as to be unjust" (*Human, All Too Human*, 39) since human judgement is always partial and generally uncritical of its instrumental and unconsciously anthropomorphic presuppositions.[16]

But, Nietzsche argues, we also want knowledge. We want truth even as we become aware of our limitations and the questionable origins of the desire for truth. The consequence of this is that we are creatures moulded and enfolded in paradox: we are beings in error who are desirous of truth, unjust creatures seeking the justice of honest self-understanding. This is the case in part as a consequence of the unforeseen ramifications of the pragmatics of primitive social life (*The Gay Science*, 110). In the primitive community some judgements may be deemed "good," some "bad," but there are also those which seem to be neither. In this ambiguous space the first experiments in thinking occurred, the playing with propositions that appeared to have neither a beneficial nor damaging consequence. Here is the origin of metaphysical speculation and its undoing. Eventually, Nietzsche suggests, this speculative tendency became part of us, too, and with this came the need to enquire, to ask questions about the nature and limits of the conditions constitutive of the social bond. We are the inheritors of this condition. In us, the need for custom, stability, and law (the preservers of human social life) comes into conflict with the desire to question the assumptions upon which they

16 That is why, Nietzsche comments, it is difficult to see any particular thing in the world impersonally, "I mean to see it as a thing, *not as a person*" (*Assorted Opinions and Maxims*, 26). Our injustice is bound up with our being creatures who are dominated by a "person-constructing, person-investing drive": we are anthropomorphists through and through.

rest. To find oneself in such a situation exemplifies, for Nietzsche, the dilemma of being a philosopher, of being one who is driven by habits of judgement yet capable of bearing witness to their habitual and hence unjust nature: "two lives, two powers, both in the same human being. A thinker is now that being in whom the impulse for truth and those life preserving errors clash for their first fight, after the impulse for truth has also proved to be a life-preserving power. Compared with the significance of this fight, everything else is a matter of indifference: the ultimate question about the conditions of life has been posed here, and we confront the first attempt to answer this question by experiment. To what extent can truth endure incorporation? That is the question; that is the experiment" (*The Gay Science*, 110). The philosopher is a battleground of a contest between inimical inclinations – an open-ended experiment concerning the possibility of a synthesis of contraries. Nietzsche thereby ends up asking about the extent to which it is possible for us to criticize our most deeply held presuppositions, even though such beliefs constitute a necessary condition of our existence.

It is now clear enough how Nietzsche can answer the question first posed as the beginning of *Human, All Too Human.* The "need" for truth springs from "error" – and it has become an essential feature of human life. To be human means to be prey to the desire for truth that has developed contingently out of our customary, law-like propensities. Yet, at the same time, such a desire for truth is not something that finds its source in mere utility as customary, metaphysically sanctioned belief does. Rather, from the utility of the primitive customary inheritance of beliefs that helped preserve the species arises a need that transcends them. This is the need to question metaphysics – the need for historical philosophy. Nietzsche can now ask about the degree to which it is possible for us to strive for truth and objectivity given that such striving may mean sacrificing the metaphysical errors upon which our lives rest. Pursuing "truth," in this sense, involves becoming a historical philosopher and criticizing metaphysics, recognizing as one does so that one is inexorably trapped within it. To do so means engaging in a form of sustained criticism of the very conditions of one's own life. Out of epistemic injustice, therefore, has emerged the relentless demand that we somehow do justice to our beliefs and thereby ourselves. As Nietzsche puts it in the 1887 addition to *The Gay Science*, the only way to pursue justice in this sense is through scepticism. In other words, one must refuse to allow "convictions" any "rights of citizenship [*Bürgerrecht*]" in the domain of knowledge (*The Gay Science*, 344). Nietzsche's use of the language of law and invocation of the legal subject is no accident here. The realm of the law-like that has given rise to us can now be turned against itself in us.

One does not, Nietzsche adds, thereby escape from metaphysics. However, a new moral demand concerning the value of truth comes to take its place in our table of values: the "'will to truth' does *not* mean 'I will not allow myself to be deceived' but – there is no alternative – 'I will not deceive, not even myself'; *and with that we stand on moral ground*" (ibid.).

This insight provokes the conclusion that human judgements need to be evaluated according to new criteria inspired by a new conception of the will to truth. These criteria concern the degree to which judgements are "life-advancing, life-preserving, species-preserving, perhaps even species-breeding" (*Beyond Good and Evil*, 4). Having charted out the domain of law-like custom that gives rise to us, Nietzsche seeks to go beyond it. He wishes to take the sense for truth and justice that we have unconsciously cultivated and turn it against its own presuppositions and hence ourselves, with the aim of discovering the degree to which a new humanity can thereby be given form, one which is capable of taking an affirmative stance with regard to its being a creature of earth and erring. It is a matter of taking the perilous path of resisting "customary value-sentiments" and thereby situating one's thought in a domain that is "beyond good and evil." This is the domain of naturalism.

Naturalism, as Nietzsche will come to call historical philosophy, means rethinking not only what it means to be human but what nature too signifies when it has been divested of metaphysical significance.[17] Understood ontologically, that is, from the standpoint of becoming affirmed at the beginning of *Human, All Too Human*, law at its outset is lawless accident, justice is unjust imposition. That we are law-like at all is something whose origins, like those of our desire for justice and truth, reside in the contingencies and vicissitudes of history. Creatures that

17 There is for Nietzsche no natural order of things that precedes the development of humanity, guiding its path into becoming the kind of being it now is. Any rigorous rumination on truth and justice must, it follows, begin with the realization that it starts with error and injustice. Nature is essentially lawless insofar as it contains no moral teleology. Even the modern scientific notion of the existence of an overarching realm of natural laws (that is, of an iron rule of lawfulness to which the natural world conforms) is just a more recent example of our kind's propensity for ancient mythological feelings. All utterances of faith (including those of the sciences) in a natural world that behaves in a way corresponding to our concepts of legitimacy and regularity are words of mere "*superstition*," incantations (*Assorted Opinions and Maxims*, 9). The notion that a "necessity" of this kind exists in nature is another form of metaphysical delusion, a last nook of refuge in which the "mythological dreaming" of speculative and superstitious fantasy takes shelter. "Laws" are better understood as "conventional fictions": they are useful as markers that can be used with a view to arriving at understanding, not as denoting something that "really" exists in the world (see *Beyond Good and Evil*, 21).

looked like our dim and distant ancestors might have turned out differently, or not at all, with the consequence that we might never have been. No first and privileged principle or concept can be placed at the beginning of the process that leads to our ancestors being seized and transformed by the law-like regularity of social order and custom into creatures that demand truth and justice in some form or another. Yet we are, for Nietzsche, creatures seized by the demand for truth and justice. We have been shaped inexorably by forces that place this demand within us as a condition of life. It is not, however, at this primitive level alone that Nietzsche's naturalistic account is applied most forcefully. Rather, Nietzsche's naturalistic paradigm is applied inexorably to his consideration of the institutions, concepts, and dominant understandings of law and justice. It is to these areas that we must now turn.

3

Justice Talk, Community, and Power

1. Our nature, for Nietzsche, is the cumulative outcome of the prehistoric mastering of drives through practices. Culture is thus a synthesis of the organic and the normative. It is in this synthesis that the sources of justice lie. Here, too, Nietzsche's thoroughgoing naturalism is evidenced. Justice, prudence, indeed, all the Socratic virtues, he argues, originate in animality and the pragmatic demands of life.

As we have seen, Nietzsche develops a naturalism that holds the primeval, normative force of custom and tradition to have shaped the human animal in a decisive manner. To be human is to be a being of law-like propensities, i.e. of custom and tradition moulded by a shared realm of habits and conventions. We are creatures of law, morality, and the sacred because we are creatures of norms. Nietzsche's emphasis here is on living and doing, i.e. on practices. Activity is the decisive feature of valuing, and valuing means holding true, desiring to know, deeming good and bad, considering just, fair, and the like. On this account, there is no gap separating our epistemic and normative propensities, which means that our origins and identity are more animal-like than the metaphysician would ever assume.

Naturalism means emphasizing the animal origins of the human and re-integrating humanity into the wider world of natural history. Every animal, Nietzsche tells us (*Daybreak*, 26), needs to escape its predators and facilitate the capture of its food and does so by adapting itself to environmental demands: "one wishes to elude one's pursuers and be favoured in the pursuit of one's prey." For this reason, the animals "learn to master themselves and alter their form, so that many, for example, adapt their colouring to the colouring of their surroundings … [or] pretend to be dead, or assume the forms and colours of another animal or of sand, leaves, lichen, fungus." We are no different. Our concepts, however transcendent their ambitions may be, are elaborations of practical, animal import rather than of metaphysical significance. Nietzsche here naturalizes the germinal aspect of "the sense for truth." The desire for truth is not an exclusively human possession. Like us, no animal benefits practically from being deceived by what it confronts, or by deluding itself, or by responding precipitately to the prompting of its passions. Every animal wants "truth," in this limited and practical sense, no less than we are inclined toward it in a more extravagant, all-too-human sense. Provoked by environmental demands, the non-human animal, too, becomes aware of the effects that its presence has on other beings. It thereby "learns to look back upon itself, to take itself 'objectively.'" Here, albeit in brute form, Nietzsche locates the roots not only of the desire for truth but of our other virtues, too: "The animal assesses the movements of its friends and foes, it learns their peculiarities by heart, it prepares itself for them: it renounces war once and for all against individuals of a certain species and can likewise divine from the way they approach that certain kinds of animals have peaceful and conciliatory intentions. The beginnings of justice [*Die Anfänge der Gerechtigkeit*], as of prudence, moderation and bravery – in short all that we designate as the *Socratic virtues*, are *animal*: a consequence of that drive which teaches us to seek food and elude enemies" (*Daybreak*, 26). Characteristics that we have come to esteem (being just, resisting temptation, courage) are presented here as the result of a drive directed instrumentally toward practical demands. Virtue is thereby naturalized, the appeal of metaphysics as a means of explaining it denuded. What we think of as a matter of high principle that sets us apart from the rest of what lives is in fact the product of pragmatic considerations as common in humanity as in dogs. Nietzsche's conjoining of culture and nature exposes the supposedly autonomous Socratic virtues as complex refinements of the drive to survive. What "nourishes" – in the refined sense that exemplifies the world of culture – is not mere nutrition, however, but the self-understanding that accompanies a life of cultivation. What is dangerous likewise becomes, through culture, transformed into one's understanding of what is antithetical to one's cultivation. Strictly speaking, Nietzsche concludes, "it is not improper to describe the entire phenomenon of morality as animal" – at least in so far as its origins are concerned. Our virtues of justice, truthfulness, and prudence spring from inclinations no less animalistic and instrumental than those underlying the invention of hammers.

2. *Justice talk emerges as an articulation of our law-like, communal nature. Justice begins, Nietzsche argues, as a kind of exchange that springs from relations of power. Power is central to Nietzsche's theory even in his earliest "middle-period" writings, as something constitutive of the communal social realm: the human*

community has its origins in the struggle of the weak to preserve themselves against forces that would overwhelm them individually. The community is a majoritarian structure. Its founding principle is an equality that is governed by the dominance of the whole over the individual. It is a realm in which the norm is enforced relentlessly with regard to all its members in order to achieve a state of equilibrium. Communal equality, it follows, is an achievement rather than a given condition derived from natural principles: there is no "natural law," as liberalism might assume. Nietzsche offers an illustration of this conception of communities in The Wanderer and His Shadow *(22). A community, Nietzsche argues, will respond to threats posed to it by seeking a state of equilibrium, either in the form of the playing off of parties against one another or by increasing its collective power to match that of the perceived aggressors. This pursuit of a state of equilibrium characterizes the communal creation of justice. It likewise reveals why there is no such thing as "natural justice."*

The crude beginnings of justice, as we have seen, reside for Nietzsche in the extrapolation of pragmatic demands common to the animal and human worlds. He interprets the origin of justice in its specifically social and political forms as coming out of a subsequent re-elaboration of the logic of these demands by law-like, normative beings (i.e. creatures rather like us) endowed with language and culture:

> *Origin [Ursprung] of justice* ... Justice (fairness) [*Gerechtigkeit (Billigkeit)*] originates between parties of approximately *equal power* ... where there is no clearly recognizable superiority of force and a contest would result in mutual injury producing no decisive outcome the idea arises of coming to a mutual understanding and negotiation over one another's demands: the characteristic of *exchange* is the original characteristic of justice [*der Charakter des Tausches ist der anfängliche Charakter der Gerechtigkeit*]. Each satisfies the other, inasmuch as each acquires what he values more than the other does. One gives to the other what he wants to have, to be henceforth his own, and in return receives what one oneself desires. Justice is thus requital and exchange under the presupposition of an approximately equal power position: revenge therefore belongs originally within the domain of justice, it is an exchange. Gratitude likewise. (*Human, All Too Human*, 92)

Justice emerges from out of the play of exchanging practices. Questions concerning giving and receiving, the calculation of costs and benefits – in short, forms of negotiation – must all enter into play when one contemplates the nature of being just. Most especially, as this passage makes plain, power is central to Nietzsche's view. The notion of something counting as having the same value as something else, the logic of substituting one thing for another in a symbolic relation of equivalence that is deemed "just," is coterminous with the manifestation of power. Justice and power are thereby inextricably entwined. Exchangers who meet in the domain of culture as opposing parties with conflicting interests encounter one another locked together in a power relation that demands resolution – and the only resolution where neither party can overcome the other will, by necessity, be a "just" one.[1]

Nietzsche comes only later to develop a full-blown philosophy of will to power, but it is notable that even in *Human, All Too Human* power patterns his understanding of the social realm in a decisive way. Justice, on this conception, flows from relations of power – more specifically from the notion of an equality of power between two mighty forces. Justice, one should note, is above all characterized as "justice talk." It is negotiation, an engagement between law-like disputants with initially heterogeneous interests and purposes situated within a common sphere (the realm of exchange and culture). Each side finds itself forced into discussion and compromise by its own *lack* of a decisive advantage. Power, it follows, defines and shapes social relationships in such a way as to be an essential precondition of the emergence of justice. One should add that even here in the book that announces Nietzsche's first embracing of psychology, power is not relegated to the status of a mere psychological trait of the individual (i.e. a second-order feature). Rather, power is constitutive of relations between selves, of the conditions in virtue of which beings capable of meeting as disputants exist at all.

Power is in the first instance the power of shared custom and tradition over the body and it is this that gives rise to the possibility of any disputation between powerful camps arising. It follows that power is normative in its essential aspect.[2] Power is internal to communities; power radiates out from communities; and power radiates through the elements out of which they are constituted, coalescing around their formation and creating the conditions for designating what is designated as "outside" them (what is deemed "other") just as much as what falls "within" them (individuated subjects). The reason for this resides in the conditions under which communities originated and in the fact that these conditions abide so long as communities exist. In their beginnings, Nietzsche tells

1 Presumably, parties can also fail to reach such a just resolution. In such a case, conflict becomes interminable and is characterized by the strife and waste that epitomizes ceaseless feuding.

2 See Sedgwick, "Nietzsche, Normativity and Will to Power."

us (*The Wanderer and His Shadow*, 22) communities came about as structures that enabled the "weak" to organize themselves in such a way as to counter any powers that threatened them. They emerged, in other words, as a means of exerting a counter-form of power. Just as our distant ancestors' lack of sharp teeth and claws drove them to this collective solution to the problems posed by creatures endowed with very sharp teeth and claws, so more sophisticated proto-human and human social formations answer the same basic need. Communities exist because they satisfy the vulnerable, ever-threatened individual's need for safety (*The Wanderer and His Shadow*, 31).[3] As befits any organization of the weak, communities are majoritarian structures. They are established "on the basis of [their members] positing themselves as being *equal* to one another." The condition of equality is therefore the founding condition of communal relationships, but such equality is a kind of imposition.[4] In terms subsequently expressed in *On the Genealogy of Morality* (II, 1–2), the community is the site of regulation, the place where the norm is established (by unrelenting force if necessary). Should a community collapse into anarchy, Nietzsche adds, it ought to come as no surprise that there will straightaway erupt "that condition of unreflecting, ruthless inequality that constitutes the state of nature ... There exists neither a natural right nor a natural wrong [*Es gibt weder ein Naturrecht, noch ein Naturunrecht*]" (*The Wanderer and His Shadow*, 31). Communal equality is not a given, natural condition. Its authority does not reside in the universality of a timeless natural law but in the dynamic of the socially constituted realm from which it springs. Equality is posited as a precondition of a certain form of life (a shared life) being possible.

The discussion offered in section 22 of *The Wanderer and His Shadow* illustrates these points. Nietzsche envisages a situation in which a robber and powerful individual are both in a position to benefit from what they can get out of a weaker, communal group. The difference between baron and robber, Nietzsche notes with typical irony, resides not in their respective moral status, but only in the different ways they seek to obtain their incomes. The person of power can get what they want in tribute from the local community by promising to defend it from incursions

3 The word "individual" here does not necessarily designate a fully self-conscious subject endowed with all the faculties we conceive of now when we use the term "human." As has already been said, an individual can be just one organism, a member of a species. "Individual" in this sense does not denote individuality, which is for Nietzsche an achievement of culture.

4 Nietzsche adds in *The Wanderer and His Shadow*, 31, that the individual does not necessarily sit happily with the imposition of this communal compromise.

threatened by the robber. The robber attains their ends through threats and force. Both are more or less subtle brigands. What is "essential" in differentiating the two, Nietzsche argues, is the nature of the promise that the powerful person makes to the community. This promise states that he or she will enforce a state of "*equilibrium* with the brigand." It is in the space of possibility opened up by this balance of power that the grouping of the "weaker" detects the possibility of scraping out some kind of living while avoiding destruction at the hands of two equally threatening forces. The person of power exists in a relationship with the population of the locality that depends upon his or her ability to counter the threat posed by the robber and achieve a state of equality of power that ensures they will not be overrun and terrorized. For the community, the powerful individual is a means to the end of resisting the robber; and it is a means that is preferable to the more dangerous alternative of a weak community actively resisting both and thereby situating itself precariously between two aggressive and powerful parties. The community's strategy thus "holds *two* dangerous beings in check: the former through the latter, the latter through considerations of advantage." The community in this way repeats the logic that governed its primeval originating conditions. Just as the origins of communities reside in the weak gathering together in a domain of equality to guarantee mutual protection, so the community operates as a structure of power enabling the weak to impose by any possible means a state of "*equilibrium*" on an unequal and unstable situation.[5]

5 Seyla Benhabib makes the following comment: "For Nietzsche, morality is a sublimation of the life drive of the stronger to dominate the weaker; the origins of morality are internalized controls imposed upon the strong by the weak such that the weak cannot be damaged" (*Situating the Self*, 195). A similar view is expressed by Irving Zeitlin, who argues that Nietzsche, following so-called "pre-Socratic" thinkers such as Callicles (Zeitlin calls them "proto-Nietzscheans"), holds law and morality to be a construction of the weak designed to restrain the strong (see Zeitlin, *Nietzsche: A Re-Examination*). As is clear from the account offered here, from the outset Nietzsche has more nuanced conceptions of power, strength, and weakness in mind than the former view accords him. *All* human beings are, for Nietzsche, in their origins "weak" animals: our ancestors' lack of sharp fangs and claws is what impelled them into communal life. The proto-human community, as an assemblage of the vulnerable threatened by overwhelming nature, survived by way of the imposition of conformity on its individual members. In other words, as the second essay of the *Genealogy* argues, those who are subject to strong impulses that threaten the community are either mastered or spurned by it. The community is thus the original condition of human life which, at the same time, through various means unconsciously cultivates those who are subsequently able to turn on it and subjugate it (the "strong" – the tyrants who are the originators of bad conscience and the state, see chapter 5, section 5). It should be noted, however, that Nietzsche considers weakness to be productive (it gives rise to

Needless to say, the demand for equilibrium and security that constitutes an essential condition of communal existence means that any community will also seek other recourse to overcome existential threats if possible. This is because the state of subjection to one more powerful "is the least desirable one for the community, since it must deprive them of the time they need for the provision of their subsistence with the regularity it requires and be attended by the ever-present threat that they will be deprived of all the products of their labours. That is why the community prefers to bring its power of defence and attack up to precisely the point at which the power possessed by its dangerous neighbour stands and then give him to understand that the scales are now evenly balanced: why, in that event, should they not be good friends with one another? *Equilibrium* is thus a very important concept for the oldest theory of law and morality; equilibrium is the basis of justice"[6] (*The Wanderer and His Shadow*, 22). The very condition of equilibrium that forms the basis of communal life now forms the condition out of which justice (i.e. a fair exchange between disputing parties) emerges. When faced with danger, the community reasons economically (as one might expect of a population of workers and exchangers). If possible, it will sacrifice sufficient expenditure to raise itself up to a situation of power equivalent to that of the aggressor. However, Nietzsche argues, once the "scales" are balanced, once the community attains equality of power, what is sought is not unproductive, pre-emptive violence, nor vengeance for past wrongs suffered, but a just and law-like relationship that replicates the logic of the community's constitutive conditions.

What is revealed here, Nietzsche argues, is one of the essential preconditions of the ancient theorization and teaching of law, right, and morality: *the striking of a balance.* The epistemic injustice that, we have seen, Nietzsche holds to lie at the root of primitive human ancestry is thereby articulated into a domain of fairness. Equality of power is taken to supply the necessary condition for a just calculation of competing interests. The community applies the logic of equality that constitutes the internal condition under which its members relate to one another to what it encounters "outside" itself in an attempt to bring them into the power of its own

---

the intellectualization of humanity, and hence to all that is worthy of celebration in culture – see *Genealogy*, I, 7: "The history of mankind would be far too stupid a thing if it had not the intellect of the powerless injected into it"). Nietzsche's castigation of the weak (the herd) and his valorization of the strong (the individual) is therefore a more complex matter than at first it appears to be.

6 "*Gleichgewicht* ist also ein sehr wichtiger Begriff für die älteste Rechts- und Morallehre; Gleichgewicht ist die Basis der Gerechtigkeit."

domain. Equilibrium (which, amongst other things, is the precondition of being equal before the law and thus an extrapolation of custom and tradition) is an *achieved condition* of communities. It is essential to them, since their survival turns upon it. Justice, in turn, is possible in virtue of this state of balance. The reasoning underlying Nietzsche's consistent scorn for conceptions of natural justice is revealed here. If justice is a created thing, a matter of culture, practices, and interests, then any attempt to assert for it an origin within the natural order of things is an act of violence that distorts its reality. A "justice" that is an extrapolation of purportedly timeless, natural principles is one that ignores the judgement of historical, naturalistic scrutiny. A timeless justice is not something to be pondered, it is not something that has been struggled over; it cannot be questioned since its principles are taken to be always already given in their totality. Nietzsche's own justice, as we will see in the following two chapters, is prefaced on the contention of the necessity of such struggling, pondering, and questioning.

3. *For the metaphysician, justice involves the application of pre-existing and universal rules denoting right. In reality, justice is actively constructed: it is an extrapolation of the logic of equilibrium and exchange that characterizes communities. A pragmatic balance is struck. This balance is always a balance of power that expresses the regulation of costs and benefits necessary to maintaining social order. There is, consequently, no "natural justice." The condition of the "rule of law" likewise expresses a balance of power. The sources of these normative notions reside in the fact that communities are domains of power relations that impose equality, conformity, and regularity.*

Cruder metaphysical conceptions of justice, Nietzsche notes, grasp neither the nature of communal equilibrium nor the justice that characterizes it with sufficient subtlety. They fail to note that it is *not found but made.* On a crude conception, being just is taken to signify the conservation of an existing natural order of things. The principle of equivalence ("an eye for an eye") is simplistically presupposed to be something that merely preserves an already existing condition of justice by imposing a limit that the fury of the wronged party must not transgress when seeking recompense.[7] The crude conception thinks that when one exacts

7 Such a view is exemplified by Locke's liberalism. For Locke, natural right is at work even in the state of nature. The transgression of natural right legitimates a victim's desire for compensation for a wrong suffered. In turn, the victim's partiality in this regard justifies the creation of a civil pact and the invention of government as the impartial enforcer of principles of right. The role of the state is in this way given authority by natural law.

retribution in the form of "an eye for an eye" this means that the principle of justice is conserved in the retributive act itself.[8] Against this, Nietzsche claims that retribution does not preserve an already existing condition of being just, but actively constructs it. The assertion of a victim's right to *jus talionis* (the right to pay back in kind) re-establishes "the equilibrium of the disturbed power relationship": it *makes just* rather than merely conforming to a pre-existent universal state of justice from which the act of wrongdoing represents an unfortunate deviation. In other words, justice presupposes the creative striking of a balance; it is a matter of achieving an equal relation of power, not the mere conservation of an already established situation. Justice must be created; and it must be created within the productive tensions that characterise power relations.

To the extent to which equilibrium, on Nietzsche's conception, is not merely something given, it likewise cannot be taken to denote a naturally existing state of neutrality that gets disrupted by an illegal incursion when injustice occurs. Equilibrium (the balance of power) must be striven for and attained. It is for this reason that in the primitive, original states of early human societies, retaliation in the form of an eye for an eye was sought – "one eye, one arm *more* is [considered] one piece of power more, one weight more in the scales."[9] That is why in all communities there exist forms of discipline (in the shape of public shaming and penalties) that serve "as measures against transgressions, that is to say against disruptions of the principle of equilibrium." Punishment reflects this in so far as it usually takes the form of a loss of equality, "the transgressor is *reminded* that through his act he has *excluded* himself from the community and its moral *advantages*: the community treats him as one who is not equivalent" (*The Wanderer and His Shadow*, 33). In this regard, punishment is never mere repayment: it "contains something *more*, something of the *harshness of the* [*unforgiving inequality of the*] *state of nature*; it is precisely *this* that it wants to *recall*" (ibid.). Law, Nietzsche argues here, is once again best conceived of as an expression of the power of social forces and relationships. In such a world, costs and benefits as they relate to the collective social body regulate behaviour.

Justice ensues as the consequence of the human propensity to weigh and measure – it expresses an understanding of difference and equality.

8 This exemplifies what Gillian Rose calls the "classic definition of justice" (*The Broken Middle*, 143). This definition is, in Rose's words, "purely formal" and holds "that fairness consists in treating like cases alike. It implies that justice has always meant ... the re-establishing of differences judged to be just."

9 One could add here that power on this conception is embodiment. The body itself is power made manifest as an entity situated within a social domain.

It follows that when one encounters situations in which the rule of law has been established, the fact of its having been established does not spring from natural principles of justice, even if it is associated with conditions of equality. The state of equilibrium that the presence of the rule of law indicates is, rather, the sign of the forming of a social contract as a consequence of establishing an equality of power relations. The rule of law is thus a means rather than an end (*The Wanderer and His Shadow*, 26), since it ultimately rests on contracts between those who are *equal*. The rule of law consequently exists for as long as the power of those who have made the contracts remains "equal or similar." Pragmatism, not high principle, rules here: "prudence created law to put an end to feuding and to *useless* squandering between forces of similar strength." Because of this pragmatic condition, Nietzsche notes, should one party later attain dominance formal legality is easily overturned, "subjection enters in, and law ceases." We may be law-like beings, but each formally articulated instance of law and justice is at best a temporary condition, a contingent articulation of law-like propensities.[10]

We are, then, as a rule, creatures of community and, because of this, beings subject to the condition of equality. In terms Nietzsche will come to use increasingly, human beings are sophisticated "herd animals" (cf. *Beyond Good and Evil*, 199). Sophisticated herd animals are self-interpreters gripped by the power of norms; they obey the commands of custom, tradition, and law because the commands are what they are, because that is the norm, because that is how "we" do things here, and how we do things is sanctioned by the uncanny and frightful power of the sacred. It is this obedience that serves as the guarantor of the equilibrium upon which all human forms of communality depend if they are to endure. Here lies the source of the balance of power. Communities are structures permeated by the power of custom, the power of the sacred and what the sacred sanctions: the power of law. So long as the community remains relatively stable so does the law that characterises it. Custom, the sacred, and the law all point to the power of conformity that accompanies this stability: to the power that makes equal and

10 However, the consequence of the negation of law is "the same as that previously attained through the rule of law" since the dominant party needs to be careful to ensure that the strength of the subjected should be conserved and not pointlessly wasted. Nietzsche thus draws a distinction between the historical outcroppings of our primitive, law-like sensibility and that sensibility itself. The latter is the condition of the rule of law, but such formal conditions of legality are not themselves given as permanent structures. Their existence depends upon the balance of power within a community, or between different communities, and is historically contingent.

alike. The more that human psychology has been forged by this power, the more that human communities in the shape that we come to recognise them – i.e. as realms of shared values and practices populated by subjects endowed with socio-psychological propensities and abilities (e.g. promising, entreating, offering) and (not infrequently conflicting) interests – come into existence. With this we enter the realm in which the making of justice and rights happens.

4. Justice has the initial characteristic of an exchange because it emerges as the consequence of the nature of communities and the relations between them. We are exchangers, and negotiation is second nature to us. The idea of justice as fairness is hence a development of the primitive legal domain of exchange (like for like). Here lie the origins of personhood; likewise, the ancient view of justice as vengeance.

As has been noted, on Nietzsche's interpretation, what comes to be called "justice" has the initial characteristic of an exchange. It has this characteristic because it emerges as the consequence of the nature of communities as modes of organizing the weak and because stalemates arise between communities of exchangers and estimators. Such beings are creatures imprinted with normative propensities and they cannot help but unthinkingly bring these propensities to bear upon their situation. For an exchanger and estimator, negotiation and the giving of one thing for another is a natural extrapolation of the order of things wherein purposes can be pursued and wants satisfied according to the governing norms that ensure social equilibrium and stability. The notion that justice is a matter of fairness, Nietzsche adds elsewhere, is a further articulation of this (*The Wanderer and His Shadow*, 32). Fairness is a more nuanced extrapolation and enhancement of the principle that demands like be treated as like, "a subtler regard for equilibrium which looks before and behind and whose motto is 'as thou to me, so I to thee.' *Aequum* [equitable] means precisely 'it is in *conformity with our equality*'" (ibid.). Fairness, in short, presupposes the elaboration of crude, communal conceptual understanding into a richer web of self-interpretation: it requires each of "us" be counted as one amongst equals. Justice is hence deemed "fair" so long as it involves the exchange of like for like, so long as each party receives by way of repayment what it can claim an entitlement to in virtue of the demand for recognition of its equality, i.e. so long as power is balanced. Justice, one should therefore note, is from the outset of *Human, All Too Human* understood in terms of characteristics that signify a primitive legal realm composed of possession and barter. This is the realm in which,

Nietzsche argues in the second essay of *On the Genealogy of Morality* (II, 8), person encounters person for the first time. Personhood, exchange, equivalence, equality, and justice thus all emerge together as a battery of related and defining elements of the human world.

We can also note on the basis of this why vengeance, which often sounds to modern ears like irrational and unjust cruelty, also belongs to the most primordial sphere of justice. Revenge, the extorting of the most violent requital in compensation for a damage by a wronged party, is no less a form of estimation that springs from the notion of repayment than more recent and refined conceptions of fairness. That we moderns are no longer inclined to think in such hard and fast terms, Nietzsche notes, reveals the extent to which the meaning of justice pertains to an unpredictable fluidity, for meaning is a matter of historical development and such development is contingency through and through. The rank order of valued things and actions is neither stable nor eternal: "if someone prefers revenge to justice, according to the standard of an earlier culture, he is moral, according to that of ours he is immoral" (*Human, All Too Human*, 42). The meaning of the word "immoral," it follows, merely articulates an un-thought but constantly observed norm: it denotes someone considered "backward" from the standpoint of contemporary standards. The rank order of "higher" and "lower" on the moral scale does not, it follows, represent something that is established according to autonomous, timeless moral principles; but once it is in place this assumption comes to look like the universal basis upon which judgements are made. Cruel people, Nietzsche comments in line with this last point, strike us as a kind of living archaeology, throwbacks to earlier cultural stages in the development of humanity. Cruel human beings are a window on our ancient inherited identity: "They show us what we all *were*" and the gap that has opened up between them and us reveals the contingent and constantly shifting status of standards of value.

5. *Talk about justice is a consequence of there being creatures like us. Such talk emerges as an historically unfolding discursive practice that articulates relations of equivalence and power that are themselves rooted in a blind, organic drive to self-preservation. The power in question is not, however, a matter of individual psychology or brute force. It is a condition of possibility for equitable exchange and compromise. We can dispense with the kind of bodily sovereignty presupposed by Locke's "state of nature" theory (the body as possessor of inalienable natural rights). The body is possessor and possessed only in so far as it is a product of community, culture, history, and power. It is in being fashioned through these that the body becomes a bearer of rights.*

As we have seen in relation to section 92 of *Human, All Too Human,* Nietzsche envisages justice to be the consequence of a blending of necessary and contingent conditions. Justice presupposes exchange, and exchanging presupposes the kind of animal forged by the power of the morality of custom into the shape of a measuring esteemer. Given the power dynamic of this created human social world and the vicissitudes of life, conflicting parties of exchangers will sooner or later meet in a situation where none has the decisive upper hand that allows for the domination of one by the other. Justice talk is thus a necessary consequence of there being creatures like us. But the terms in which such justice is initially formulated, the terms that state what is equivalent (and hence what is subsequently open to being deemed "fair") rather than the relation of equivalence itself, will always be coincidental. Justice, it follows, cannot be defined in terms of the determinate content of timeless propositions. It is, rather, an historically unfolding discursive form that springs from the relation of equivalence being applied to otherwise intractable situations. Justice likewise stands revealed by Nietzsche as something that has a hidden history: justice talk springs directly from power differentials. Moments of "justice," it follows, do not consist in the negation of power but are in each case its exemplification. In this sense, justice can be traced back to an organically conceived self-interest (to the body as a field of drives) underlying the most primitive demand for self-preservation that compelled our ancestors into communal life. With this revealing of a hidden terrain of power, and in line with the ambitions of historical philosophy, justice is (rather casually) demythologized: "So much for the origin of justice," Nietzsche says, concluding the account in section 92 of *Human, All Too Human* elaborated above (cf. section 2). Revealed thus, justice is now something that originates in the cultural articulation of a blind egoism, an egoism without an ego, one that goes back to the drives and the body rather than self-consciousness. It is the expression of self-preserving powers, the origins of which have come to be forgotten due to layer upon layer of historical over-interpretation being pasted on top.

At the same time, it is worth noting what Nietzsche's demythologizing achieves here and what it does not. Although even in *Human, All Too Human* power is an essential component of Nietzsche's account of values, power is never mere imposition and domination any more than it is ever a matter of merely individual psychology.[11] Under the right

11 As Nietzsche will put it later in *Twilight of the Idols,* what matters about our habits is that they are *species habits,* rather than merely individual propensities. It is this contention that divides him decisively from Hume, who tends to consider habit to be above all a matter of personal psychology.

conditions, power gives rise to the need for negotiation, balance, and the attainment of settled outcomes rather than forced ones. Power is the condition that, for Nietzsche, creates the space within which something like fair and equitable discourse is made possible. Justice talk is not anchored in Kantian transcendental conditions. It is not governed by a power-free transcendental structure of possibility akin to an "ideal speech situation";[12] indeed, this kind of talk springs from a compromise that is not ideal in any sense. The notion of a settled compromise is a matter that concerns questions of power. In such a situation, however, there is no mere imposition of power or will. An equilibrium of power frustrates the capacity of brute willing (i.e. the drive of interests that motivates the organism, conceived here in terms of the high and mighty, the group who are the wielders of power[13]) to achieve its aims. What is required is discussion, a meeting of exchangers' egoisms and consequently compromise. The equality that underlies justice talk, it follows, is not a neutral space akin to the Lockean "state of nature."[14] No "state of nature" is presupposed here in the sense of a realm where right of possession springs from the isolated individual's claim to a natural sovereign legitimacy over his or her own body. Rather, the body is for Nietzsche a possession only in so far as it is situated and already worked upon in the domain of culture. It is an exemplification of the community, a kind

12 See Habermas's claim that legitimacy is not merely a matter of dominant norms, but concerns the manner in which such norms are rendered acceptable (*Communication and the Evolution of Society*, 188). Nietzsche's claim here would be that the very conditions of rendering norms acceptable are articulations of power. Power in this regard becomes something akin to a transcendental condition of social possibility.

13 Nietzsche specifically has in mind here the discussion between the representatives of the Athenian Empire and the Melian oligarchy that occurred during the siege of the island of Melos in 416 BCE, as dramatized by Thucydides. The Athenians wished to incorporate the Melians into the Empire of Athens, and the leaders of the island (not unreasonably, one might think) resisted this. In Thucydides's dialogue, the vastly outnumbered Melians are told in brutal enough terms about the reality of power. Questions of right, the Athenian representatives contend, concern only those who are in a relation of equality. A somewhat strained justification for this is given: this is the way of the world, for nature dictates that whoever has power behaves in similar fashion. The Athenians say they are merely an exemplification of this principle and so cannot be judged for what they do. The threat is then hammered home: in the absence of such equality the powerful do whatever they can do and the weak suffer what is imposed upon them. The Melians, who refused the terms of surrender offered during this discussion, finally capitulated to siege. The victorious Athenians responded by murdering all the Melian men they had captured, enslaving all the women and children, and subsequently colonizing the city. The slaughter that ensued was held to be an outrage in much of the Ancient Greek world and was the cause of much Athenian fear and anxiety when they themselves were overrun by the Spartans around a decade later. See Thucydides, *History of the Peloponnesian War*, 400–9.

14 See Locke, *Second Treatise of Government*, in *Two Treatises of Government*.

of illustration of its logic. The body is possessed only in so far as it already represents the communal human rebellion against the chaotic, lawless inequality of nature. The body is something fashioned, a conjoining of primitive organic self-interest with crude communal norms that ultimately serve to fashion the human animal into the kind of being capable of striking a compromise. With compromise, in turn, we enter the domain of rights talk.

6. Nietzsche's anti-metaphysical naturalism concentrates on natural historical articulations of rights, duties, and the like. Rights emerge when inequalities of power are created within or between social orders. Even subjugation creates conditions conducive to rights, since what is subjugated is of value to the subjugator – as the establishment of slaves' rights in the ancient world reveals. Rights, like justice, emerge from power relations and struggle. They are a form of power rooted in notions of exchange and contract and historical contingency. Rights are also, consequently, fluid. Any arbitration between competing interests is hence never a matter of the mere application of a universal rule. Fairness involves balancing interests in terms of the particularity of context in which they are at stake. Humanity's measuring propensities are fashioned in accord with the power relations that give rise to rights. We are sensitized to power differences as a hound is to scents. Our acute ability to sense power differences reveals culture to be driven by power relations. Power is normative, hence power is for Nietzsche the condition of historicity itself.

Conceptions of rights originate in power relations wrought within the primitive social structure of customary conformity. Rights came from tradition and tradition emerges from "*agreement.*" In other words, rights talk presupposes a form of social equilibrium no less than justice talk does. Once, Nietzsche argues in *The Wanderer and His Shadow* (39), people arrived at an agreement that worked well enough for them. It came to pass that the agreement became adopted continuously and unconsciously. The agreement became "natural" – that is, it became second nature, tradition. As the origin of the tradition faded, so it became sanctified: "Tradition was now a *compulsion*, even when it no longer served the purpose for which the agreement had originally been concluded." Notions that arose out of the necessity imposed upon our ancestors by their living conditions thereby became detached from their instrumental origins as a sign of the new, formative power these notions had acquired over the human soul. Once the self has been fashioned in this way, new forms of struggle and negotiation become possible.

Rights are established when two groups meet in a relation of unequal power (*Human, All Too Human*, 93). Under such conditions, the weaker is compelled by circumstance to submit to the stronger. However, with this submission comes the instituting of another kind of power: the threat that the weaker can always destroy itself, thereby depriving the victor of the spoils. Thus, even under conditions of subjugation there is a sort of equality "on the basis of which rights [*Rechte*] can be established."[15] Slave and master, too, exist within this framework: the slave is a possession, but as property the slave is valuable to the master. Correspondingly, certain limited rights accrue to the slave. "*Rights* originally [*ursprünglich*] extend *just as far as* one *appears* valuable, essential, un-losable, unconquerable and the like, to the other" (ibid.). It is for this reason that Spinoza's maxim hits home: "*unusquisque tantum juris habet, quantum potentia valet* [each man has as much right as he has power] (or more exactly: *quantum potentia valere creditor* [as he is believed to have power])." Rights, like justice, thus spring from relations of power in which acts of imposition, negotiations and, above all, the beliefs that form the conditions of such negotiations, serve to bind competing parties already locked together in new ways. Under such conditions, Nietzsche adds, a limited mutuality can even come from the subjugation that characterizes the ownership of the slave.[16] Rights are hence "a kind of power" (*The Wanderer and His Shadow*, 251). This struggle over power, which is an extension of the conjoining of natural drives and cultural norms that make human identity, forms the basis of Nietzsche's most powerful naturalizing critique. In a gesture that will be repeated elsewhere,[17] *Daybreak* talks of constructing a "*natural history*" of duties and rights. This means that such things can be accounted for in terms that do not require a metaphysical explanatory framework, only an historical one focused on the conditions of emergence and transformation of norms and the practices associated with them.

The duties we have, Nietzsche tells us, are the rights of others over us. As with justice, such rights exist because the notion of equilibrium allows each of us to be regarded as similar in terms of our ability to engage in "contracting and requiting." One is given rights because of what one is considered to be able to do with them. Such rights are not God-given.

15 Nietzsche again clearly has in mind here Thucydides's account of the Athenean and Melean dialogue. One of the Athenian arguments in favour of their opponents surrendering that is presented here is the contention that this course of action actually bestows a dual advantage: the one who surrenders does not suffer unnecessary loss and pain, while the subjugator gains by not having to destroy what will become their possession in any case.

16 A point reminiscent of Hegel's account of the master-slave dialectic in the *Phenomenology of Spirit*.

17 Most famously in part 5 of *Beyond Good and Evil*, "On the Natural History of Morality," and in the *Genealogy*.

They are contracted within social structures to individuals by others as a kind of precaution. They are given on the basis of the judgement that the person given rights can return by way of repayment something akin to what one has been granted to them when need be: "We fulfil our duty – that is to say, we justify the idea of our power on the basis of which all these things were bestowed upon us, we give back in the measure in which we have been given to" (*Daybreak*, 112). Typically for Nietzsche, a rights holder is an exchanger, a being capable of understanding and giving back in kind the equivalent of what has been given to them. I am given my rights because it is believed that, if needs be, I am in a position to return the favour in kind. Equally, I might be given rights because I am feared, since granting rights secures the means of avoiding a dangerous struggle. The possession of rights and their defence can also be an expression of self-interest: one party's loss of advantages might be held injurious to the party that gives them the rights they have. Finally, rights can be a gift of the powerful, something granted by those who feel sufficiently strong to be able to donate to another who is weaker. In each instance, however, the same principle applies: rights arise as "acknowledged and guaranteed degrees of power." If one were to construct a history of rights one would therefore be marking out tracings of struggles involving the enlargement or containment of forms of domination and the complex of negotiations that arise from such struggles.

All bestowing of rights, it follows, takes place on a plane of relationships patterned by power. If it should happen that "power-relationships undergo any material alteration" the rights associated with that initial state vanish, and in their place "new ones are created – as is demonstrated in the continual disappearance and reformation of rights between nations" (*Daybreak*, 112). The loss of a group's rights, by the same token, is a sign of loss of power. In this regard, rights and the talk of justice and fairness that accompanies their assertion and denial are, for Nietzsche, sites and symptoms of political struggle. On such an interpretation, prevailing social and political conditions determine the precise nature of the content of rights and duties. Rights are foremost signs of the workings of the social forces that cultivate equilibrium. The person who considers rights considers matters of balance in a manner akin to the calculations involved in using the scales with which one measures out ingredients for cooking or assesses the precise value of a precious metal in relation to a norm (e.g. a "gold standard"): "Where rights *prevail*, a certain condition and degree of power is being maintained, a diminution and increment warded off. The rights of others constitute a concession on the part of our sense of power to the sense of power of those others. If our power appears to be deeply shaken and broken our rights cease to exist: conversely, if we have grown very much more powerful, the rights of others, as we have previously conceded them, cease to exist for us" (*Daybreak* 112). Thus, what characterizes rights most acutely is their fluidity. They spring from the contingency of history and can be easily swept away when forces flow in a different direction. It follows from this that the person who wishes to be scrupulously fair stands in thrall to the vicissitudes of history and must be "in constant need of the subtle tact of a balance [*Wage*]." Fairness, in other words, involves the ability to calculate "degrees of power and rights" with a sensitivity that transcends the thoughtless application of a predetermined rule. Nietzsche here reveals himself as uncompromising in his rejection of the complacent belief that fairness is the mere application of a general rule. To be fair means to be aware of the limitations of what one conceives of as universal and indubitable: judgements are legitimate only in so far as they are determined within specific contexts. Like the relative values of stocks and shares on a modern-day market, the equilibrium that one may look to in order to supply the rule for the calculation of rights will never stay where one thought it was for very long. Fairness, it follows, is "difficult and demands much practice and good will, and very much good *sense*" – but it does not demand mere principles.

On Nietzsche's account, then, justice, right, and fairness all spring from normative conditions that are articulations of power relations. Out of these conditions human identity is wrought. Since we are beings fashioned by power it should come as no surprise that we are for Nietzsche worshippers of power (*The Gay Science*, 13). Nor should we be surprised that Nietzsche consistently holds "great politics" to be driven by a deep-seated need to cultivate the feeling of power (*Daybreak*, 189). This feeling for power constitutes, for Nietzsche, the domain of human sensibility to its innermost degree. The dim and distant past of human prehistory is again in no small measure responsible for this. The constant feeling of threat that our ancestors experienced when faced with a threatening world of inanimate objects, Nietzsche notes, led them to conceptualize inanimate nature as motivated by the powers of spirits, and to create "the most superstitious practices."[18] One sought to make oneself secure against the dangers posed by unseen forces in the same way as one did "against men and animals, by force, constraint, flattering, treaties, sacrifices" (*Daybreak*, 23). As a consequence of the constant provocation and cultivation of this state of fear "the *feeling of power* has evolved to such a

18 For the primitive human being, Nietzsche comments in *Human, All Too Human*, 111, "When one rows it is not the rowing which moves the ship: rowing is only a magical ceremony by means of which one compels a demon to move the ship."

degree of *subtlety* that in this respect man is now a match for the most delicate gold-balance." We are beings sensitized to power – our social instincts fashioned so as to be responsive to the most delicate and subtle differences of power. This betrays who we are and the nature of the primitive communal realm we emerged from in equal measure. The ability to sense differences of power has become the tendency that most strongly characterizes humanity, and the "means discovered to create this feeling" practically amount to the history of culture itself (ibid.). Culture, it follows, is driven by power and is, properly speaking, unthinkable without this insight.

Humans are compelled to cultivate the feeling of power because the threat of nature has been transformed through culture into a condition of existence. Norms create the human sensitivity to differentials of power, and power relations thereby get expressed as feelings. In the distant past, the primitive supplicant sought to appease the spirits by invoking the power of the conventions that animated and influenced the primitive social world. The so-called "civilized" person of modernity still does much the same.[19] In this way, norms stand as both the expression of primitive feelings and, in turn, a means whereby such feelings are refashioned into new forms of significance. Cultures are thereby stamped with identity by the power of norms. In social environments, power is always normative power – the power of command and convention. This is, for Nietzsche, akin to a transcendental condition of culture: without this condition, culture could not be an object of thought. This condition amounts almost to the opening up of historicity itself. Along with the notion of becoming, this condition is central to Nietzsche's conception of historical philosophy and hence his account of the conditions under which justice, the rule of law, fairness, and notions of rights and duties emerge.

19 To recall a passage from *Daybreak* (section 99) our habits dominate us because they are linked inexorably with primitive feelings. The realm of feeling is the realm of the unconscious, of evaluative tendencies that we simply act on without a thought. We are thus concatenations of relations of habits which gain their force due to the power of the feelings that have been cultivated both with and by way of these habits. One must be careful to grasp the subtlety of Nietzsche's position here. Feelings are manifestations of the body, of the fact that we are organic beings and hence creatures of the drives. But they are also fluid in significance. With culture, the realm of drives and feelings is subject to the power of norms. Norms harness, modify, and reinterpret the drives and feelings associated with them. Culture, in short, fashions the body and with it the self. It is a domain characterized by the tension between primitive feelings and norms. This uneasy coexistence of feelings and norms in unstable but productive relationships shows power to be what it is: a condition of life. Power does not, on this view, lurk behind things as a kind of essence in a manner akin to the forms of Platonic ontology. Power is manifest; it is the surface, it is lived – and *living something*, for Nietzsche, is the measure of what counts as reality.

7. Historical naturalism requires that the origins and significance of our moral world and the terms that populate it be reconsidered. This requires a comparative historical evaluation of the diverse moral forms, discourses, and practices (e.g. concerning love, conscience, law, punishment, relaxation, even nutrition). In this way, it is possible to make explicit the nature of norms whose usual justification resides in no more than unthinking familiarity and to thereby initiate an era ruled by the demands of scholarship. It is in the midst of this trajectory of thought that Nietzsche begins to develop further his philosophy of power. Power reveals the senses that accrue to dominant practices – an insight that reveals power to be a social and cultural rather than subjective phenomenon. Power thus invites us to reconsider the nature of subjectivity. Understanding, for example, can be analyzed in terms of a struggle and ensuing negotiation between contending drives rather than as an expression of conscious will. Understanding is a symptom of harmony that ensues when a balance of power is struck in social and political orders – it involves the formulating of "a kind of justice and a contract" akin to that between disputants endowed with rights. In this way, the social and individuated realms conform to a common logic of power: "inside" and "outside," community and subject, self and body, are conjoined, the latter being a community in microcosm. Any history of law or punishment, on this account, must be a social history of the body and its fashioning into forms of second nature.

Nietzsche's historical naturalism demands that the origins, nature, and significance of the elements that constitute the terrain of our moral world – law, justice, fairness, right and wrong, rights and duties – be rethought. Perceived from this standpoint, the study of morality now opens up an enormous field of labour for the curious. It requires first and foremost, Nietzsche tells us in *The Gay Science*, an engagement in the historical study of all the various forms of morality and evaluation that have hitherto existed. Up to now, every notion that has so far coloured human life with meaning lacks a corresponding historical narrative. Who hitherto, he asks, has sought to offer histories of love, greed, and jealousy, of conscience, piety, or cruelty? "Even a comparative history of law or at least of punishment is so far lacking completely. Has anyone made a study of different ways of dividing up the day or of the consequences of a regular schedule of work, festivals, and rest? What is known of the moral effects of different foods? Is there any philosophy of nutrition?" (*The Gay Science*, 7). In short, although we live through them we are ignorant of the nature of our norms. We do not exactly know what law is, nor what punishment might truly signify, nor how the regulation of work and play modifies those subject to it. We take our own norms for granted and all too readily fall prey to the bogus belief that we are adequately equipped with an understanding of these things and consequently of ourselves.

The world ought, on Nietzsche's view, to seem stranger to us than it generally appears to be. Our pretence to knowledge, he notes in part 5 of *The Gay Science*, needs to be unmasked as being nothing more than mere casual familiarity (355). History is unmasking, demythologizing, the stripping away of the layers of ignorance that conceal and protect the authority of what is in reality illusory. Imagine that the histories of our key evaluative practices and norms were somehow, someday done. What would happen then? The consequence, Nietzsche notes, would be the destruction of the goals stipulated by these practices. Scholarship would have to seek to replace them with itself, an endeavour that would require "centuries of experimentation" that "might eclipse all the great projects and sacrifices of history to date. So far, science has not yet built its cyclopic buildings; but the time for that, too, will come" (*The Gay Science*, 7).

It is in the context of such ruminations that Nietzsche begins to consider power to be a "teaching" (*The Gay Science*, 13). Power has a special explanatory value. The consideration of power is what reveals the significance of a practice within any comparative history one might construct. Take the example of cruelty, which Nietzsche has already listed as being amongst those things that demand the attention of the naturalistic historical philosopher. Beneficence and cruelty to others, Nietzsche notes, are equally effective ways of extending our feeling of power. Hurting a person whom one wishes to feel under one's power is the most efficient and crudest means of doing so, since pain is a simple and economic means of achieving the desired effect. However, more sophisticated ways of cultivating the feeling of power also exist for social animals like us. For example, we can cultivate the feeling of power by seeking to benefit others who are already in some manner dependent upon us, since an increase in their power brings to us a reflected glory. The more powerful we are, the more we demonstrate to others the usefulness of their being under our power – why it is good for them: "that way they will become more satisfied with their condition and more hostile to and willing to fight against the enemies of our power" (*The Gay Science*, 13). We willingly sacrifice much for the cultivation of this feeling, for it is the altar at which we unthinkingly worship.

Power, as is clear from each of these examples, always concerns others: it is socially mediated rather than a simply "subjective" issue confined to the ruminations of a mind on its own contents and dispositions. In the light of this insight, subjectivity and its attributes are open to being rethought. Take, for example, what is commonly held to be amongst the most characteristic of human attributes: understanding. For Spinoza, Nietzsche tells us (*The Gay Science*, 333) understanding means not laughing, lamenting, or despising. The Spinozist path to knowledge entails an overcoming of the passions, an absence of the turmoil associated with power struggles, that through this overcoming promises to take us into a neutral realm of pure reflection that spurns judgmental feelings. Understanding is calm, reflective consciousness. For Nietzsche, in contrast, understanding is a matter of the logic of power relations (of the passions, the feeling for power that characterizes us most acutely) working itself out through the interplay of drives and norms. The conscious state of my feeling that I have understood something is in reality mere testimony to the fact that I am in a condition of subjection to something more powerful than my consciousness. This "something," Nietzsche notes, is generally not even badly interpreted by us, since it is not as a rule even noticed. Understanding denotes the consequence of negotiation between the drives. It is the state in which one feels the outcome of the passions at work – of laughter, lamentation, rancour, and the like – in a manner co-ordinated under a kind of contract. To understand is to be in a state of harmony akin to the condition of the balanced equilibrium that characterizes the agreements constitutive of socio-political orders. When we evaluate (which for Nietzsche is what thinking and understanding amount to) the drives are at play within us, making competing claims, seeking dominance. In the aftermath of this staking of claims and the ensuing struggle there sometimes comes "a mean, one grows calm, one finds all three sides right, and there is a kind of justice and a contract" (*The Gay Science*, 333). This is because "by virtue of justice and a contract [*vermöge der Gerechtigkeit und des Vertrags*]" each of the drives is able to preserve its existence and hold itself to be in the "right [*Recht*]" with regard to the others. What we call "understanding" is merely an after-effect, the becoming conscious of this moment; it is the conclusion of a struggle, the ease-inducing sense of justice that reflects a state of equilibrium achieved as a consequence of the resolution of conflict between competing elements. The social and the individual realms, right down to the conditions that govern the workings of one's private thoughts, thus conform to the same logic of power.

We presuppose understanding to be "something conciliatory, just, and good," to be something that stands in opposition to the realm of the drives. In reality, however, understanding is no more than "*a certain behaviour of the drives toward one another.*" The feeling of comfortable optimism that accompanies understanding generates the illusion that the state of consciousness associated with it constitutes the core feature of thought. Consciousness, however, is insensitive to the drives and their combat, which takes place on another, deeper plane of feelings. On this plane, Nietzsche argues, the drives seek to assert dominance by exerting force and causing grief to one another. The account of their struggle thereby parallels on two levels the mode of struggle that Nietzsche holds to take place between competing social groupings when arriving at a just resolution to a dispute. First, the same logic is at work in the sense of ease that characterizes understanding as when justice and rights are fashioned in social orders. The same conditions of struggle, competition, and attained equilibrium used to characterize the one epitomize the other. Second, the attribution to the drives of the aim to injure replicates the "teaching" outlined in section 13 of *The Gay Science.* The social and the personal are intimately conjoined. The subject (the "individual") is an extrapolation of the body. The body, however, is on this conception never something that can be purely individuated and endowed with a fixed and unified core identity. It is a society in miniature, a nexus of evaluative propensities, a communal order in microcosm composed of multiple elements. Indeed, it is nothing less than a "social structure" made up of many souls (*Beyond Good and Evil,* 19).[20] To write a history of law or punishment means, on this view, to construct a socially aware account of the power relations inherent within different practices and different communities and the effects of these relations on the socially synthesized unity of the body. The history of humanity is, in this sense, always the history of second nature, of struggles between drives and cultural norms on the one hand and environmental conditions (amongst which may be included the norms of different cultures and communities) on the other.

8. Nietzsche's approach provides the basis for an account of the development of juridical norms, which are determined by power relations in a social context. It is in power relations that Nietzsche finds the genesis of herd morality: the rejection of what is "other" because it is a threat to the conformity conducive to communal survival. Nietzsche's approach throws light on how ethical norms, lawfulness, and a sense of justice develop out of realms of practices situated in webs of power. This approach also reveals how the will to conformity produces social orders that are not simply smooth spaces of harmonious obedience but domains of contradiction and resistance. Here, too, is demonstrated Nietzsche's naturalistic approach to morality, politics, and the social realm – an approach that is exemplified by his treatment of punishment.

Consider, in the light of this, how juridical norms develop within a community. What counts as "moral" and comes to be sanctioned by the content of law, deemed "just" and hence considered to be something that is

20 "*ein Gesellschaftsbau vieler Seelen*" (*Beyond Good and Evil,* 19).

a matter of right and duty, will always depend in some part or other upon the situation in which a community finds itself (*Beyond Good and Evil*, 201). If the community is faced with danger posed by what lies outside it (and for Nietzsche this condition underlies the constitution of all human communities since, as has been noted, they are essentially arrangements for the preservation of the weak), then its values will spring from this extra-moral need for self-preservation. The universal fear of the outsider, the conceptualization of the one deemed an "enemy," exemplifies this principle. The expression of this fear can take on two forms. The first is the fear already mentioned: the fear of what is purely other, of those who are not members of the community. The second is the fear of dangerous individuals located within the community who have themselves been cultivated there as a means of countering the dangers posed by outsiders. Thus, communal development gives rise to internal contradictions. In order to survive external threats the community encourages the development of individuals whose strength can be as risky to its internal order as it is essential for the community's defence. As life gets safer and more predictable, social structures become more stable and durable and the fear of the alien, the outsider-enemy, increasingly gets focussed inward upon these dangerous individuals. In short, the very success of the community in cultivating violent and risk-taking drives for defensive purposes means that those in whom such drives receive their most powerful expression now pose a problem. Although their initial necessity is outlived, the unruly individual endures as a dangerous threat to the "equality" that is the condition of social order. Here lies the genesis of what Nietzsche calls "herd morality" or "herd conscience." The logic of survival gets extrapolated to include all deviance, however pragmatically harmless. Anyone who looks as if they are independent, who appears to be dangerously "individual," comes to be regarded with suspicion and hatred from the standpoint that is the norm. The community senses in self-possession and independence of intellect a desire for independence that threatens its identity and self-confidence. It consequently deems such "individual" things to be immoral and ultimately "evil."

Things, however, get easier and more tolerant when "very peaceful conditions" come about. Now the community no longer feels overly threatened by much at all, and feels the bite of conscience at the slightest example of its own harshness. Even the hitherto "evil" criminal is forgiven, and sympathized with, due to the state of extremity they are placed in as a result of the force of the law being brought down upon them. The power of normative understanding (the "herd"), which from the outset hates anything that makes it feel threatened and uncomfortable, draws its own self-destructive conclusion. Even the "severity in justice" of punishment provokes discomfort and comes to be avoided as much as possible in favour of simply making sure the miscreant can no longer cause harm. The community thus draws the logical conclusion of its herd premises. What makes it feel unsafe should be abolished – including the very morality that states this ought to be the case, since this morality itself has the propensity to provoke this feeling, as in the instance of the harsh treatment of the criminal.[21] One sees in this account how the inner tensions of power relations at work within communal structures are productive of moral norms and a sense of justice. Likewise, Nietzsche also accounts for the way in which these norms can create individuals antithetical to them in terms of relations of power. As soon as one conceives of the social domain as a realm of power it is possible to grasp the manner in which social differentiation, tension, strife, and instability flow from the attempt at regulation and the imposition of unity. In order to survive, the community is driven to cultivate contradictory tendencies.

The account discussed above is presented in part 5 of *Beyond Good and Evil*, "On the Natural History of Morals." Here, as the very title makes manifest, Nietzsche's naturalistic conception of the moral, political, and social realms is writ large. Common conceptions of the true and the just are rendered open to doubt. If one might be tempted to consider Nietzsche's discussion of the self-destructive justice of the herd community as merely speculative, as concerning something fanciful and distant from us, the following section (*Beyond Good and Evil*, 202) aims to quash such a view. Modern European political ideals, Nietzsche argues, be they democratic, revolutionary, socialist, or anarchist, embrace the idea of the total superiority of the "*autonomous* herd." They all seek equal rights, praise the morality of pity, and reject the concept of "punitive justice" in just the way the herd community outlined in the previous section (201) does. Naturalistic historical critique is thus also a political tool in Nietzsche's hands – albeit an unsettling one. Its aim is to show how our conceptions of right, the good, morality, justice, and fairness have arisen in such a way as to challenge what is today taken for granted when it comes to the principles that are held to form the basis of good governance. Here, too, lies the motivation of a key aspect of Nietzsche's view of punishment – a problem that, from *Human, All Too Human* to *On the Genealogy of Morality*, is a constant presence in his writings. It is to Nietzsche's post-metaphysical account of punishment, therefore, that we turn next.

21 In Nietzsche's view, modern Europe is going through this latter stage of nihilistic judgement: it is in the process of taking its Christian morality to its logical conclusion and abolishing it.

4

The Punishing Animal

1. Metaphysics holds us to be creatures endowed with free will. This, for Nietzsche, forms the basis of a metaphysical distinction between humanity and nature. We presuppose that natural events carry no moral accountability, whereas human actions do. One is a sphere of mere necessity, the other of choice. The "criminal" is, in line with this distinction, deemed "evil" and "immoral" because they are considered capable of choosing otherwise than they did, i.e. they are held to be endowed with "intelligible freedom." Nietzsche's naturalism seeks to challenge this conception of accountability and the opposition between humanity and nature. He does so by seeking to show how the origins of the popular conception of responsibility spring from false inferences concerning the nature of values, selves, and actions. Originally, Nietzsche argues, values were communally determined. The consequences of some actions were frowned upon because of the damage or danger they threatened the community with. Actions with such consequences were deemed "bad." By degrees, however, the evaluations associated with the damaging consequences of deeds came to be associated with the deeds themselves, then with the motives associated with such actions, and finally with the person who does the "bad" deed. Responsibility, in other words, has a history, and that history begins with questionable assumptions concerning the link between doer and deed. Free will, Nietzsche argues, is in fact an error, as is the notion of responsibility that it justifies. This view informs Nietzsche's interpretation of justice, as it is commonly conceived. Such a conception is doubtful since no "justice" in any persuasive sense of the term can be served by foisting a false guilt on the undeserving.

Metaphysics, on Nietzsche's conception, has always drawn a dubious distinction between humankind and nature. For the metaphysician, the question of what makes us truly human has an answer that resides in the contention that we are endowed with characteristics and abilities whose integrity and autonomy cannot be doubted. We are held to be beings that have souls; who think; to be creatures of consciousness, conscience, morality, knowledge, and truth. According to the metaphysical way of thinking, all these attributes point back toward the human essence that underlies them: we are characterized first and foremost as beings endowed with *free will.* It is the attribution of such features and the spiritual freedom that grounds them that allows metaphysics to draw the kind of distinction that it does between humankind and the natural world. This distinction operates on an everyday level – which is another way of saying that we are all, to a greater or lesser extent, unwitting metaphysicians. Nature, Nietzsche notes in *Human, All Too Human,* sends us thunderstorms and various forms of stress, chaos, even disaster, but no one would be so foolish as to charge it with immorality because of this.[1] People do not as a rule hold nature accountable for what it does, however terrible, but they invariably do hold their neighbour to be responsible for his or her actions. The person who causes us harm (the "evil" human being, the criminal) we seldom hesitate to judge as "immoral." The reason we judge differently in each case comes from the fact that we attribute mere necessity to nature, but always feel the actions of the wrongdoer to be the consequence of free will, to be a matter of autonomous decision and unhindered choice (*Human, All Too Human,* 102). From the outset of his naturalistic turn Nietzsche wishes to challenge the presuppositions that underlie this conception of freedom, a conception that asserts an unproblematic causal link between individual choices and actions separated from society, the body, and its history. What he argues must be questioned is, in short, the "*fable of intelligible freedom*" (*Human, All Too Human,* 39).[2]

How, Nietzsche wonders, does it come to be the case that people presuppose that both others and they themselves can be held responsible for their actions? As one might expect from the kind of naturalism that Nietzsche endorses, the preliminary answer to this question offered in *Human, All Too Human* is given by way of a "history," i.e. an experimental narrative that turns round the formative power social norms exercise

1 For Nietzsche, even religious consciousness does not hold nature to be immoral on account of what it does. Storms might betray the anger of the gods, but the guilt that has aroused such ire is of human origin.

2 The phrase "intelligible freedom" refers to the conception endorsed by thinkers such as Schopenhauer. The latter's "On the Freedom of the Will" argues for the view that a noumenal, ahistorical will is the foundation of human action. On this view, my will is a pure faculty, unencumbered by the vicissitudes of history in a manner akin to the Platonic notion as it is used to distinguish between the sensible and intelligible realms. In Platonic metaphysics, the first is associated with sense experience and is removed from reality; the second with the pure apprehension of reality by thought. Nietzsche also associates this conception with Kant.

over the individual (*Human, All Too Human*, 39). It tells a story that depicts a sequence of dubious inferences. One begins with the initial stage of valuation. First, values are in their origins communal norms. Communities, not individuals, collectively evaluate actions on the basis of their utility. Actions were initially deemed "good" or "evil" not, as one might think, by way of reference to the motives that might underlie them but according to the consequences they have for the social body. Such values, in short, are instrumental judgements.[3] This leads to a second stage. Values, as we have seen, are for Nietzsche always already a matter of practices and customs. As layer upon layer of practices and customs accrues, the utilitarian origins underlying the community's evaluations get obscured, become over-written, and finally are all but obliterated.[4] The prehistoric pragmatic source of valuation is forgotten and the evaluative terms "good" and "evil" come to be taken to signify properties inherent in actions themselves, irrespective of the consequences these actions might have. This condition allows for the third stage, in which the designations "good" and "evil" come to be assigned to the motives that supposedly underlie actions. The attribution of motive allows for the fourth and final stage in which the attributed values and motives are conjoined in an act of identification wherein one now takes the predicates "good" or "evil" to signify the person doing the action. In this way, Nietzsche argues, the social order that governs human relations "successively makes men accountable for the effects they produce, then for their actions, then for their motives, and finally for their [own] nature" (ibid.). As soon as one appreciates that this nature is a constituted thing rather than something given and "natural" – that it is a product of concatenations of drives and cultural forces and consequently metaphysical presuppositions concerning it are questionable – one begins to realize that possibly nobody can be held ultimately responsible for their feelings, motives, and actions. Indeed, Nietzsche argues, if it is the case that a series of errors of reasoning underlies the attribution of responsibility, then the notion of responsibility as it is commonly conceived is another example of metaphysical mythology.

3 This, of course, does not mean that such values have to be true. They can be false (i.e. rooted in error and mythology) and function perfectly well instrumentally.

4 The signs that point to the origins of our value judgements are for Nietzsche to be found in our psychology (i.e. our evaluative inclinations, including our rational and logical capacities – whose origins are famously irrational and illogical) and in the hidden testimony of language, revealed by etymology. The latter, famously, is the key to the unfolding of the project of the *Genealogy*.

This myth fuels self-misunderstanding and fashions self-interpretation while we yet remain oblivious to the reality that abides behind it. What we hitherto considered deep, what counted as fundamental insight into the anatomy of the human soul, is not even superficial. It is pure error, bad interpretation that allows a chain of questionable inferences to generate belief in a mythical individual autonomy and personal responsibility. Trace these inferences back and one is in fact confronted with no more than "the history of an error, the error of accountability, which rests on the error of freedom of will" (*Human, All Too Human*, 39). With this insight, a new and strange moral-free world opens up before us. This is a world of uncanny innocence, one in which we are all delivered from the burden of being responsible for who we are. Here nobody "is accountable for his deeds, no one for his nature; to judge is the same thing as to be unjust [*richten ist soviel als ungerecht sein*]. This also applies when the individual judges himself." As this passage implies, Nietzsche's overturning of responsibility is intimately allied to the contention explored earlier[5] that error and injustice are inevitable components of human identity. However, the implications of this insight are such as to terrify the faint-hearted conformist. For, if there is no such thing as responsibility, then there can be no guilt – and no genuine justice can ever be served by acts of retribution for a guilt that is a mere chimera.

One immediate consequence of this questioning of what has hitherto set the terms of justice talk must be a new modesty with regard to the value of one's own judgements. Such modesty demands the suspension of the egotistical faith that one's own values and the presuppositions of one's own times are infallible. If people are not responsible for what they do, then one must not too readily judge the past for its violence and cruelty (*Human, All Too Human*, 101). Past societies that engaged in "the injustice [*Ungerechtigkeit*] involved in slavery" and subjection are, for Nietzsche, cases in point. In such times, "the instinct for justice [*Instinkt der Gerechtigkeit*]" that we moderns have refined so greatly, an instinct that underlies the trajectory of Nietzsche's own thought, was far less evolved. We must be prepared to admit that, taken on their own terms, even the torturers of the Spanish Inquisition had reasons to consider their violent acts to be in the right. The same goes for children (and also, for some reason, for "Italians"[6]), who Nietzsche considers to have a

5 Cf. chapter 2, section 2.

6 One Italian, a certain Herr Zuan, is said to have admitted to being a member of a gang of children in Sils Maria who devoted a good deal of time to pursuing and persecuting Nietzsche as he walked around in the rain under the shelter of a red umbrella. They would fill his closed umbrella with stones which would then fall on his head when he

highly developed propensity for deriving pleasure from cruelty to animals. As we will see, Nietzsche's refusal to judge in such cases is no mere nihilistic indifference to the question of judgement. It is, rather, rooted in an unrelenting commitment to the view that we must interrogate the grounds of our own propensity to judge; that what we take to be self-evident is always open to being rendered as alien and strange as the judgements of the past seem now to us – and in fact usually deserves to be revealed as such. In this regard, what looks like a trenchant form of sceptical cultural relativism in Nietzsche's writings is often something whose significance needs to be grasped polemically, in terms more closely associated with a tool than a method. It is a means to the end of critical self-questioning, something open-ended in its implications and consequently an invitation to further reflection rather than to nihilistic abandon. As, for example, when Nietzsche contends that we ought not to judge too readily those who are or have been cruel to animals but at the same time makes explicit what underlies such cruelty and thereby challenges it. Cruelty can be diagnosed as a sign that something is absent: it is a symptom of lack of understanding, that shows "the animal has ... been placed too far below man" (ibid.). It is not individuals who must be placed in question for dubious behaviour, but the culturally constructed relationships between drives and norms that speak through them and license or condemn their actions. In this regard, a refusal of the temptation to judge in simplistic terms is the essential precondition of rigorous social and moral critique.

2. Human, All Too Human *shows Nietzsche pondering a causal justification for his denial of free will. Like the twisting play of water rushing down a waterfall, actions appear complex and irreducible, but in both cases this complexity conceals something that is in principle calculable. Human actions are determined; there is no metaphysical "free will" motivating an ahistorical self or soul concealed behind our actions that is ultimately responsible for them. The person who seeks knowledge must begin by affirming the lack of individual responsibility and refuse the temptation to indulge in moral censure. Nietzsche attempts the dissolution of the very distinction that licenses moral censure: that between good and evil. For him, since the origins of value judgements are instrumental (serving the practical needs of communities) the differences between such judgements are differences of degree, not differences in kind. In turn, a person's ability to make appropriate judgements in a social context cannot spring from either a specifically "moral" or "immoral"*

---

opened it (see Theodor Adorno, "Aus Sils Maria" (1966), in *Ohne Leitbild: Parva Aesthetica* (*Adorno: Gesammelte Schriften*, vol. 10:1, 328ff; cited in Clausen, *Theodor Adorno*, 333).

source. Its origins reside in the heritage of a primitive dynamic of communal relations and bodily drives. Only by degrees, Nietzsche adds, might a "knowing humankind" of the sort exemplified by historical naturalism supplant this more primitive, "moral humankind." A knowing humanity would be such that it could affirm the essential innocence of human identity and affirm the amoral necessity at work in human life. In affirming such necessity, Nietzsche's new creed for knowledge seeks the cultivation of new habits of thought that spurn moral censure. This vision of a comprehending and wise humanity illustrates Nietzsche's conception of justice. This justice rejects the hegemony of what has hitherto counted as "morality."

In section 106 of *Human, All Too Human,* Nietzsche experiments with providing grounds for his view. The conception of freedom of the will that is commonly adhered to is, he argues, a misinterpretation. We have a powerful tendency to consider the relatively complex realm of human comings and goings to be a matter of autonomous action grounded in free choice. As a rule, it does not deserve to be characterized in this way, any more than the behaviour of water plunging from a waterfall, exhibiting twisting patterns that appear to be redolent with the kind of spontaneity characteristic of freedom of the will, would tempt us to attribute free will to water. What is at work in falling water is only iron necessity. The appearance of hazard and arbitrariness conceals something that is "calculable" (at least in principle). Human actions are no different. Here, too, an "all-knowing" gaze would be able to compute and measure every act, every gain in knowledge, every deed of evil or good. The agent may feel him or herself to be "fixed in the illusion of free will," but freeze this moment and an all-encompassing intelligence could calculate from it the future of every being down to the smallest detail. "The actor's conception of himself, the assumption of free-will, is itself part of the mechanism it would have to compute." Such a god's-eye view, Nietzsche knows, is impossible for us; but its invocation here allows for the denial of the moral right of even a god to judge. In the same way, the person who seeks knowledge must take as their starting point an innocent humanity, one that is utterly unaccountable for what it does (*Human, All Too Human,* 107). What has hitherto counted as a key motivation underlying the desire for knowledge, the urge to judge, must be discounted. The philosopher must become someone who "may no longer praise, no longer censure, for it is absurd to praise and censure nature and necessity." The person of knowledge must stand in front of humanity in the same way as the botanist confronts a plant, the aesthete a musical artwork: the object of contemplation may fascinate, it may be loved for its elegance or beauty, but neither fascination nor beauty endows either botanist or aesthetician with the right to sit in moral judgement of what lies before them. Why, then, treat people differently? Are we not also as blameless as the plant in the field or a melody? Are we not as morally unaccountable as the complex intertwining play of water as it cavorts and tumbles down a precipice?[7]

What are taken to be good or evil motives, Nietzsche contends, must consequently have their origins somewhere other than in the individual's will and choices. Indeed, it is possible to conclude that good and evil are much closer kin than is generally believed, for they share a similar social utility. Apparently opposing moral judgements are marked by differences of degree, not by differences in kind: "Good actions are sublimated evil ones; evil actions are coarsened, brutalized good ones" (*Human, All Too Human,* 107). It is only the level of an individual's "competence for judgement," which is not a *morally* accountable matter, that determines the degree to which he or she is driven by brute desire or by what are taken to be "higher," normatively determined social goals. All of us possess "an order of rank of things considered good" with reference to which we judge our own actions and the actions of others. But the "standard [*Maßstab*]" of measure according to which the individual judges is limited, and hence partial, due to its primitive origins. In any case, "the highest degree of human intelligence which can now be attained will certainly be exceeded in the future: and then all our actions and judgements will seem in retrospect as circumscribed and precipitate as the actions and judgements of still existing primitive peoples now appear to us." To think of this may be painful, but we should be consoled by the fact that the pangs experienced in such thoughts are "labour pains": "The butterfly wants to get out of its cocoon, it tears at it, it breaks it open: then it is blinded and confused by the unfamiliar light ... It is in such men as are *capable* of that suffering ... that the first attempt will be made to see whether mankind could *transform itself from a moral to a knowing mankind.*" Morality, in other words, must give way to "wisdom." With

7 Of course, one may ask about the status of the philosopher in all this. Is he or she any less prey to the illusions they unveil at work elsewhere? Such obvious problems will lead to Nietzsche later developing the notion of the "will to truth" as a means of further explicating the meaning of the pursuit of knowledge. This, as we will see in the next chapter, is a component in Nietzsche's mature conceptions of freedom and justice. For the moment it is enough to note that Nietzsche's position in *Human, All Too Human* turns on the contention that there is a significant difference between moral and critical-historical discourse: where the one is mythology, the other, if properly articulated, is a demythologizing critique that spurns any claim to an absolute standpoint on the world. As such, its task is essentially negative. It performs a kind of ground-clearing for the more positive philosophical project Nietzsche begins in the early 1880s with *Thus Spoke Zarathustra.*

this a new "gospel" will be in the ascendant. This new gospel is one that brings with it a paradoxical feeling of elation and despair, for it is at one and the same moment a dawn and twilight. "Everything is necessity – thus says the new knowledge; and this new knowledge is itself necessity. Everything is innocence: and knowledge is the path to insight into this innocence. If pleasure, egoism, vanity are *necessary* for the production of the moral phenomena and their finest flower, the sense for truth and justice in knowledge [*des Sinnes für Wahrheit und Gerechtigkeit der Erkenntniss*]; if error and aberration of the imagination was the only means by which mankind was able gradually to raise itself to this degree of self-enlightenment and self-redemption – who could denigrate those means?" (ibid.) It may be, as the opening of *Human, All Too Human* avers, that everything is in a state of flux. But it is also contended that "*everything is also flooding forward*, and towards *one* goal." This goal is one that the mature Nietzsche endorses no less than his more youthful self, although he may cease to consider its occurrence to be quite so inevitable. It is the goal of cultivating in ourselves "a new habit, that of comprehending, not-loving, not-hating." What will happen thereby is that this new habit may after millennia "perhaps be strong enough to bestow on mankind the power of bringing forth the wise, innocent (conscious of innocence) man as regularly as it now brings forth – *not his antithesis by necessary preliminary* – the unwise, unjust, guilt-conscious man" (ibid.). Here, for the first time, is presented the vision of Nietzsche's new justice. It is a justice that embraces innocence as its starting point: the innocence of becoming and the innocence that marks a return to what is natural, the assertion of naturalism as the only means of explicating the potential offered by the human animal to overcome itself and thereby be transformed into something better.

3. If we are not morally responsible for what we do, any "justice" that seeks to praise or blame, reward or punish, is a sham. This view leads Nietzsche to question further the moral value attributed to punishment. If punishment serves only the pragmatic purpose of ensuring the continuation of society, then its significance must be reconsidered. Punishment needs to be acknowledged for what it is: a powerful social tool, not something concerning matters of desert. So long as one thinks of punishment in moral terms one is, ironically, being unjust. The philosopher thus needs to stand beyond the temptation of moral judgement. In doing so, he or she becomes more truly a person of justice than the one who exemplifies the social norm in their indulgence of the urge to judge others as morally wanting. Nietzsche calls this refusal to judge wisdom. Wisdom demands that the criminal be decriminalized. This view stands in stark contrast to the modern administration of justice, i.e. the world of penal law replete with its formal conditions and institutional functionaries. The practice of law and justice as it is now understood is, for Nietzsche, erected on the dubious assertion of free will. It presupposes that the criminal is always already able to distinguish between good and bad reasons and, for reasons of irrational assertiveness, chooses bad ones reasons over good and so commits evil. Such an account is absurd. It presupposes the primary motivation for action is intelligence and that the criminal is someone who perversely elects to flout their own best insight into what constitutes the right course of action. If this were so, then an individual's guilt would reside in a pure, irrational wilfulness that flies in the face of pragmatic and moral reasons alike. Such a view, Nietzsche argues, is contradictory. A wilfulness of this sort would, by definition, exceed the conditions that serve to specify an agent's rational competence and so render them blameless.

If one comes to follow the teaching that holds us to be essentially unaccountable in moral terms for our actions, then it follows that one can no longer consider a "so-called justice that punishes and rewards [as falling] under the concept of justice at all: provided, that is, that this [justice] consists in giving to each what is his own" (*Human, All Too Human,* 105). Here, the value of values is placed in question; likewise, the justification of punishment. Punishment, as we have seen, is held by Nietzsche to be a matter of social usefulness. The one who is punished does not "deserve" to be punished but is simply the means of advertising the consequences of acting as they have in order to predispose others against doing likewise. Nor, by the same token, does the "good" person deserve reward for what they do, since they simply act as they must in any case, not from any moral superiority. Thus, it is "mankind's utility [that] requires their continuance," not any overarching conception of the just and the good. A powerful instrumental necessity drives the normative realm of human culture. If we were to get rid of punishment and reward we might well lose some of the strongest influences that incline us to act or not act in certain ways, but we would not be morally worse off. We are driven to judge, to punish and reward, as a condition of being here at all, but such judgements as we make have no meaning independently of the environmental and social conditions out of which they are articulated. This attitude illustrates Nietzsche's contention that the philosopher's role is to furnish a commentary on the realm of human affairs that refuses to succumb to the temptation to precipitate moral censure. The philosopher is someone who seeks to be just, which means they must not judge with a view to censure: this is the hallmark of their wisdom. This is why a philosophical mind reveals itself in its "unbelief in the metaphysical significance of morality" (*Assorted Opinions and Maxims,* 33). The philosopher happily accepts that there is no way out of the prison of causal necessity, no exit leading out "into the air of free will" and the responsibility that would accompany it, for "we can only dream ourselves free, not make ourselves free." There is, it follows, no tribunal of judgement on the world or those in it that could warrant anyone being held morally accountable for anything. Neither humanity nor the universe of becoming is blameworthy: "the philosopher thus has to say, as Christ did, 'judge not!'"[8] It is here, in this refusal to judge, that the philosopher is for Nietzsche a being of justice. One must spurn the temptation to hold anyone accountable simply for being who they are, for there are no moral grounds for such a condemnation. Consequently, one must de-criminalize the criminal.

With this last claim Nietzsche places himself in opposition not only to the common conception of justice, but also the functionaries and forms of authority associated in modern culture with notions of legality and right: those who administer systems of criminal law and punishment. The prescribed roles of the professional judges and punishers of modern society presuppose the very conception of freedom Nietzsche questions. The legal functionary must always seek "to establish in each case whether an ill-doer is at all accountable for his deed, whether he was *able* to employ his intelligence, whether he acted for *reasons* and not unconsciously or under compulsion" (*The Wanderer and His Shadow*, 23). Being deemed a miscreant means being taken to be a person who, in a given situation, freely decided that bad reasons were preferable to better ones. The central presupposition is that the criminal "must therefore have *known*" about and understood the difference between better and worse reasons. Only with this knowledge can a person be held responsible for what they do. By the same token, only a *lack* of this knowledge that was not the result of some kind of wilful neglect of the duty to learn would serve to mitigate responsibility. The law, it follows, holds people accountable for their wrong-doing because it presupposes a person endowed with the ability to know better, someone who can grasp with sufficient clarity the nature of doing wrong even as he or she does it. The evil person, in other words, is taken to be capable of judging him or herself to be evil, which is to say that the person who engages in wrong-doing can be legitimately punished because he or she "intentionally acted contrary to the better dictates of his [or her] intelligence." The problem with this conception, for Nietzsche, is revealed by a contradiction: "But how can anyone intentionally be less intelligent than he has to be? Whence comes

8 Nietzsche points out here that where Christ says this on the basis of the belief that we are all equally sinful and hence guilty, he does so because he asserts the fundamental innocence of all.

the decision when the scales are weighted with good and bad motives?" Here, Nietzsche notes, the usual answer to this quandary steps in: one calls upon the concept of free will. The evil person *chose* to be evil. The miscreant's acting in the way they did is taken to be an expression of "*pure wilfulness.*" What matters is their intention and it is the will that is thereby held to account in the court of law: "It is this supposed wilfulness which is punished: the rational intelligence which knows law, prohibition and command, ought to have permitted no choice, and to have the effect of compulsion and a higher power. Thus the offender is punished because he employs 'free will,' that is to say, because he acted without a reason where he ought to have acted in accordance with reasons" (*The Wanderer and His Shadow,* 23). Why did the miscreant do what he or she did? The account that invokes free will now actually does so in a manner that pushes this very question to one side. To claim in this way that a deed is an act of free will, Nietzsche points out, is to make of it something that originates in unreason. The evil deed has no source and no purpose that accords with the conditions of rational intelligence – it is pure wilfulness. But if this is the case, then it follows that the perpetrator committed their act without any intention of doing so, and if this is so then they cannot legitimately be held to account for what they have done. Thus, the very thing that is invoked to justify punishment is left in tatters. The person who endorses to the concept of free will has "*no right* to punish."

4. An action's meaning is a matter of context and of the evaluations that predominate in a particular social realm or milieu. In modern society, the law court is best understood as the exemplification of the dominant normative sphere. It consists of rules specifying the conditions in virtue of which a person is to be held responsible for committing "bad" actions and the measures appropriate to punishing them for doing so. The sphere of law clashes with the alternative normative milieu of the criminal, who is obliged to step out of a violent social sphere where the justification for sometimes appalling acts is not too difficult to find, and give reasons for doing so in terms acceptable to the norms of the legal sphere. This fact, Nietzsche adds, is why the law court is often a place where mitigation is sought on the grounds of extenuating circumstances. The gulf separating the realms of criminal action and legal judgement cannot, however, be bridged in the law court. Fully grasping the conditions that mediate and condition the significance of a person's actions would mean abandoning the desire to find anyone guilty, and this is something no court can do simply in virtue of being what it is. Nietzsche argues that the habitual criminal is less blameworthy than the habitually good person because they are more entrenched in their habits. If one wishes to apportion blame for a misdeed, it might be better to trace the deed back from the doer to the forces (parenting, education, and the like) that shaped them, in short society as a whole. At the heart of the penal system lies a lust for protracted vengeance that circumscribes the social realm. Our notions of legality and just punishment represent the enactment of an impersonal and repressed form of revenge on the miscreant who represents a threat to social order. Public virtues are, on this view, always avenging virtues. All virtues that are public, it follows, depend upon enforcing the condition of an exchange in which recompense is made for a wrong. Other virtues exist, Nietzsche notes in a manner that prefigures his later writings, that spurn this logic of exchange.

For Nietzsche, action is essentially a normative issue. If one wants to know what it means when a person commits a wrong it makes sense to look at the everyday world they inhabit and the conditions constitutive of that world. The criminal who is completely cognizant of what he or she has done, Nietzsche suggests, often does not regard their malfeasance as so very out of the ordinary and beyond rational comprehension as do those who judge and rebuke him (*The Wanderer and His Shadow*, 24). What occurs in the law court is a clash of normative worlds mediated by power. The criminal steps from one normative realm into another; in the one they simply act, in the other they greet their fate at the hands of authority. The punishment that the criminal receives is determined in exact accordance with the degree to which those who judge and condemn lack an understanding of the wrong doer: "Our crime against criminals consists in the fact that we treat them like criminals" (*Human, All Too Human*, 66). The game played out in the court of law usually involves the defence seeking to illuminate all the elements of the case that excuse the accused, that show the extent to which he or she was not able to do otherwise given the conditions they inhabited. In principle, if the mitigating circumstances of the crime are sufficiently well known by an accused person's counsel then this knowledge ought to end up melting away any sense of the criminal's guilt. "Or, more clearly: the defending counsel will step by step *ameliorate* that *astonishment* which condemns his client and metes out his punishment, and finally expunge it altogether, by compelling every honest auditor to confess to himself: 'he had to act as he did; if we were to punish, what we would be punishing would be eternal necessity'" (*The Wanderer and His Shadow*, 24). The problem with the legal process, however, is that such an ideal bridging of normative spheres is impossible. The judge can never grasp fully the kind of knowledge of a crime that would allow it to be understood completely. "Fairness [*Billigkeit*]," Nietzsche argues, ought to decree the equal treatment of like cases – but given that the mitigating circumstances of one case may be much better known than those of another, it follows that the possibility of fairness and therefore justice is compromised from the outset.

To enter the criminal's world, to grasp the conditions that give rise to their self-interpretive acts,[9] requires an ability to slough off the urge to hold accountable. Nietzsche does not shy at attempting to take such a step, starting as one might expect with the grounding condition of action: habit. Criminals, he argues, are like everyone else: they act on habit. This insight ought of itself to incline us to consider someone less blameworthy for a crime than we might otherwise consider them to be, "for it happened as the result of a tendency the criminal has acquired and which he would have found hard to resist" (*The Wanderer and His Shadow*, 28). In practice, however, the opposite is the case. In the law courts of his times, Nietzsche notes, a person who has had a hitherto blameless life is more likely to be treated leniently than the habitual criminal: the previous serviceability of the blameless conformist is weighed against his single harmful act and this person's punishment limited accordingly. Thus, what in reality occurs when law is administered is that a person's past is generally rewarded or punished, which is absurd. Why, Nietzsche asks pointedly, stop at the point where one does with regard to a person's past? Surely "one ought to go back even further and reward or punish the causes of such or such a past, I mean parents, educators, society, etc.: in many cases the judges will then be found to be in some way involved in the guilt." The individual is ultimately as innocent or blame-worthy as the social-historical order out of which he or she has sprung[10] – but who would dare to hold to account an entire society?

What is at stake when the criminal is brought to account? What lies behind the pomp and regal ritual of the court of law and the punishments it deals out? Nietzsche's short answer to such questions is that, as things stand, in most cases what matters is vengeance, in one form or another. Revenge, of course, is a word that can have many meanings. It is akin to a catchall, a convenient pouch that, as with all words, one can use as a place to store a wide variety of things (*The Wanderer and His*

9 To act, on Nietzsche's account, is to interpret, and interpretation is a kind of activity. There is for him no sense in differentiating between theory and practice in hard and fast terms. All attempts to do so, beginning with Platonism, have merely contributed to the unfortunate conceptual aberration called metaphysics.

10 Nietzsche's endorsement of this view, and many passages from the *Genealogy*, render questionable claims that for him politics "must *first* be individual, and only then social" (Strong, *Nietzsche and the Politics of Transfiguration*, 217). Such a view, as I argue in the final chapter of this book, tends to presuppose a liberal conception of the political that the general tendency of Nietzsche's thought seeks to overturn. For Nietzsche, the individual is constituted out of the communal domain of custom and tradition, and the political emerges as something that shapes individuals as much as something that might be shaped by them (consider in this regard the politics of slave morality discussed in the first essay of the *Genealogy*).

Shadow, 33). Vengeance can be a simple, honest, and direct response, such as occurs when one hits out having suffered a blow from someone or something – its purpose is limited to averting further damage. It can also, and more sinisterly, mean acting with a view to causing hurt. The latter generally requires time and planning: one must consider the best means to cause the greatest harm. This means that one does not, as in the first case, simply seek to avoid more harm for oneself but, on the contrary, knowingly invites the possibility of yet more harm. Nietzsche notes that this form of revenge "is a question of restitution." It is a repayment dependent upon the familiar logic of exchange that assumes one can determine a relation of equivalence between acts and things. The extent to which one can think oneself into the position of the victim upon whom the revenge is to be discharged will determine how extreme it is, how it can cause maximal pain and loss and satisfy the equivalence-lust for restitution. It follows that revenge requires a sense of social status, for the victim must be deemed "worthy" of the pain or embarrassment that is destined for them – one would not consider it worthwhile to take revenge on someone who is already despised.

We are, as a rule, a society of avengers – a rule that has few exceptions. The law court, likewise, is a sphere of revenge on two levels. One can pursue someone individually by means of a private litigation – a pursuit compounded and enriched by the fact that the court of law necessarily invokes "the revenge of society." Thus, by way of "judicial punishment, private honour as well as the honour of society is thus restored: that is to say – punishment is revenge. Undoubtedly there is also in it those other elements of revenge already described, insofar as through punishment society serves its own self-preservation and delivers a counter-blow in self-defence" (*Human, All Too Human*, 33.). One cannot, for Nietzsche, properly comprehend the nature of the court of law, likewise the modern penal system that lies behind it or the realm of public virtues that surrounds it, unless one acknowledges that it is circumscribed by the notion of revenge in all possible guises. Revenge is, in this regard, a matter of impersonal social utility. The public virtues demand equivalence (payback time) as the price that is to be paid for subversion of the order of things because subversive criminality creates social instability. For this reason the practising of clemency cannot be a public virtue. The person who shows mercy acts in a manner that is inexorably private. They embrace a virtue that stands beyond the bounds of the ruling norms of the social order. That is why "No bench of judges may conscientiously practise mercy," which is constitutionally usually a privilege of the sovereign (*The Wanderer and His Shadow*, 34). The social order acknowledges as virtues only those forms of action that have social utility or are harmless to it, "those that can be practised without its incurring loss, for example justice." Hints of Nietzsche's mature conception of individual autonomy are scattered in this observation. Any virtue which does not conserve, which is costly and involves loss, does not have its origin "*within society*," since loss contradicts the utilitarian principle of the preservation of equilibrium that is a grounding condition of communal and social life: "They are thus virtues belonging among non-equals, devised by the superior, the individual; they are the virtues of *rulers* bearing the sense: 'I am sufficiently powerful to put up with a palpable loss, this is a proof of my power' – and are thus virtues related to *pride*."

5\. *For Nietzsche, the sources of action are largely mysterious and consequently any claim to know them exhaustively is wholly mythical. "Moral realism," the view that holds free will to be the cause of human action, must be subverted. Just as the value of a person's labour can never be fairly assessed, for it would demand the impossible achievement of placing the entire person into the reckoning, so any attempt to estimate the degree of a person's moral culpability founders on the same impossibility. Justice, as it is practised, is really a game of consequences – it is purely pragmatic and instrumental. Consequently, like Christ, Nietzsche urges us to withhold moral judgement of others. This lack of moral accountability entails a rethinking of our presuppositions and habits: a re-examination of the value of punishment is needed. The criminal needs to be regarded as a helpless innocent, as someone no different from the person who has lost their sanity. Not punishing vengeance, but understanding and treatment is the appropriate response to the wrongdoer. The primary aim should be to restore the criminal's self-respect rather than denigrate them according to the logic of compensation demanded by "shopkeepers' scales." The concepts "sin" and "punishment" need to be done away with. In short, the utilitarian logic that dominates the social realm must be challenged in favour of a vision of a state that regards those who damage it with mildness and toleration. What is needed is an ethic of mercy.*

As we have seen, the belief that we know "*how human action is brought about*" is for Nietzsche a "primeval delusion" (*Daybreak*, 116). Nietzsche's condemnation of "moral realism," of the belief cleaved to by Socrates and Plato that right knowledge will always be followed by right action, of the attitude that endorses a conception of free will that allows for the wrongdoer to be held responsible for their actions, springs from this. Nietzsche's view is that we must begin with the assertion that none are guilty and that the assumption of guilt conceals this reality. Justice as it has been generally conceived is, it follows, not about morality and responsibility but concerns the practical requirements of social life. Take the parallel example of how work is evaluated in modern society. The value of work can never be fairly evaluated by the degree of time and effort, good intentions, idleness, etc. put into it – such an approach "can never be *just* [*gerecht*]" (*The Wanderer and His Shadow,* 286). A fair analysis of this would require putting "the entire person on the scales [*Wagschale*], and that is impossible. Here the rule must be 'judge not!' ... no personality can be held accountable for what it produces, that is to say its work: so no *merit* can be derived from it." The labourer works from utility and is never free to decide upon what he does or how he does it – and only the practicalities of social life determine its worth: "That which we now call justice is in this field very much in place as a highly refined instrument of utility." As soon as one perceives the degree of utility in such things, one is driven to question the attribution of responsibility in all its forms. "Worldly justice [*Die weltliche Gerechtigkeit*]" is in this way threatened with being turned upside down and emptied of its normative content by Nietzsche's teaching that no one is guilty, no one accountable for their deeds (*The Wanderer and His Shadow,* 81).

Christ, Nietzsche notes, likewise sought to abolish this worldly justice, but he did so not by affirming our essential innocence but rather with the opposite teaching. For Christ, we are all accountable; we are all sinners before God and hence each and every one of us is culpable: "*All* judges of the realm of secular justice were thus in his eyes as guilty as those they condemned" (*Human, All Too Human,* 81). Every kind of judge is, on this view, "hypocritical" through and through. Nietzsche shares Christ's suspicions, but not his metaphysics. It is not that we are all equally sinful and so all unfit to cast the first stone, but that we are all equally innocent and undeserving of having stones thrown at us at all.[11] The individual is part of a whole, an element within a complex of relations in constant flux – a world of becoming that includes the sphere of relations that make up the social world of human experience. We must hence rethink our moral presuppositions concerning the criminal and his or her acts. The way in which modern society deals with criminality by seeking to hold the person who commits evil accountable in the sternest possible terms is regressive. It is as if the criminal brings out the more primitive aspects of social relations. Look, Nietzsche exhorts, at the means that are resorted to in order to deal with criminality: "the sly police agents, the prison warders, the executioners; do not overlook the public prosecutors and defence lawyers; and ask yourself, finally, whether the judges themselves, and punishment, and the whole process of the

11 We are, says Nietzsche, no more morally accountable for what we do when awake than we are for what we dream (*Daybreak,* 128).

courts, are not phenomena much more likely to produce a depressive than an elevating effect on the non-criminal: for no one will ever succeed in covering self-defence and revenge with the cloak of innocence; and whenever man is employed and sacrificed as a means to an end of society's all higher humanity mourns" (*The Wanderer and His Shadow*, 186). Here is the epitome of the "punishing justice" – the kind of justice that is for Nietzsche exemplified by the judgemental attitude of the Christian church (*Daybreak*, 78)[12] and which must be "rooted out" (*Daybreak*, 13). This is the attitude that has signally failed to educate us to cultivate the sense for genuine "honesty and justice" (*Daybreak*, 84).

Rather than seeking to judge and condemn them, Nietzsche considers criminals to be close kin to invalids who suffer from mental illness. Indeed, he goes so far as to say that there is no "essential difference" between the two (*Daybreak*, 202). What is warranted in such cases is *understanding*. The criminal, like someone who suffers from an imbalance of the mind, should be approached in a spirit of tolerance and sympathy. Not punishment but treatment is what is needed: a change of living conditions, of company; the criminal may even find it useful to live incarcerated for a while, as a means of securing him- or herself "against a burdensome *tyrannical drive*." Criminality is thus conceived of here as a kind of indiscipline. If a person is incurable and suffers from themselves they should be allowed the honourable route of suicide. However, above all "one should neglect nothing in the effort to restore to the criminal his courage and freedom of heart; one should wipe pangs of conscience from his soul ... and indicate to him how he can make good the harm he has done perhaps only to a single person, and more than make it good." Present society still wants revenge on the criminal, "and for the time being the courts continue to maintain our detestable criminal codes, with their shopkeepers' scales and the *desire to counterbalance guilt with punishment*: but can we not get beyond this? ... Let us do away with the concept *sin* – and let us quickly send after it the concept *punishment*!" Like the invalid, the criminal is someone who takes much from society but cannot return the effort expended on his or her care. Yet, Nietzsche asks, would anyone today want to punish invalids for this – which means punishing invalids simply for being invalids? This sounds "inhuman," yet was once the norm. Once, primitive societies treated the insane person in a primitively metaphysical fashion, that is to say

12 "*Die strafende Gerechtigkeit.*" Christianity, Nietzsche holds, has made of the earth "a dreadful place," one in which "'the just man [*der Gerechte*] is *tortured* to death'!" (*Daybreak*, 77)

> as a danger to the community and the abode of some demonic being who has entered into his body ... here the rule is: every sick person is a guilty person! And we – are we not ready for the opposite view? Can we not yet say: every "guilty person" is a sick person? – No, the hour for that has not yet arrived ... no thinker has yet had the courage to evaluate a society or an individual according to how many parasites it can endure, nor has there yet been a founder of a state who has wielded the ploughshare in the spirit of that generous and mild-hearted dictum: "if thou wouldst cultivate the land, cultivate it with the plough: then the bird and the wolf who follow behind the plough shall rejoice in thee – *all creatures shall rejoice in thee.*" (*Daybreak,* 202)

One should bear in mind here that Nietzsche originally worked on *Daybreak* under the title *The Ploughshare* – a title he also initially considered for *Human, All Too Human.* The image of the plough proposes a mode of thought that opens up and overturns norms, which shatters the stale formality of institutionalized customs and the values associated with them. In place of the logic of a justice that stipulates tit for tat, compensation by way of like-for-like, punishment determined as repayment, Nietzsche suggests an ethic of mercy that spurns revenge and consigns punishment to oblivion. Behind this is a characteristically Nietzschean point about symptoms. Just as a runny nose indicates the possible presence of a cold virus, or the excessive urge to control denotes a pathological fear of lack of control,[13] so the manner in which a society treats its miscreants tells us perhaps rather more about the nature of social order than it does about wrongdoers. The best thing to do for the criminal and society alike is to desist from thinking too much about "punishing, reproaching, and improving" people (*The Gay Science,* 321). We seldom alter them thereby; indeed, as often as not, those who indulge in the lust to punish are changed by it, and changed for the worse. Mercy means letting go, allowing things to pass one by in a state free of rancour. "Let us not contend in a direct fight – and that is what all reproaching, punishing, and attempts to improve others amount to ... Let us sooner step aside. Let us look away" (*The Gay Science,* 321). It is better, Nietzsche concludes, to seek to direct others by example, or to do nothing beyond turning one's gaze elsewhere, than to indulge in punishment.

13 Consider the example of Socrates offered in *Twilight of the Idols.* His excessive rationalism, his faith in dialectics, points for Nietzsche to a deep fear of overpowering passions, one whose capacity to grip and over-run him means that Socrates must resort to any means of control possible. See *Twilight of the Idols,* "The Problem of Socrates," 1ff.

6. The ethic of mercy Nietzsche proposes does not rest on timeless, universal moral principles. It springs from his contention that moral judgement is a matter of historical contingency. When one judges others what is in reality being affirmed are the conditions necessary for one's own existence. No moral necessity can be deduced from this. The significance of our actions and the values they enact needs a proper decoding, one that begins with an acknowledgement of the essential opacity that surrounds them. Willing thus stands in need of an appropriate mode of interpretation, which will allow for a rethinking of the nature of freedom. This insight returns Nietzsche once again to the question of power – as exemplified by a discussion presented in book 5 of The Gay Science. *Two kinds of power need to be distinguished: power that takes the form of standing-reserve, i.e. awaits being used up; and power that directs, i.e. endows something with a sense of purpose. What directs is usually misidentified as being the most powerful and typical aspect of a thing. But what is decisive is, rather, the "quantum of strength" that lies in wait for a means of actualizing itself. Nietzsche argues that having purposes may be a necessary condition of being human, but which purposes one has is a contingent matter. Power, it follows, is not in its essence purposive any more than the primitive normative structure that gave rise to punishing was purposive, or punishing itself pertains to a moral teleology.*

The claim that one must teach by example and spurn revenge in favour of mercy is not rooted in some abstract conception of right grounded in an eternal standard set by a universal reason. Questions of right are raised and answered for Nietzsche by the concrete conditions that make a person who he or she is, i.e. by the historical conditions that determine a culture and society being what it is. This, as has already been noted,[14] is a matter that concerns the concatenation of drives and norms that is constitutive of human identity. Our normatively settled judgements about what is right, the power that lurks behind the pull of the so-called "call of conscience" that most people are prone to from time to time, rests upon this tangle of forces that in each case makes us who we are. One's judgement that something is right has its "prehistory" in the drives and their organization into instincts. Likewise, moral judgement rests upon other historical contingencies, such as what one has experienced and what one has not. Whenever conscience speaks out one must ask what it was that gave rise to this call. If one does not, if one responds to conscience as an obedient servant answering to the command of something whose authority is simply beyond question, this is evidence of a lack of critical independence. One thereby merely uncritically affirms

14 See chapter 2.

what one is and one's cultural world. "[Y]ou consider it 'right' because it appears to you as your own 'condition of existence' (and that you have a *right* to existence seems irrefutable to you)" (*The Gay Science*, 335). But we can never prove the goodness, nobility, and validity of our beliefs concerning rightness any more than we can demonstrate the fact of our own existence to be an inalienable right. What lives is at stake in the living and is placed in question by what it does and does not do. Its value and rights are not assured in advance. Living, consequently, is not simply an expression of belief and will. What speaks through us is in need of decoding; it requires proper interpretation, which means accepting that ultimately "every action is unknowable," since the origins of actions cannot be traced back to the conscious states of belief that we tend innocently to assert as their causes. This does not imply that human consciousness is completely powerless, any more than Nietzsche's questioning of the will implies that he rejects all talk of willing. But what it does imply is that values and beliefs are always necessarily opaque. Thus, it is the case that "our opinions, valuations, and tables of what is good certainly belong among the most powerful levers in the involved mechanism of our actions, but that in any particular case the law of their mechanism [*das Gesetz ihrer Mechanik*] is indemonstrable." One should note here a development in Nietzsche's conception of human identity and the nature of willing in comparison with the earlier text of *Human, All Too Human*. There, in section 106, the degree of causal determination that underlies actions is, in principle at least – by way of a kind of thought experiment – determinable. Now, for Nietzsche, the notion of an all-knowing gaze able to survey and predict the mechanics governing all possible outcomes of choice and action is no longer possible even in principle. Willing is in essence impenetrable in its complexity. The notion of an objective eye being cast upon the realm of human self-understanding is another chimera, since beliefs do not have the transparent causal relation to actions that is generally assumed to be the case. Consciousness, in short, is not the direct cause of values and beliefs and certainly cannot police their domain of meaning, although it remains an element in the play of forces that speak through values and beliefs. The "causes" are multiple, the significances likewise.

Willing, it follows, stands in need of a new interpretation, one which will allow for a more nuanced understanding of the nature of freedom. As Nietzsche will put it in book 5 of *The Gay Science*, dealing with such issues as this comes down to a matter of understanding the nature of power in a new way. One must be astute with regard to distinguishing between different modalities of power. There is, above all, a distinction to be noted between the kind of power that gives rise to actions, generally, and the kind that is associated with goals and purposes (*The Gay Science*, 360). One must learn to render distinct the "cause of action," i.e. that which gives rise to actions, from what brings about "acting in such-and-such a way," i.e. what stimulates action in a particular direction and endows it with a particular purpose. The first of these concerns "a quantum of dammed-up strength [*Kraft*] that is waiting to be used up somehow." This is like a packet of power sitting in wait for some means of being brought forth: it must necessarily discharge itself, but how it does so is a contingent matter. The second (the "how") is minor by comparison. It is, when set against the first cause, "a matchstick in relation to a powder keg." Strength (necessity) thus lies in wait for the contingent conditions that allow it to express itself. Second order causes include purposes; they are directive. But it is the first kind of cause that matters, that which awaits being ignited and expended in one way or another. As part of his challenge to the hegemony of consciousness, Nietzsche thus also challenges the view that purposes are initiating as well as directing forces. Purposes do not motivate actions; they do not lie behind deeds pressing them on to their goal. The purpose is coincidental. The confusion that generally occurs regarding the strength-that-drives and the strength-that-directs[15] means that one is all too inclined to mistake "the steersman for the steam." People, it follows, generally "act" simply because they are at any one time the prey and expression of a dammed-up quantum of energy that needs to be discharged: the "quantum of strength" is decisive in all doing. How someone acts and toward what end (i.e. the direction in which a pocket of strength is discharged) is a coincidental issue: the person goes the way they do because, like a ship caught in a current, they are compelled by the power that expresses itself through any purpose that just happens conveniently to come along. Power is no more inherently purposive than the prehistoric social mechanism that gave rise to humanity was. For this reason, Nietzsche concludes in *The Gay Science*, what is really needed is "a critique of the concept of 'purpose.'"

7. *Consciousness, Nietzsche affirms in his early and late writings alike, needs to be rethought in relation to the notion of purposes. Its over-estimated significance is a product of our own bad and egotistical habits of self-interpretation, habits that incline us to interpret the world of nature in terms of laws and purposes that do not pertain to it – an error that is recapitulated uncritically by modern physics. There is no free will and there is, likewise, no unfree will. Both conceptions of will*

15 "*treibende Kraft*" and "*dirigirende Kraft*."

are errors. What matters with regard to willing is the question of strength, the distinction between strong and weak wills. In this way, Nietzsche's conception of will replicates the differentiated structure of power that, from Human, All Too Human *onwards, characterizes his view of the social realm and the self alike. The will is always a matter of the affects of a sensible body in a community. On this conception, the notion of a pure libertarian agency must be abandoned. With this, one must refuse the temptation to indulge in moral censure, since what is being censured is an illusion. It is this refusal to censure that is the precondition of an ethic of mercy. The overcoming of morality, for Nietzsche, is really its self-overcoming: it does not involve the abandonment of questions of moral judgement, merely the equation of the good with vengeance, and it does so out of a sense of honesty that is derived from morality. Moral values need to be dealt with symptomatically. They are signs that reveal the form of life that extols them in a manner that trumps mere self-understanding. Penal laws can be treated in the same way. They do not exemplify a society's view of itself but what it feels itself not to be. Thus, what a society deems criminal always epitomizes those customs associated with its enemies. The criminal is the other, the alien, the outsider; one who does not accord with the norm This claim reflects Nietzsche's contention that the nature of law is a historical and normative issue. What is punished, what is deemed "criminal," are those norms that are regarded as falling outside what a community deems as good and proper. Criminality, it follows, is always a cultural and political matter.*

Like Kant's *Critiques*, Nietzsche's critique of the notion of purpose is much more intent on detailing the misuses of concepts than generating positive knowledge of them. It is important to understand the limits of our conceptual abilities. We must become more careful with regard to the manner in which we speak and think about speaking and thinking and, consequently, willing and doing.[16] The doer needs to be rethought, for, as we have seen, it does not possess freedom of will in the "superlative metaphysical sense" often attributed to it – which is the conception of "rustic simple-mindedness" (*Beyond Good and Evil*, 21). By the same token there is also no such thing as an unfree will. The latter point compels us to refuse to adopt the views of those "natural scientists" who falsely reify our concepts of cause and effect, turning them into substantives that mislead us into thinking of the world as something that can be represented by them. As with words like "law," "freedom," "necessity," "willing," "thinking," or "doing," so talk of "causes" and "effects" is also only meaningful in relation to human communicative needs, and has a

16 One should note that Nietzsche does not distinguish between thought and deed, concept use and action, theory and practice.

primarily social and instrumental function: "In the 'in itself' there is nothing of 'causal connection,' of 'necessity,' of 'psychological unfreedom'; there 'the effect' *does not* 'follow the cause,' there no 'law' [*Gesetz*] rules. It is *we* alone who have fabricated causes, succession, reciprocity, relativity, compulsion, number, law [*Gesetz*], freedom, motive, purpose; and when we falsely introduce this world of symbols into things and mingle it with them as though this symbol world were an 'in itself,' we once more behave as we have always behaved, namely *mythologically*. 'Unfree will' is mythology: in real life it is only a question of *strong* and *weak* wills" (ibid.). The law-like animal is, in short, prey to the tendency to the anthropomorphic projection of its regularized nature. Law is a human propensity, a product of the realm of culture (i.e. a fusion of drives and practices) that expresses the need to negotiate the environment in order to cope with it. To take the realm of culture to be a clear lens through which it is possible to see an undistorted nature is pure mythology. A non-mythological form of thinking would seek to conceive of the will not in terms of pushing and being pushed (i.e. mechanistically), a mythical notion that, perhaps necessarily, seduces the natural scientist, and brings with it the sense of willing as something unified and directed. Rather, one must interpret willing in terms of the multiplicity of elements at work in the power relations that inhere between sensations and feelings of command and obeying. The word "will" for Nietzsche thus denotes a mode of relations that is paradigmatic of the realm of social relationships that gives rise to human nature as something concatenated out of the fusion of drives and cultural norms. The world, as understood in terms of power, thereby becomes a great web of sensibility, a patchwork of relations between various modes of power-feelings. That is why it makes sense for Nietzsche to talk in this context of strong and weak wills. This is a distinction that depends upon feelings, not concepts: it is not conceptuality that defines the will (at best our concept of the will is a weak and attenuated sketch of something loosely akin to the affects that accompany doing) but rather *affectivity*, the sensibility of the embodied self (which is a community of hierarchically organized organic elements, i.e. drives) and of the social community within which the self is necessarily embedded.

Nietzsche would not accept the predictable response that might be raised against this view, i.e. that in order to draw the distinction between strong and weak he is already privileging a formal and hence conceptual order no less rigid and determined than the ones concerning such things as freedom, law, and motive that he rejects. The tendency in his thought is from the outset to attack such claims as manifesting a conceptual fetishism and self-deception. For Nietzsche, thought is not necessarily "conceptual" any more than all language is "philosophical": thought transcends our conceptual abilities. Concepts characterize the kind of thought we call consciousness and are related to the realm of language. Not all thought is conscious[17] any more than all thought is ever merely language. Thought is (amongst other things, possibly even at its base) feeling; and the conditions of this precede it. These conditions are underwritten into the world as embodiment, community and power relations encoded as a hierarchical realm of sensory differences. Feeling, which underwrites our awareness and understanding of power, is essentially differential: power is always that which is "stronger than" or "weaker than" and can never be thought about or spoken of independently of this relational condition. It is an economy of relations. Power is always a matter that concerns a hierarchy of command

17 Consider, for example, *The Gay Science*, 8. There are different "laws of development [*Gesetzen der Entwickelung*]" at work in the conscious and unconscious qualities that every person has. One set is visible, the other invisible in its workings. Nietzsche likens the latter to the patterning on the scales of reptiles. Seen from a distance this pattering is invisible, but viewed close-up under a microscope they look like "ornaments or weapons." It would, nevertheless, be an error to interpret the significance of scales on the basis of what is revealed close-up. The detail on the scales cannot be viewed in nature by those other animals for which they are supposed to exist. The camouflaged skin is what it most truly is when seen (or not seen) from a distance. Our moral qualities, Nietzsche notes, are similar. Those that are visible ("and especially those we *believe* to be visible") go their own way, as it were, "and the invisible ones that have the same names but are in relation to other men neither ornaments nor weapons, also follow their own course – probably a wholly different course." Take the examples of "our industry, our ambition, our acuteness." The visible qualities that these terms signify denote something essentially public in nature. When considered in this public sense, my ambition is the ambition that finds its meaning in the norm. Such qualities are conscious because they are a matter of the community, they are known in terms of one's relations with others. On the other hand, however, there may be "*our* industry, *our* ambition, *our* acuteness" (note the stress here on the individuated, personal "*our*"). Such things are unconscious, hidden, and defy crude conceptualization. For these no direct means of detection has yet been devised for they are instinctive qualities that remain hidden "as it were, behind nothing." In contrast to these hidden elements, consciousness is the least developed feature of animal life (*The Gay Science*, 11) and for this reason it gives rise to errors that would probably lead to the individual's destruction all too often were it not for the "conserving association of the instincts." "Before a function is fully developed and mature it constitutes a danger for the organism, and it is good during the interval if it is subjected to some tyranny. Thus consciousness is tyrannized ... One thinks that it constitutes the *kernel* of man; what is abiding, eternal, ultimate, and most original in him. One takes consciousness for a determinate magnitude. One denies its growth and intermittences. One takes it for the 'unity of the organism.'" Such an overestimation of the role and value of consciousness has had the good consequence of preventing it from developing too rapidly, for our faith in our actual possession of it in its ultimate form prevents us from exerting ourselves to develop it further. Consciousness, in other words, is a mere fraction of thought, for Nietzsche, and cannot therefore be taken to be its defining paradigm.

that has inherent within it a mode of exchange characteristic of our normatively determined willing nature.

When framed within the context of the above conception of willing, the notion of a pure, libertarian agency whose essence resides in the kind of moral accountability that serves to sanction the moral legitimacy of punishment simply shrivels up. Punishment, on this view, can never be defined in terms of a "moral" practice – it is neither specifically directed by moral ends nor does it achieve a specifically "moral" end. Punishment is understandable only as a practice that has its roots in the unthinking play of social forces. The assertion that agents are endowed with a moral status on the basis of their ability freely to make choices is simply, for Nietzsche, a piece of bad interpretation typical of the unhistorical frame of mind of the metaphysician. What is needed is a new inversion – a more enlightened "*extra-moral*" era, an era of post-moralism, must be ushered in. This would involve the initiation of a culture endowed with a rather different normative shape, one in which the value of an action comes to be understood in terms of the manifold elements that give rise to it. The question needs to be posed as to whether "the decisive value of an action resides in precisely that which is *not intentional* in it, and that all that in it which is intentional, all of it that can be seen, known, 'conscious' still belongs to its surface and skin – which, like every skin, betrays something but *conceals* more? In brief, we believe that the intention is only a sign and symptom that needs interpreting, and a sign, moreover, that signifies too many things and which thus taken by itself signifies practically nothing" (*Beyond Good and Evil*, 32). The common-sense understanding that has dominated thinking about morality up to now privileges intentions because it misunderstands the nature of willing as a matter of free choice rather than as a struggle between strong and weak elements. What must be advocated, Nietzsche urges, is the overcoming of this error, that is, the overcoming of morality.[18] This overcoming can also be made intelligible by the paradoxical formula "the self-overcoming of morality" (ibid.), for it is done out of a residual sense of morality, i.e. as a result of the sense for truthfulness that morality has developed in us that has so much become part of us that it compels us to turn on morality itself and find it wanting. Nietzsche's transcendence of morality does not propose an abandonment of ethics – for mercy does not stand outside

18 In the words of Terry Eagleton, "in Nietzsche's resolutely naturalistic view, morality is a function of biology, psychology, physiology, anthropology and the ceaseless struggle for domination. Its roots lie not in the spirit but the body ... Like Marx, Nietzsche is concerned with the natural history of material conditions of morality." (*Trouble with Strangers*, 171).

the realm of ethics: it merely seeks to transcend the desire to find reasons that justify vengeful feelings.

Our conscious judgements and values are, as the above account reveals, for Nietzsche defined by an essential opacity. This opaqueness of our judgements ultimately provides the impetus for Nietzsche's turn to a more symptomatic approach to values. Taken on their own terms, Nietzsche will come to say,[19] values signify nothing. The values I unthinkingly endorse are best read as signs that betray who I am, my cultural world, the hierarchy of my drives (my instincts), my form of life. The same goes for criminal laws. Penal laws neither express individual will nor "the will of the people" – if such a thing exists. Their significance is unconscious: they betray a great deal more about what a community considers itself *not* to be (*The Gay Science*, 43). Laws of punishment betray a society's hidden side, that aspect of its normative self-description that eludes its overt self-understanding, for such laws present its negative image of itself, the dominant view of what and who is deemed alien and worthy of being despised. Punitive law betrays the propensity of any society to regard what is antithetical to it as "bad." It is criminal to be *like them*. In this regard, a nation's "laws refer to the *exceptions* to the morality of custom, and the severest penalties are provided for what accords with the customs of a neighbouring people." Formalized punitive laws are never expressions of an internally adhered to ideal of the good. Their function is not to endorse what is possessed in common, but to outline what is prohibited and lies beyond the compass of such possession. It is for this reason, Nietzsche concludes, that one must understand the paradigm instance of the criminal to be made manifest in the despised condition of the outsider, the one for whom, simply in virtue of their being thus, the severest treatment is reserved. Social norms, legality, right, the realm of the just, are expressions of cultural identity and symptomatic of the tensions that abound whenever, as must always be the case, neighbours dwell in proximity to one another. What, then, is really being punished when the criminal is subjected to the consequences of condemnation? What, in short, is the sense of punishment? It is one of the tasks of the *Genealogy* to pose some possible answers to these questions.

8. The Genealogy *stands as the fruit of Nietzsche's naturalistic labours. It provides an account of human identity that turns on the conception of power, which*

19 See *Twilight of the Idols*, "The Problem of Socrates," 2. See also the discussion of this in the conclusion.

is now called "will to power," already outlined in a provisional way in the middle-period writings. Nietzsche seeks to show how being human has always meant being fashioned by norms that weave together notions of punishment, suffering, and guilt. We are the punishing animal. This tendency springs from our prehistoric inheritance and is a consequence of the nature of the most primitive proto-human communities being founded on the relationship between creditor and debtor. Against this backdrop two forms of competing moral discourse emerge: noble and slave morality. Noble domination creates the impotent slave's desire for a revenge that can only be taken in thought rather than deed. This is the source of the morality of ressentiment. *What the slave calls "justice" is in reality the expression of a desire for vengeance that sanctifies punishment by giving it moral respectability. The* Genealogy *challenges the hegemony of this ethics.*

On the Genealogy of Morality, in may ways Nietzsche's most mature and certainly his most experimental text, seeks to articulate the implications of the "historical philosophy" first outlined in *Human, All Too Human*. As such, the text of the *Genealogy* bears the fruit of Nietzsche's initial naturalistic philosophical labours (see Preface, 4, 2–3). The *Genealogy* seeks to develop a post-metaphysical account of how valuing, esteeming animals like us came into being. Where metaphysics responds to the nature of values by holding them to pertain to a pure and unchanging meaning that springs from a miraculous origin, the *Genealogy* embraces the implications of affirming the shifting domain of history as the source one must look to in order to decode the terrain of the values we unthinkingly inhabit and thus enact. Given the interest in the social dimension of power evidenced in Nietzsche's earlier texts, it should come as no surprise that the domain the *Genealogy* explores is one inexorably constituted out of relations of power. "Will to power" lurks within the notions of right, fairness, equilibrium, equality, and justice that make up the vocabulary of moral discourse. The three essays that comprise the *Genealogy*, arranged in an order almost designed to defy the reader by privileging polemic over interpretive ease, seek through this power analysis to challenge metaphysical presuppositions concerning the origins of such notions. We are in this way urged to reinterpret our evaluative abilities and the role that values play in human culture. In short, Nietzsche urges us to consider a new approach to questions of truth, right, and justice.

These elements are bound together in the text by a common thematic thread that Nietzsche constructs by a careful uncovering of the degree to which the notions of suffering, punishing, and valuing are entwined with one another. We are, the third and final essay of the *Genealogy* concludes, the suffering animal, for it is the human lot that each of us is overwhelmingly susceptible to suffering from its own existence (*Genealogy*, III, 28). We suffer in this way because, as the second essay tells us, we are the punishing, guilt-conscious animal (*Genealogy*, II, 4ff). In other words, we are creatures of norms – that is, creatures that both fashion and are fashioned by norms. We are driven to judge and in doing so come to judge ourselves also. We are the punishing animal because of the evaluative legacy we inherit from our ancestry. Punishment, the second essay of the *Genealogy* argues, was the means whereby primitive, proto-humanity inadvertently imposed rules of behaviour upon itself and thereby initiated the break from nature that led to its inhabiting the domain of culture. This was achieved at the cost of the creation of the feeling of guilt engendered by the fact that our ancestors had their natural drives subjected to the tyrannical power of communal norms – to the containing and constraining power of custom and law. It is in the context of this account of culture that the first essay, "'Good and Evil,' 'Good and Bad,'" offers its account of two forms of competing moral discourse, those of the noble and the slave (*Genealogy*, I, 2–6, 10). These moral discourses, Nietzsche argues, spring from the creation of a social order in which the enforcement of power becomes conjoined with notions of suffering and punishing in a specific way. The noble's assertion of power (expressed as self-affirmation, as "noble morality") gives rise to the suffering and guilty impotence of the subjugated. The suffering experienced by those who are on the receiving end of noble assertiveness generates a form of ethically expressed resistance in which the deep-rooted conjoining of suffering, guilt, and punishment is given expression in the moral discourse of the victim ("slave morality"). The powerful noble's domination of the slave constitutes them as suffering beings denied recourse to all practical means of countering their suffering condition. The consequence of this is that the victim takes succour in the form of a spiritual-moral discourse – a discourse that springs from a dispossessed faction of the nobility, the class of the priest (*Genealogy*, I, 7). Priest and slave conjoin to counter noble tyranny in the guise of the morality of "*ressentiment*" (I, 10). Under the guiding power of the priest, the noble is cursed as evil and condemned to everlasting suffering in a hell sanctioned by the pursuit of a "just" world in which the downcast will be empowered eternally.[20] Here, for Nietzsche, lies the source of the morality of revenge that finds its fullest flowering in the shape of Christian ethics. The slave's conception of justice is in fact an urge to revenge that draws on deep and dark

20 Nietzsche makes it clear enough in the third essay of the *Genealogy* that in reality it is not the subjugated who are empowered by this morality but the class of the priest (I, 11–15).

propensities underlying the prehistoric conditions of humanity's emergence from nature. Just as punishment fashioned human identity in a decisive way during its primitive, formative stages so punishment and the pleasure in punishing reasserts itself in slave-inspired Christian moral discourse as "justice": this so-called "justice" is in fact masked vengeance.[21] The *Genealogy* aims to challenge the hegemony of this ethics of revenge. Its primary justification for this resides in Nietzsche's contention that justice, properly understood, cannot be served by endorsing punishment since punishment cannot be justified in moral terms and is therefore strictly speaking unjust.

9. Punishment is a notion peculiar to humans, and a precondition of the development of cultural life. It is rooted in the communal demand that anti-social drives be mastered or liquidated and is indelibly stamped into the history of the emergence of our promising nature. Here lie the origins of "moral memory" and the path that leads to human culture. Punishment has, however, no moral justification at its roots. Its violence underlies much we hold to be worthy.

What is peculiar about punishment is that it is a form of behaviour unlike anything exhibited by other animals. Only the "animal man," as Nietzsche calls us (*Genealogy*, II, 3), punishes. The reason for this is in some respects simple enough. Proto-humanity began to punish as soon as primitive individuals began to live together. Punishment is a precondition of human sociality. Without it the social bond that holds communities together could not be forged, for it enforces the law of tradition and custom. It is because of this need for social cohesion, Nietzsche tells us, that humankind emerges as a species of promisers (*Genealogy*, II, 1).[22] Envisage a group of proto-human creatures forced into communal existence by circumstance. What matters when it comes to the question of survival in such a community is not the life of any individual member but the continuance of the community itself. Herein lies the problem that

21 Slave morality "[a]s the will to the truly non-existent 'second world,' which guides the weak, is a disguised will to power in the only real world, [and] it is also a disguised will to nothingness, in the radical sense of the word." (Müller-Lauter, *Friedrich Nietzsche*, 49). In other words, metaphysics and politics are, for Nietzsche, bedfellows.

22 For Gillian Rose, the opening to the second essay of the *Genealogy* is ironic in tone. The irony in the passage in *Genealogy*, II, 1 where Nietzsche talks of nature "breed[ing] an animal that is able to make promises" lies in the knowing invocation of a nature that cannot, on Nietzsche's own account, possibly exist: a "contract presupposes complex social and ethical relations … and in turn, contractual relations give rise to, or form, internalized identities – the moralization of legal concepts" (*The Broken Middle*, 185). Clearly, the reading offered in the present volume is indebted to this insight.

the community must face: the primitive individual is initially merely a bundle of drives, a body whose sociality is confined to its inner organization, i.e. to the relationship stipulated between cells and functions. Such a body is endowed with dispositions that it acts upon with a view to their fulfilment. Sexual desire and hunger are cases in point. They are responsive drives constituted out of the relationship any organic body must have to its environment if it is to survive. Both serve to ensure the continuation of the individual and thereby the species. But if unhindered, such desires do not necessarily harmonize with the conditions that ensure the continuance of community (*Genealogy*, II, 3). Communal survival is something long-term, a thing that necessitates limiting the short-lived immediacy of desires replete with anti-social propensities. The "primitive requirements of social life" must be satisfied (ibid.), which means that the individual must somehow be prevented from acting in such a way as to bring about harm to the communal whole. A special kind of memory must be made (*Genealogy*, II, 1–2). The individual must be made to conform. Conformity is an achievement – albeit an unconscious one. It is also an achievement that is mired in blood (*Genealogy*, II, 3). Social actors must be rendered predictable, they must be made akin to their fellows, and able to take on commitments and then follow them through. This requires, amongst other things, the development of temporal understanding, for without it no memory of something now past could be acknowledged as having a claim on one's present and future actions. As Nietzsche notes, this memory is attained simply and laboriously enough through sustained punishment: it is beaten and battered onto the body through violent discipline, so that, through the stimulus of pain, the individual comes to remember what is prohibited and to refrain from doing it.[23] Through the administration of punishment we stand on the doorstep of culture.

Community begins with punishment, with "that particular instinct [*Instinkt*] which discovered that pain was the most powerful aid to mnemonics. The whole of asceticism belongs here as well: a few ideas have to be made ineradicable, ubiquitous, unforgettable, 'fixed' in order to hypnotize the whole nervous and intellectual system through these 'fixed ideas'" (*Genealogy*, II, 3). Thus, sociality is the conduit through which drives are concatenated into determinate relations. Only thereby is human sensibility possible, for sensibility is rooted in the propensity to respond to environmental conditions that arises from the imprinting by

23 The means to this end is torture: "'A thing must be burnt in so that it stays in the memory: only something which continues *to hurt* stays in the memory' – that is a proposition from the oldest (and unfortunately the longest-lived) psychology on earth."

social forces of specific interpretative tendencies ("fixed ideas") on the individuated body. Pain takes on significance because it fulfils a social function – it pertains to "meaning" because it has a normative content determined by its amenability to serving the power of social demands, e.g. "I suffer because I am guilty of breaking this or that custom." Nietzsche thereby develops the thesis already formulated in *Human, All Too Human,* which holds punishment to have only instrumental value. In the *Genealogy,* however, the complexity and richness of the thesis is expanded. What is addressed concerns not merely the moral value – or lack thereof – of punishment, but the constitutive role that punishing practices play in forging the normative sphere. Punishing is the instrument by way of which what is subsequently called "moral commitment" (the ability to promise) is rendered possible. It is the condition in virtue of which the human world as a world of norms is brought about. What is usually referred to as our "rationality" is one of the consequences of this unconscious, instrumental fashioning of the socialized self: "With the aid of such images and procedures, man was eventually able to retain five or six 'I-don't-want-to's' in his memory, in order to enjoy the advantages of society – and there you are! With the aid of this sort of memory people finally came to 'reason!'" (*Genealogy,* II, 3). Our rationality is not grounded in thought understood as abstract reflection, but rather develops out of an activity that is always already concrete, an intervention that jangles nerves, slices flesh, and snaps bones as it is refracted through practices. Thus, the human ability to reason, to reflect on emotions and desires rather than merely act upon them – i.e. one of the things that makes up the great privilege and "splendour" of being human – has its origin in violence: "how much blood and horror lies at the basis of all 'good things!'" Nietzsche adds with characteristically acid irony.

Nietzsche's irony hints at the fact that there is something uncanny about this violence. It is impersonal and takes the form of a collective reaction to an individual who has transgressed the bounds of the social bond and thereby threatened the unity that is a prerequisite of survival. Yet this violence is at the same time something that is acted out on the individual with results that are (albeit unthinkingly and unintentionally) creative. From the outset of Nietzsche's narrative, the individual is rendered a being equipped with the potential for individuality by way of the imposition of the regularized discipline of communal order. Individuality, in other words, is attained only at the price of punishment.

10. Out of punishing practices our ancestors sculpted the contractual relationship wherein promises were made that refined the practical concepts of equivalence, exchange, possession, and personhood. With this the notion of justice emerged: a wrong can be compensated for by an exchange of something equivalent to the damage suffered. Speaking in this crude sense, we are always already legal beings, i.e. subject to the law of exchange and compensation. Cruelty and power thus reside at the historical core of the legal and moral spheres. Behind such things as the feeling of human superiority over animals, formalized legal relationships, the ability to compare and count, equity, equality, even thought itself, can be found the legally constituted condition of power relations known as "justice." "Power," here, is not mere domination but domination within a realm of rule-like behaviour, the realm of law. All human communities emerge on the basis of this condition of domination, which fashions selfhood. Conceptions of others, of those who are "like us" but alien or enemies, likewise originate in this condition: the outsider relative to the community is one beyond the law, a non-person for whom the brutality of war is reserved. War provides the template for all forms of punishment. This does not, however, entitle us to draw conclusions about the meaning of punishment. Something's origins do not determine its meaning and purpose. Purposes are signs: they are symptoms of one thing's being put to use by a superior power. Punishment needs to be interpreted with this in mind. It has two aspects: the "relative permanence" characteristic of practices, rituals etc., and the meaning, aim, and anticipatory feelings that accompany it. Punishment, as procedure, conceals a plurality of meanings. It cannot, consequently, be necessarily connected with morality or justice.

Punishment is, for Nietzsche, the basis of culture (*Genealogy*, II, 3). Its centrality to human life is revealed by the fact that we have been nothing if not inventive when it comes to the task of giving pain to our own kind. At the hands of their own kind, people have been stoned, broken on the wheel, impaled, trampled, drawn and quartered, boiled alive, burned, and flayed – and all with collective, official, and even divine sanction. One can hardly ignore this violence unless one is wilfully inclined to skip over the less amenable aspects of history and write a sanitized and sickly fantasy in place of genuine history. Punishment is a legacy. It is not merely the means whereby our primitive proto-human forbears were rendered fit for social life and in turn became open to being transformed into beings like us; its influence permeates the domain of culture, constituting its fundamental conditions. Punishing practices generate the kind of precepts we subsequently come to deem "moral." Punishment is, in this sense, autochthony. It marks the passage of humanity from living clay into lived culture, the transformation from mere organic becoming into the history that gives birth to the self. The first selves meet, Nietzsche argues, on terrain marked out by punishment. The inflicting of pain in requital for a wrong characterizes the initial exchanges between persons. The basis of the model Nietzsche develops here resides in the notion of law and contract. More specifically, it resides in the legal concepts of credit, debit, and the rights that pertain to one who is a possessor of goods – especially, the rights such a possessor has over the body of another who is indebted to him (*Genealogy*, II, 4).

Moral discourse generally (rather than specifically noble or slave discourse) owes its origins to the creditor-debtor relationship. What we call "guilt," the abstract feeling of being morally culpable, springs from the concrete condition of indebtedness to another. Punishment and debt are thus entwined from the outset. But this entwinement does not initially include the kind of guilt that is associated with any conception of the "freedom of the will." To think of punishment as retribution for a misdeed on the part of someone endowed with freedom of choice presupposes a vast array of concepts that could not have sprung up fully formed in primitive societies. The seemingly "inescapable thought" we feel compelled by, the one that holds that a miscreant is punished because he or she could have acted differently, is "an extremely late and refined form of human judgment and inference" that does not have a place in the "psychology of primitive man" and hence in any account of the origins of punishment (*Genealogy*, II, 4). Against the view that punishment was originally directed at someone who was responsible for his or her actions, Nietzsche argues that for the majority of "human history" punishment was in fact directed at wrongdoers in the same manner that "parents still punish their children." A wrongdoer was punished simply as a corrective to unacceptable behaviour. Underlying the development of punishment, law, and justice, Nietzsche argues, is the idea not of freedom but of equivalence, which is something "primeval, deeply rooted and perhaps now ineradicable." This notion got its "power [*Macht*]" from "the contractual relationship between *creditor* and *debtor*," a thing that is "as old as the very conception of a 'legal subject' [*Rechtsubjekte*] and itself refers back to the basic forms of buying, selling, bartering, trade and traffic." Contractual relationships of a legal nature, ones that spring from the socially mediated realm of punishing practices, are of central importance to the evolution of promising and thus moral responsibility because they are *constitutive* of it: "Precisely here, *promises are made*; precisely here the person making the promise has to have a memory *made* for him" (*Genealogy*, II, 5). The debtor has to guarantee the promise of paying back the debt and the duty of this obligation must be etched into the debtor's understanding to ensure this. This is done by way of the imposition of a substitute payment if the promise is not kept. Failure to repay the debt brings with it a forfeit on the part of the debtor: "in particular, the creditor could inflict all kinds of dishonour and torture on the body of the debtor, for example, cutting off as much flesh as seemed appropriate for the debt." Nietzsche's central point is now hammered home. What is really at stake within this notion of compensation is not just desert but the pleasure of power exercised in a social hierarchy. The creditor, in exercising their right of compensation, "takes part in the *right of the masters*: at last he, too, shares the elevated feeling of despising and maltreating someone as an 'inferior'" (ibid.). This is also the case if punishment has become a formalized legal matter and is meted out by "the 'authorities.'" Punishment is in its origins a formally sanctioned (legal) inflicting of pain, and it is in this respect that it is an essential element in the emergence of human self-understanding. We are, in this cruel and primitive sense, already legal beings, i.e. subject to the disciplined imposition of law, before we even begin to talk of responsibility, freedom, law, justice, and the like. The sphere of legality outlined above gives rise to a host of moral notions. It is here that the human "moral conceptual world" is fashioned (*Genealogy*, II, 6). Only once this legally encoded ordering of social space is articulated do notions such as "guilt," "conscience," and "duty" arise.

Nietzsche is happy to admit that the above account is a matter of conjecture – after all, it concerns a hidden world that is difficult to interpret (*Genealogy*, II, 6). He is also keen to develop the account further. The legally constituted relationship between creditor and debtor underlies our self-understanding and even our mental capacities (*Genealogy*, II, 8). The origins of thought itself, perhaps, reside in the observances that bind creditor and debtor together in this "most primitive" of personal relationships. Only with the refinement of this communally articulated condition of human life does the world of formalized social relationships begin to appear. One begins with the activities of buying and selling, calculating and comparing power with power, which provide the basic conception of individual right. These, in turn, are transferred to the coarsest of initial social complexes. Thus, ideas of duty, right, debt, and compensation are subsequently given a socio-legal dimension. The notion of a person as the possessor of a legal entitlement to rights and compensation for suffering a wrong finds its origins in this transference. With this development of the concept of entitlement, a "great generalization" emerged: "'Everything has its price: *everything* can be compensated for.'" Here, says Nietzsche, echoing the discussions presented in *The Wanderer and His Shadow*,[24] can be found "the oldest, the most naïve canon of morals relating to *justice*, the beginning of all 'good naturedness,' 'equity,' all 'good will,' all 'objectivity' on earth. Justice at this first

24 See chapter 3.

level is the good will, between those who are roughly equal, to come to terms with each other, to 'come to an understanding' again by means of a settlement – and, in connection with those who are less powerful, to *force* them to reach a settlement amongst themselves" (ibid.). Justice, properly understood, presupposes the kind of equilibrium and equality of power that typifies Nietzsche's earlier discussions in *The Wanderer and His Shadow* and elsewhere. Justice, once again, is inextricably linked to relations of power. Power, in turn, is no simple matter of the strong dominating the weaker by subordinating them to the capriciousness of an arbitrary will. It is, rather, the sphere where capriciousness ceases, where the condition of settling disputes and struggling against those who have power over one is rendered paramount. It is the sphere in which rules trump brute force.

The legally encoded creditor-debtor relationship is, on the view Nietzsche now develops in the *Genealogy*, the basic condition of all communities. From the outset, the most primitive community is akin to a creditor, its individual members akin to debtors. So long as one lives in such a social world, one enjoys the benefits of the community's protection and thereby stands in a relation to it of indebtedness. The one who breaches the terms of this relationship is the villain, the breaker of the social bond "who has broken his contract and his word to the *whole* ... The lawbreaker is a debtor who not only fails to repay the benefits and advances granted to him, but also actually assaults the creditor." The community takes revenge for this. The criminal is punished, which means he or she is subjected to something akin to the savagery that lies outside the protective domain of the community's power: the power of communal protection is withdrawn from them. Punishment is an expression of reactive sentiment. One should again note the continuity of this observation with Nietzsche's earlier comments, for example in section 43 of *The Gay Science*.[25] The identity of a community does not turn on its understanding of itself but on those who it regards as its antitheses – the enemies or aliens, those who are culturally other. Punishment within the community is a "copy" of the treatment usually reserved for enemies defeated in war, i.e. those who have no rights, who lack even the entitlement to mercy since they do not qualify for the status of personhood. From the outset, the community looks outwards and greets the other with war and the war-like practices and rituals of war directed towards obliterating what lies "outside" the community. The community's relation to its enemies gets refracted back into it in a decisive manner. War,

25 See this chapter, section 7.

Nietzsche argues, is the source of all ways of punishing: "war itself (including the warlike cult of the sacrificial victim) has given us all the *forms* in which punishment manifests itself in history" (*Genealogy*, II, 9). The history of punishment, it follows, is entangled with the merciless propensity to wage war.

War endows us with the *forms* of punishment, just as credit and debit endow us with the conditions of personhood that get articulated into the legal subject. However, one ought not to feel emboldened to derive any determinate meaning about the nature of legality or punishment from this. To recall section 360 of *The Gay Science*,[26] one must distinguish between the power that awaits expression and the power that directs and gives meaning. Questions about origins and questions about purposes are separate matters (*Genealogy*, II, 12). It is possible to see in law and punishment today, Nietzsche notes, the enactment of purposes, such as those of "revenge or deterrence." However, when properly understood, punishing practices teach us something quite different. When viewed in terms of their historical origins and development, punishing practices and rituals do not have a determinate sense. One cannot discover a purpose from simply narrating the story of a thing's emergence into history – which is, after all, the narration of the emergence of a ritual or practice, not a meaning associated with it. Thus, whatever one may discover about the history of law's emergence[27] one cannot derive a fixed meaning concerning the law that has come about with it. History is a chain of differing and competing interpretations. The interpretation of a thing necessarily reinterprets and so overwrites the previous senses that may be attributed to it. Moreover, a reinterpretation can be so radical that the earlier meanings associated with something become irretrievable. Interpretation is thus akin to inscription in so far as a thing's earlier meaning can be almost literally scratched out. This is why one has to learn different ways of telling stories about life. The current utility of anything, whether it be a bodily organ, religious ritual, or "legal institution," tells one nothing about its origins. Purposes are not to be confused with origins. All purposes are signs. Every purpose is akin to a symptom, i.e. is something that reveals the putting to use of one thing by another, superior thing. A stipulated end reveals the immanence of power or "will to power."[28] Our view of history must change if we accept this argument. A thing's history is a "continuous chain of signs, continually revealing

26 See the discussion in section 6.

27 "*Entstehungsgeschichte des Rechts.*"

28 The will to power thus denotes the priority of *activity*, the manifestation of the "life-will."

new interpretations and adaptations, the causes of which need not be connected even amongst themselves, but rather just follow and replace one another at random" (ibid.). History is an amalgam of conflicting purposes, of power struggles, but this very variety and multiplicity of purposes means that it is devoid of the kind of conceptual unity associated with a universal purpose. History, in other words, is not going anywhere – it is unbridled contingency. It is the unpredictable playing out of relations of power.

Punishment, which is the practice that most decisively fashioned the human animal, can be characterized in the light of this. It has a "twofold" character. First, there is the side to punishment that exhibits "relative *permanence*." This concerns the customary elements involved in punishing, the ritual of the punishing act and the conventionally observed order of succession that typifies it. In other words, there is the aspect of punishment that is procedural. This procedural element is what endures, relatively speaking, when compared to the second aspect, which concerns the feelings of sense, purpose, and anticipation that accompany the ritual. This characteristic of punishment is best characterized by "*fluidity*" (*Genealogy*, II, 13). The rituals that constitute punishment, in other words, precede the meanings that we might be tempted to attribute to it at any one time. The same goes for other practices.[29] We tend to make the error of thinking that the meaning and end of a thing is what defines it. The sense we today tend to attribute to the punishing act is, however, only something late and coincidental to it. The procedures that characterize punishment were not, it follows, "*invented* for the purpose of punishment" as the naïve moral and legal genealogist might believe. The attribution of a sense to punishing is something that comes much later: it does not pertain to a single sense, but a plurality of them. Indeed, the notion of punishment we cleave to today, Nietzsche now concludes, is in fact a "synthesis" of various senses – which looks like a unity simply because we have got to the point where the individual uses and attributions of uses that have accrued around it are now so densely woven together that they appear to possess a coherent unity. Strip away these uses and meanings, however, and one would be left with a nullity. The concept of punishment is like an onion: it has lots of layers, but no core. One cannot define it – as, indeed, one cannot define anything that

29 Take the example of politeness. Being polite requires the observance of ritual, e.g. knocking on the door before entering, shaking hands in greeting, etc. The "meaning" of politeness is, however, a contingent matter. What one expects from it will depend upon whether one is out on a first date, paying the bill at a restaurant, losing a game of golf to one's boss, challenging the witness in court, and so on.

has a history, since that history will always be the concatenation of a variety of uses to differing and sometimes unrelated and even conflicting ends.

It follows that the purpose of punishment can never be given in absolute terms. In considering punishment one always discovers a plurality of purposes, the multiplicity of different senses that constitute its history. In the past this would have been an easier issue to resolve, the "synthesis of meanings" would have been simpler to disentangle. It is, even now, still possible to see how the history of punishment is characterized by a range of "elements," whose syntheses "change valence" so that "now this, now that element stands out and dominates, to the detriment of the others, indeed, in some circumstances one element (for example, the purpose of deterrence) seems to overcome all the rest" (*Genealogy*, II, 13). The point, however, is that what punishment signifies is always going to be an "uncertain, belated and haphazard" matter so long as one thinks in moral or teleological terms. One can at various points see a variety of purposes at work, with one dominating at any given time, and Nietzsche concludes his discussion with a long, but by no means exhaustive, list of such possible purposes.[30] What is notable, Nietzsche is telling us, is that the confusing of punishment with justice is one of the typical errors that the naïvely moral interpreter will make. Punishment is not intrinsically linked to being just, since why one punishes is one of those questions that will produce an at best obscure answer.

11. Punishing does not conform to a "moral" purpose – it does not make people "better." It is a tool of social utility. The real historical significance of punishment concerns its role in transforming the nature of the creditor-debtor relationship and hence the legal subject. As the communal creditor gains in wealth and power it relaxes its hold on the miscreant because he or she is less of a threat. Powerful societies hence tend toward leniency in matters of justice. Power, which initially constitutes the forces of equilibrium that determines the sphere of right, now tends to conditions that outstrip the exchange logic underlying the law itself. Out of one conception of justice another emerges that is antithetical to it, spurning equivalence and vengeance in favour of generosity and mercy. Legal systems epitomize this kind of generous power when they treat issues of right and wrong as rule-like matters and thereby foster an impersonal ethos that protects the wrongdoer from

30 Punishment as deterrence, as a means of making harmless, as repayment to the victim, as a means of ensuring social stability, as inspiring the fear of those endowed with the power to punish, as a means of weeding out those persons deemed unacceptable, as celebration of power over the vanquished, as a means to assisting memory, as compromise, as warfare against the one who threatens the peace of the social body.

revenge. Genuine justice stays the vengeful hand of the victim and thereby transcends the logic it emerges from. Taking such a view is an attitude characteristic of the freethinker who resists the power of custom. Such free thought is creative in its challenging of the norm. As such, it is, from the standpoint of conventional authority, a form of criminality. What is needed, Nietzsche argues, is a new order of legislation grounded in the non-conformist and "criminal" attitude characteristic of the freethinker. The illusory nature of conformist conceptions of justice must be exposed and, in turn, the kind of freedom necessary for the experimental attitude of the freethinker demonstrated.

One thing is fairly certain, Nietzsche adds. Punishing people hardens them (*Genealogy*, II, 14). It does not make one "better" and is consequently very unlikely to serve a "moral" end, although it certainly serves to intensify the power of the intellect and refine the ability to master one's own desires. It is for this reason that one needs to look to the realm of practices and the manner in which they function if one is to glean anything useful about punishment. Its significance, as has already been noted, resides in the fact that punishing does not serve an exclusive meaning or goal, but is rather a social function, an instrument that satisfies the utilitarian requirement that social order be secured from forces that endanger it. Such a functional instrument also shapes the self. The most primitive community is erected on the creditor-debtor relationship, a relationship in which the communal order itself stands as creditor and the individual member of the community as debtor. For Nietzsche, what is interesting about punishment is found in the developments and refinements of this relationship as they occur in the context of the conception of the legal subject. Initially, the primitive creditor claims what is their due according to the rules of calculation that stipulate what is the "just" (i.e. equivalent) compensation for a wrong suffered. What is at stake here is the feeling of power generated by the force of social hierarchy. The creditor gains pleasure from inflicting pain on the debtor and the higher the latter stands in the hierarchy the greater the pleasure to be derived from his or her misery. But as culture develops, things change. Credit takes what is due to it and increases in wealth. As it does so, limitations come to be placed on the amount that can be demanded of the debtor in virtue of the possession of that wealth (*Genealogy*, II, 10). The wealthier I am, the more damage I can withstand; and the greater the damage I can withstand the less I am inclined to make of my entitlement to recompense. Power, in other words, is a key determiner of the extent to which punishment is the hallmark of the sphere of justice. The more impoverished a community, the more it is inclined to punish with harshness. The more powerful a community becomes the less the lawbreaker appears to represent a danger to the social whole and the lesser its inclination to harshness. Indeed, Nietzsche adds, the law even begins to protect the wrongdoer from the wrath of the victim. Penal law thus develops under the sway of the notion of equivalence, which holds that wrongs can be compensated for, that "every offence ... [is] something which *can be paid off*, so that, at least to a certain degree, the wrongdoer is *isolated* from his deed." Justice, in short, is liable in the end to take the form of the generosity of the powerful. A powerful society, in other words, will not demand of its wrongdoers that they are rigorously punished. It may be inclined even to go so far as embracing mercy as the most appropriate response to the criminal.

With this claim Nietzsche returns us to the ethic of mercy already outlined in *The Wanderer and His Shadow* and *Daybreak*. One can imagine a society "*so conscious of its power* that it could allow itself the noblest luxury available to it, – that of letting its malefactors go *unpunished* ... Justice, which began by saying 'Everything can be paid off, everything must be paid off,' ends by turning a blind eye and letting those off unable to pay, – it ends like every good thing of earth, by *sublimating itself*. The self-sublimation of justice: we know what a nice name it gives itself – *mercy*; it remains, of course, the prerogative of the most powerful man, better still, his way of being beyond the law" (*Genealogy*, II, 10). Power, which is at work from the outset in the constitution of the forces of equilibrium that determine the spheres of rights and just treatment, sublimates the social code of penal law into something that now outstrips the domain of the law itself. Nietzsche thereby offers us a standpoint *beyond* the realm of formal legality that spurns the vengeance that was hitherto enshrined in it. The modern law court described in *The Wanderer and His Shadow* is a sphere of revenge, a space of policing and misinterpretation in which the criminal is held to account for his or her deeds according to a mythical standard of responsibility grounded in the error of free will. In contrast, in the *Genealogy* an ethic of mercy flows from a generosity possible when one is in a state of empowerment sufficient to spurn vengeance. Understood in these terms, being just becomes something affirmative (*Genealogy*, II, 11).

Two conceptions of justice thus emerge from Nietzsche's texts that span the period from *Human, All Too Human* to the *Genealogy*. One conception of justice confines itself to the realm of tradition, to the securing of repayment for a wrong, and comes to cleave to a metaphysics of free will that sanctions vengeance. The other conception turns its back on this logic even as it emerges from it. "Justice," properly speaking, means for Nietzsche precisely *not punishing* the wrongdoer. Given the degree to which revenge has shaped human psychology and culture anyone who ceases to view the world in a manner dominated by the feeling that they are the victim of a personal injury of some kind (especially if they happen to be such a victim) would represent "a piece of perfection, the highest form of mastery to be had on earth, – and even something which we would be wise not to expect and should certainly find difficult to believe" (*Genealogy*, II, 11). Legal systems, Nietzsche now argues, can thus be read as manifestations of this kind of power, as the attempt by those most powerful in a social milieu to circumvent the spirit of revenge that permeates it. When a legal system is set up that treats a wrong in terms of rules, it cultivates an impersonal ethos that resists the temptation to view the wrongdoer through the eyes of the injured party:

> Everywhere that justice is practised and maintained, the stronger power can be seen looking for means of putting an end to the senseless ravages of *ressentiment* amongst those inferior to it .... the most decisive thing ... that the higher authorities can invent and enforce against the even stronger power of hostile and spiteful feelings – and they do it as soon as they are strong enough – is the setting up of a *legal system*, the imperative declaration of what counts as permissible in their eyes, as just, and what counts as forbidden, unjust: once the legal code is in place, by treating offence and arbitrary actions against the individual or groups as a crime, as violation of the law, as insurrection against the higher authorities themselves, they distract attention from the damage done by such violations, and ultimately achieve the opposite of what revenge sets out to do, which just sees and regards as valid the injured party's point of view –: from then on the eye is trained for an ever more *impersonal* interpretation of the action ... Therefore "just" and "unjust" only start from the moment when a legal system is set up ... To talk of "just" and "unjust" *as such* is meaningless, an act of injury, violence, exploitation or destruction cannot be "unjust" *as such*, because life functions *essentially* in an injurious, violent, exploitative and destructive manner, or these are at least its fundamental processes and it cannot be thought of without these characteristics. (*Genealogy*, II, 11)

One should compare this view with the kind of "justice" that Nietzsche has already lambasted in *Human, All Too Human, The Wanderer and His Shadow,* and *Daybreak* as typifying the law courts of his own times. The "so-called justice that punishes and rewards" (*Human, All Too Human*, 105), is now exemplified by the anti-Semitic philosopher Eugen Dühring, who advocates the view that justice originates in the feeling of having suffered a wrong (*Genealogy*, II, 11). To believe this is to regress to the most primitive of faiths in which the notions of equivalence and exchange take the ontological status of absolutes. The one who does not conform, the "evil" human being, is by way of this made into the devil personified, an object of hatred and spiteful revenge. Against this conception, Nietzsche argues for a justice that demythologizes the wrongdoer and so mitigates spite, diverting resentful feelings away from the miscreant. There is no such thing, this section of the *Genealogy* avers, as "justice-in-itself." There is no natural law, no initial violation or originary guilt that can occur outside the bounds of a formally articulated legal framework. This conception of law takes justice to be a positive force when properly understood, for it functions to shield the object of resentful hatred from the full force of the victim's spite and ultimately abandons the right to extract compensation in any form. To be "just," here, means to produce a situation in which there is an equilibrium of forces rather than to bring about the extirpation of so-called "undesirable" forces with a view to the enforcement of a fixed moral order. True justice, in so far as it has existed on earth, refuses to the wronged a free hand with regard to the fate of the wrongdoer.

Nietzsche's advocacy in the *Genealogy* of the view that justice must go beyond itself, overturning the very logic of equivalence that grounds it, represents a development connected to the idea of the role of the freethinker outlined in *Daybreak*. The freethinker thinks against norms and the power of custom and in so doing seeks to overthrow them. Such a one who acts in this way is for Nietzsche historically important, for they are the ones who create new norms and customs, the makers of values. Creators of this kind are characterized in a manner that is telling: "One has to take back much of the defamation which people have cast upon those who broke through the spell of custom by means of a *deed* – in general, they are called criminals. Whoever has overthrown an existing law of custom [*Sittengesetz*] has hitherto always been accounted a *bad man*: but when, as did happen, the law could not afterwards be reinstated, the predicate gradually changed; – history treats almost exclusively of these *bad men* who became *good men*!" (*Daybreak*, 20) The mark of "criminal," then, is something that anyone forced to think against the norm has been destined to bear. The historian of morals who does not appreciate the symptomatic nature of values and meanings fails to see this. Every value is a symptom of something having triumphed over something else, every sense a sign that the miscreant-turned-victor who has successfully overstepped the boundaries delineated by custom and the sacred has spontaneously refashioned the significance of the practices and customs that mark the space of the sacred in their own image. "The form is fluid, the 'meaning' [*Sinn*] even more so" (*Genealogy*, II, 12). The sanctioning of law as the embodiment of the dominance of custom and authority over the individual must be abandoned. The nature of the criminal must be rethought. Imagine, says Nietzsche, a world in which the criminal calls himself to account and determines his own punishment "in the proud feeling that he is thus honouring the law that he himself has made, that by punishing himself he is exercising his power, the power of the lawgiver" (*Daybreak*, 187). A situation like this presupposes a new order of legislation "founded on the idea 'I submit only to the law which I myself have given, in great things and small.' There are so many experiments to make! There are so many futures still to dawn!" (ibid.). Two conditions must be fulfilled if this vision is to be articulated satisfactorily. The first is that the bogus nature of all who claim to be the embodiment of universal goodness and justice be made evident. The second requires that the possibility of the kind of freedom necessary for such experimental living be made manifest. What must be formulated is a vision of the law-giving animal.

5

The Law-Giving Animal

1. For a consideration of Nietzsche's views on "the good and the just" one can turn to Thus Spoke Zarathustra, *a work that challenges not only accepted conceptions of morality but also conventional understandings of the genre of philosophical discourse. As such,* Zarathustra *is best read in conjunction with the work that follows it,* Beyond Good and Evil, *a text that also makes explicit Nietzsche's challenge to the conventions of philosophical thought.* Zarathustra *opens with the giving of a gift of wisdom. It is a dangerous gift (a gift of "fire"), because its acceptance entails rejecting the rule of norm and custom in one's life. This gift is the gift of the vision of the overman. The overman symbolizes a demand to rethink human identity, captured early in the text by the metaphor of a figure passing on a rope over an abyss. Humankind, Zarathustra holds, is a creature part cultured, part beast. The beast in us must be overcome. Such a path involves overcoming the merely conventional aspect of human life present in oneself in pursuit of an excellence summed up by the notion of individual sovereignty. This sovereignty comes with the demise of universalism. Its aim is the redemption of past human suffering. This vision of redemption, however, is naturalistic. It offers no "otherworldly" comforts, it denies the universal, rebuts metaphysics, and embraces the earth and history. This vision is contrasted with its antithesis: the nightmare vision of the "last man," a being who craves nothing more in life than bland contentment.*

Nietzsche's views on "the good and the just" are articulated clearly enough by his anti-prophet, Zarathustra. This semi-mythical figure – the original Zoroaster, credited by Nietzsche with the invention of morality and because of this given the privilege of bearing witness to its dissolution – enacts, sometimes in parody, the demythologization and self-overcoming of morality. The four parts of *Thus Spoke Zarathustra,* written between 1883 and 1885, form a text that begs to be read in a manner akin to the way in which one approaches a piece of music. There is an initial stage at which one neither wants nor needs critical overviews. Just as the experience of a symphony benefits from minimal information (the name of the composer and their dates of birth and death form a sufficient context) so with *Zarathustra* one is initially reduced to silence. One is driven to let the text speak first. One can ask questions after, if one wishes. Just as a piece of music can be, so *Zarathustra* is a gift. It is neither "pure philosophy" (whatever that is) nor novel ("pure" fiction). It is neither treatise nor critique, nor manifesto, nor rule book. The text of *Zarathustra* lives in the gaps that open up in one's uncritically accepted understanding of the boundaries separating genres. As befits something that slips between the boundaries of generic definition, it is, as the dedication announces, a book "for all and none." *Zarathustra* is a text for anybody and nobody, which means that it is somewhat like a letter forever condemned to being delivered to the wrong address. With such a letter, if, when you open it, you think it is specifically for you, then you are without doubt not the intended addressee. One must be a wary reader in this regard. Lawrence Lampert is surely right to see in *Thus Spoke Zarathustra* the summation of Nietzsche's philosophy,[1] but it is a deliberately frustrating summation if you are the sort of reader who wants to slice off an easily digestible morsel of something that summarizes the supposed whole that some dare to label with the phrase "Nietzsche's thought."

Thus Spoke Zarathustra is a combination of interludes, journeys, and repetitions.[2] It opens, fittingly enough, as a journey begins (*Zarathustra*, I, "Zarathustra's Prologue," 1). Zarathustra, a solitary being living in self-imposed mountain exile, decides the time has come to return to the realm of human society. He has, he announces, a gift to give to humanity:

1 See Lampert, *Nietzsche's Teaching*.

2 For an exemplary discussion of the structure of *Thus Spoke Zarathustra* see Loeb, *The Death of Nietzsche's Zarathustra*. Loeb argues that the text itself is bound up with Nietzsche's conception of eternal recurrence in its narrative structure. Zarathustra's life, in other words, is itself an enactment of eternal recurrence. Loeb's self-avowedly "literary" approach to interpreting Nietzsche is one I have much sympathy with. Such an approach means that one does not begin thinking about Nietzsche (or anything else, for that matter) by first defining one's concepts. The possibility of such a definition is fantasy – what concepts signify is determined by their role within a web of cultural practices, as Nietzsche compellingly reveals in his discussion of them in the *Genealogy* (see chapter 4). The predominance of practice in Nietzsche's writings, which is explored here especially in chapters 3 and 4, might also be well characterized as epitomizing the necessary "literary" element in all action (a term which also includes "thought"). This is why a "pure philosophy" (that is, a philosophy which is not always already something else, not always already entangled in something else – in politics, culture, history) is an impossible and dangerous fantasy. That Nietzsche is not himself immune to the temptations of such a fantasy is a thought that lies behind my discussion of revaluation and *The Antichrist* in the final chapter of this book.

the "cup" of his soul overflows and he feels driven to share the riches held within it. The text thus begins with an affirmation of the act of bestowal: "I bring men a gift" (*Zarathustra,* "Zarathustra's Prologue," 2). This is a gift of wisdom, and it truly is a gift, for Zarathustra wants nothing in return for it. A short exchange on the way down the mountain with a hermit who recalls Zarathustra's ascent into solitude reveals the source of the gift: Zarathustra has undergone a transformation fashioned by solitude and he has become full. The gift is announced on the wave of an oscillation that marks out its origin as residing in an indeterminate temporal space opened up between coming and going. It does not have an origin in the sense of being something authored. The gift, rather, springs forth from a taking leave born of despair and is announced only in its bearer's triumphant return. Zarathustra's triumph here is a kind of danger. His is a gift that must look to some like a message of searing devastation fashioned from the hot embers of burnt-out remains: "At that time you carried your ashes to the mountains; would you now carry your fire into the valleys? Do you not fear to be punished as an arsonist?" The symbolism is clear enough: Zarathustra is an inverter of the order of things. Where fire consumes itself and finishes in ashes and dust, Zarathustra conjures fire from smoking remnants. Zarathustra, an outsider, a foreigner alien to the regulated realm of social order, bears within his wisdom something incendiary. His gift brings with it the danger that it will inflame others and in doing so provoke the counter reaction of the dominant forces of conformist social order, an order all too keen to indulge in punishment and look for "justifications" afterwards for doing so.

Zarathustra's gift is the post-humanist vision of the "overman": "*I teach you the overman.* Man is something that shall be overcome. What have you done to overcome him? All beings so far have created something beyond themselves; and do you want to be the ebb of this great flood and even go back to the beasts rather than overcome man? (*Zarathustra,* I, "Zarathustra's Prologue", 3). We are almost at once offered a speech invoking the vision of a humanity that is capable of surpassing itself. What is needed, Zarathustra says, is a rethinking of what it means to be human. This forms the basis of what Zarathustra calls his love of humanity. Such love is the love of the potential humankind has to transcend its purportedly "given" nature:

> Man is a rope tied between beast and overman – a rope over an abyss … What is great in man is that he is a bridge and not an end: what can be loved in man is that he is an *overture* and a *going under.* I love those who do not know how to live, except by going under,

> for they are those who cross over … I love those … who sacrifice themselves for the earth, that the earth may some day become the overman's. I love him who lives to know, and who wants to know so that the overman may live some day. And thus he wants to go under. I love him who works and invents to build a house for the overman and to prepare earth, animal, and plant for him … I love him who justifies future and redeems past generations: for he wants to perish of the present. (*Zarathustra*, I, "Zarathustra's Prologue," 4)

Only a person who becomes a willing means of humanity "crossing over" from the customary and compliant existence that characterizes the average mode of existence in society to a new, experimental mode of life is worthy of Zarathustra's love. Such a person wills their own down-going and with it the down-going of humanity in pursuit of the vision of new conceptions of excellence. In turn, Zarathustra envisions fashioning the earth into something replete with the cultivated resources of nature that the overman, a being of supra-human futurity, will need.

The overman is, of course, a kind of metaphor for human potential. He is a representation of the most gloriously selfish creator-spirit, allied to what Nietzsche elsewhere refers to as the "Dionysian" man.[3] The overman exemplifies the self-possession, autonomy, and uniqueness of a kind of sovereign individuality, one resistant to a modernity dominated by the impersonal forces of mass production and consumption. The overman is a being of hitherto un-thought potential for freedom, for his freedom is the freedom characteristic of the creation of values. This is a freedom that marks the death of universal morality: "He … has discovered himself who says, 'This is *my* good and evil'; with that he has reduced to silence the mole and dwarf who say, 'Good for all, evil for all' … 'This is *my* way; where is yours?' – thus I answered those who asked me 'the way.' For *the* way – that does not exist" (*Zarathustra*, III, "On the Spirit of Gravity," 2). Humankind must be something that is passed through if the overman is to be attained. In this way, the collective and unimaginably vast suffering of self-inflicted punishment and self-torture that characterizes human history is open to being redeemed. The fragments that now make up the realm of human existence can then be fashioned into a new unity: all that is "fragment and riddle and dreadful accident" in humankind can, through the vision of the overman, be reassembled into something that enables the realization of humanity's potential for excellence: "To

3 See *Twilight of the Idols*, "'Reason' in Philosophy," 6.

redeem what is past in man and to re-create all 'it was' until the will says, 'Thus I willed it! Thus shall I will it – this I called redemption and this alone I taught them to call redemption' (*Zarathustra*, III, "On Old and New Tablets," 3). In this way, the past is rendered something that may be justified and redeemed by way of the overman. Such redemption is, however, naturalistic. It requires no "afterworldly" illusions in order to be communicated, it offers nothing comfortingly universal – it does not smack of metaphysics.

The vision of the "last man" that Zarathustra elucidates by way of a contrast to the overman offers a good means of understanding the vision. The idea of the overman inspires in Zarathustra thoughts of a sublime autonomy, a self-possession that expends itself in the individuality of creative expression. The last man, in contrast, is a creature of self-obsessed sterility. Zarathustra's de-humanizing description is supposed to provoke revulsion. We are presented with a creature as pestilent as the "flea-beetle," rubbing itself up against its neighbour in a search for comfort and warmth; a being devoid of any understanding of great love, creation, longing, or striving. The last man lacks even self-contempt. For him, all that matters is the prospect of a comfortable life and the stultifying happiness characteristic of one who uncritically embraces the norm: "'We have invented happiness,' say the last men and they blink ... One still works, for work is a form of entertainment. But one is careful lest the entertainment be too harrowing. One no longer becomes poor or rich: both require too much exertion" (*Zarathustra*, I, "Zarathustra's Prologue," 5). The last man typifies the dominant desire for easy living that motivates modern mass culture and characterizes communal existence generally. His is a world of short-lived, trivial mass entertainment and uncreative self-indulgence. The last man is, in short, too forgiving of himself in contrast to the self-critical hardness of those who would be a pathway to forms of living beyond the norm.

2. *The overman does not represent a form of ultimate obligation or compulsion. It is an invitation that commends to us a goal. It does so in the language of naturalistic historical philosophy. This approach embraces the body as the locus of human identity and rejects the belief in autonomous spirituality, i.e. the "immortal soul" concept. The latter belief is characteristic of the world view of the "last man," for it is symptomatic of a retreat from the traumas of life into a "better" realm beyond pain and suffering. The attack on the soul in* Zarathustra *is an attack on the metaphysical conception of free will, and hence the moralistic justification of punishment that characterizes our dominant sense of morality. The affirmation of the soul concept is equivalent for Nietzsche to the affirmation of the soul, our consciousness, as something superior to the body. With this, thought trumps the realm*

of feeling and materiality. The belief in the soul testifies to the fact that humanity is alienated from itself. In the development of human culture, becoming conscious was accompanied by a necessary degree of pain. The body, in turn, came to be denigrated as a source of suffering. The consequence of this is that we are inclined to delusion: we are subject to the soul's moralistic urge to denigrate embodiment and hence to self-hatred. Against this, Zarathustra asserts the priority of the body and its legitimate authority over the soul concept.

Zarathustra may be one who seeks to take his fire to the valleys, but his first attempt at doing so reveals that in the wrong conditions an incendiary can be a damp squib. He announces to people gathered in a market place (to the masses) the overcoming of humanity and the coming of the overman (*Zarathustra*, I, "Zarathustra's Prologue," 3). Their response is (quite understandably, one is inclined to say) epitomized by a combination of ignorance and mockery. He cannot oblige them to listen. The gift that Zarathustra bears, it turns out, is akin to an invitation (the invitation of the overman), and one can always turn down invitations. A passage from *Daybreak* provides a clue to what happens here in the text: "Only if mankind possessed a universally recognized *goal* would it possible to propose 'thus and thus is the *right* course of action': for the present there exists no such goal. It is thus irrational and trivial to impose the demands of morality upon mankind. – To *recommend* a goal to mankind is something quite different: the goal is then thought of as something that *lies in our own discretion*; supposing the recommendation appealed to mankind it could in pursuit of it also *impose* upon itself a moral law, likewise at its own discretion" (*Daybreak*, 108). In other words, it is unwarranted and unrealistic to seek to impose upon human existence any universal moral imperative. Commending us to endorse an idea of what the future could be is, however, somewhat different. If a vision appeals we can choose to endorse that vision and adopt it as our own. Zarathustra's commendation of the overman is to be taken in just this manner. It cannot be imposed by way of some superior power and remain what it proclaims itself to be. Only as an invitation does it retain its integrity as a teaching and as a gift.

Zarathustra's invitation speaks in the idiom of the anti-metaphysical naturalism Nietzsche first outlines in *Human, All Too Human.* We are asked to reconsider the meaning of our virtues through affirming naturalism, that is, through embracing the body. The majority of people, Zarathustra proclaims, believe unquestioningly in the autonomy of the soul; but such belief epitomizes metaphysical prejudice. To cleave to this belief means to look down on the body in order to glorify the soul. In such glorification Zarathustra sees the source of an illusory sense of detachment and self-determination that cultivates the un-ambitious contentment and peaceful resignation characteristic of the last man. In so far as it signifies the ideal of a thing untrammelled by the body, of an entity separated from the taint of history and becoming, the soul concept stands as a symptom of revulsion against embodied life. When one affirms the "soul," or pure thought, one affirms a realm that lies beyond the challenge and pain that are essential characteristics of existence. Life, in short, is a trauma, and one must face it for what it is. The soul concept signifies the refusal to do this. It is symptomatic of the desire to seek refuge from the traumas of life in a sense of selfhood that is immune to being stretched, scratched, sliced, maimed, tortured, and killed, as the body can be.

When he speaks of the "soul," Zarathustra's target is faith in the autonomous free will, the belief that, as we have seen, Nietzsche identifies as underlying the moralistic justification of punishment.[4] When we affirm the soul a part of us speaks and makes itself heard, but it is the weakest part – our consciousness, that part of us that does little more than bear witness to the greater strivings and struggles of the embodied self.[5] The affirmer of the soul asks, thereby, that the weaker be allowed to judge the stronger, that "pure thought" be the judge of "mere materiality" and that the body subordinate itself to the hegemony of the concept. For Nietzsche, this is akin to an illness; it is as if a part and function of the whole has sought to usurp it.[6] In reality, the soul is not fit to sit in judgement over the body, for it is a creation dependent entirely on the body. Another way of putting this would be to say that we are creatures divided against ourselves, and that the soul concept bears unconscious witness to the pain that this division engenders (see *Genealogy*, III, 13ff). Culture, which subordinates the drives to norms, is attained at the cost

4 See chapter 4.

5 See *Thus Spoke Zarathustra*, I, "Of the Despisers of the Body." Here Zarathustra draws the distinction between the self and the "I." The self is the body, a hierarchy of command dominated by a "great reason [*eine grosse Vernunft*]": "The self says to the I 'feel pain here!' Then it suffers and thinks how it might suffer no more – and that is why it is *made* to think. The self says to the I 'Feel delight here!' Then it is delighted and thinks how it might often delight again – and that is why it is *made* to think." The "I" is thus a function of the commanding self, forced into thought it is subject to the self's overwhelming authority – an authority derived from the body's having "more reason" in it than is contained in the most profound wisdom consciousness has to offer. The "I" is thus a subject of the sovereign. It is that aspect of the self that bears witness to the historical unfolding of its life.

6 See *Thus Spoke Zarathustra*, I, "Of the Despisers of the Body." As it bears witness the self-reflexive "I" interprets the life of the self, but in doing so it comes to mistake this interpretation and thereby takes itself to be the sole cause of embodied action.

of a creature whose identity is problematic. Norms act on the body to tame it, to render the brute animal a being that will conform (*Genealogy*, II, 2ff). Humanity thereby emerges as a self-interpreter and creature of will only at the cost of being alienated from its own embodied condition: it punishes itself into regularization and in doing so experiences itself foremost as pain. Becoming conscious means first becoming conscious of pain and this pain is inevitably experienced as something uncannily other, as a body in pain, one that in acceding to the dictates of webs of communal customary evaluation opens itself to suffering from the practices of punishing that are exerted upon it simply in virtue of its being a creature of society. When norms forbid, they forbid the tendency of the embodied drives to assert themselves (the tendency to anti-social behaviour) and when customs punish they punish the body, which is in this way open to being both taken as the cause of guilt and made an object of socially constructed contempt. This, for Nietzsche, underlies the human tendency to denigrate the body. Because of the necessary power of social conformity, we have an inclination to mistake the embodied source of our pain for the origin of our feelings of guilt, when such feelings are in fact merely symptoms of the power that custom energizes over the body as a condition of social life. In short, one of our dominant tendencies is the tendency to moralization.

The soul's resultant moralistic attempts to denigrate and thereby subjugate and submerge the embodied condition of its own existence give rise to something at once attenuated and ugly in its propensity for idle satisfaction. The soul hates its own embodied condition: "Once the soul looked contemptuously upon the body, and then this contempt was the highest: she wanted the body meagre, ghastly, and starved. Thus she hoped to escape it and the earth … But you, too, my brothers, tell me: what does your body proclaim of your soul? Is not your soul poverty and filth and wretched contentment?" (*Zarathustra*, I, "Zarathustra's Prologue," 3). The worship of the soul concept means denigrating the body and rendering it something starved and weak. Here lie the roots of asceticism. It is the soul, however, that is worthy of vilification, not the body. Where the body is traditionally considered a thing of pollution in opposition to the soul's purity (of processes, hunger, ingestion, digestion, excretion, desire, embarrassment, and pain) Zarathustra inverts the hierarchy. The body is pure. What is polluting are the soul's metaphysical attempts to denigrate what is in reality the embodied condition of its own existence; its desire to stand as a judge over something with regard to which it has no right to judge, as if the notion of "pure intellect" were anything more than a chimera. The body is the legitimate judge of the soul's propensities, not the other way round. Taken this way, the soul concept is found to be something wanting and corrupting, even as it is nevertheless necessary in view of the conditions under which human culture emerged. If, as Nietzsche argues from *Human, All Too Human* onwards, we are creatures who are unjust to our experiences, it turns out that this injustice is perpetrated most against the embodied condition that makes us who we are. The soul concept must be placed on trial.

3. The teaching of the overman is the teaching of the negation of both the soul myth and the myth of a free, autonomous will. Zarathustra urges us to attain the "great contempt" as a path to overcoming such beliefs. In this state, one recoils from that which hitherto has been valued and given happiness. One undergoes nihilism. This affords a glimpse of a realm of possible meaning that lies beyond conventional judgement. What is needed, Zarathustra tells an audience of listeners in a market place, is a new justification for living, a new mode of being. His audience, a crowd of instinctive humanists inclined to view themselves as the centre and purpose of things, greet him with laughter and incomprehension. The everyday world of human concerns does not condone Zarathustra's urging of a humanity that embarks upon ever more ambitious and experimental ways of life. For Nietzsche, however, such a vision is needed to steer us away from nihilism. This vision is promulgated by a reinterpretation of the law-like propensities that have made humankind what it is. A new sense of justice is needed. One must, Zarathustra holds, spurn accepted attitudes toward duty, self-respect, right, and status and reformulate them. From the standpoint of "the good and the just" Zarathustra's teaching looks like criminality. If he is to gain true listeners and followers, he notes, he must become a "robber," since he must wrestle them from a social realm dominated by conformity and unwilling to part with them. The "great contempt" is the first stage along the path redeeming the body and hence the self.

The teaching of the overcoming of humanity requires that we disabuse ourselves of the soul myth, the metaphysical belief in an autonomous faculty of free choice, of a power of consciousness immune to embodied constraints. To free oneself of the soul in this way means to overcome the sense of responsibility and guilt associated with it. For this, Zarathustra argues, the "great contempt" is needed, the moment in which one feels revulsion even toward that which has endowed one with one's greatest happiness. One must go through a moment of nihilism. What seemed to be of the highest value must now seem to be not merely worthless but repulsive. The great contempt is: "The hour when you say, 'What matters my reason? Does it crave knowledge as the lion his food? It is poverty and filth and wretched contentment.' The hour when you say, 'What matters my virtue? As yet it has not made me rage. How weary I am of my good and my evil! All that is poverty and filth and wretched contentment.' The hour when you say, 'What matters my justice? I do not see that I am flames and fuel. But the just are flames and fuel.' The hour when you say, 'What matters my pity? Is not pity the cross on which he is nailed who loves man? But my pity is no crucifixion.' Have you yet spoken thus?" (*Zarathustra,* I, "Zarathustra's Prologue," 3) Great questioning requires extravagance. It requires that one goes beyond the domain of the average everyday world of evaluations, the realm in which the invocation of the purportedly highest ideals and gods evidences nothing more than the ability to live communally, un-ambitiously, and peacefully, to do no more than take care over one's daily out-goings and in-goings, to accede to the norm without a thought. What is needed, Zarathustra holds, is a new "justification," a new way of endowing life with significance that can be encapsulated by the extravagant demand that says "my happiness ought to justify existence itself." Reason, virtue, justice, pity, ethical and political life: all must be reconsidered in the light of this demand.

It is perhaps not surprising that in the face of this onslaught on their everyday world those standing before Zarathustra when he makes this speech laugh at him. The fact is, he ruminates, that they do not comprehend that the term "humanity" denotes nothing more than an intermediate state of being (*Zarathustra,* I, "Zarathustra's Prologue," 4). They do not realize that the existence of humanity taken as it is remains a mystery, something senseless and weird, unless something can be provided that will come to embrace it through allowing it to embrace itself (ibid., 7). People have a tendency to think of themselves humanistically, i.e. in a manner that is essentially passive, as an end, as a kind of conclusion to the nature of things, as if all that has been was simply following a pre-ordained path pointing inexorably toward them as its pinnacle. To be human is for Zarathustra, however, to be a prelude. For Zarathustra, humankind is worthy in so far as it can be an overture to more ambitious experiments in living. Experiments such as that which the notion of the overman exemplifies will be capable of justifying the past not because they just happen to have sprung from it. Justification, for Nietzsche, is not passive. They will do so because they can turn on the past and, in an act of self-legislative affirmation, inscribe a sense upon it that makes manifest an act of creative will. Justification of the kind Nietzsche urges here is something that is not found but *made* and it is through its being made that it redeems humanity from the absurdity of a merely passive sense of being what it is. Such making requires rethinking the significance of our law-like propensities and it requires a new sense of justice that springs out of the older one and in doing so goes beyond it, just as a butterfly emerges from its cocoon and thereby transcends it.

To teach this, as Zarathustra does, is to risk the ire of "the good and the just" (*Zarathustra*, I, "Zarathustra's Prologue," 8). To emphasize the uncanny alienated condition that haunts the web of everyday human concerns is to place a question mark over the legitimacy of those concerns. One who does so must always be perceived as "the danger of the multitude" – as a challenger of accepted notions concerning the nature of justice itself. No surprise, then, that Zarathustra turns elsewhere, that he feels impelled to offer his teaching only to those willing to follow him to the margins of social acceptability "because they want to follow themselves" (ibid., 9). Zarathustra's wisdom now becomes something that must be communicated through acts that combine a sense of seduction and theft. He must poach from society such individuals as are suited, and hence willing, to hear his teaching. He must become outlandish, a lawbreaker, he must appear as one who rejects the norms that govern the social realm since he seeks to steal from its number: "The people shall be angry with me: Zarathustra wants to be called a robber by the shepherds." The so-called "shepherds" are none other than "the good and the just." These are the haters of the person who challenges the authority of the rules that characterize the hegemony of social conformity. To challenge such conformity means to be deemed a criminal: "Behold the good and the just! Whom do they hate most? The man who breaks their tables of values, the breaker, the lawbreaker; but this is the creator [*der Schaffende*]" (*Zarathustra*, I, "Zarathustra's Prologue," 9). Creation, that is the creation of values, always requires an act of destruction. To be a destroyer of values and to be a creator of values are two sides of the same coin, for one cannot create new ways of living, new legislations concerning life,[7] without threatening the old. Creativity, when understood from the standpoint represented by the norms that ensure the smooth operation of social order, is a form of criminality. This is because creativity shatters the faith in the norm, in the rule of custom and tradition, in what is unquestioningly accepted as demarcating the domain of the "good." The same goes for all people with faith in conformity. They hate the creator, the person who overturns established values as a necessary prelude to creating new ones. One should note thereby that the "great contempt" Zarathustra urges is not so much a state of self-hatred but the condition of suffering from what one is because of what one has valued hitherto. One can explore it further by entering with Zarathustra into a court of law and witnessing an instructive illustration of a moment of "great contempt."

7 *Das Schaffen* is legislating, producing; *schaffen*, to accomplish, to bring off, to create.

4. Zarathustra explores the notion of the "great contempt" further. We are placed in a court. A "pale criminal" is on trial. The court demands from the criminal that he acquiesce to the guilty verdict, that he undergoes the "great contempt" and feels revulsion and self-hatred at the mere thought of himself. Proper judgment of such a person must refrain from moral censure. Have not the judges themselves, Zarathustra asks, done in thought what the criminal before has done in deed? Responsibility for violence must not be placed solely at the miscreant's door. What sickens the criminal and propels them into blood-lust is the cultural milieu they inhabit. The criminal, a blend of drives and social conditioning peculiar to the vicissitudes of time and place, suffers from the fatality of simply being who he is. In other times his now unruly drives could have been put to good use. The past is replete with victims of this sort. Once the doubter experienced a similar self-loathing and sense of their own criminality because of this tendency and was made sick by being deemed a heretic and witch. Self-understanding is always already mediated by the dominant norms in a social order: the naming of characteristics as "evil" gives rise to the self-hatred of the person unfortunate enough to have these characteristics. No one is born "evil," they are made it. In the space of the law court this thought is unthinkable: the judge must affirm the normative structure of the social world they inhabit in order to fulfil their function as judge. So-called virtues, however, are in reality instrumental calculations designed to ensure the power of the norm, social stability, and a life of ease. They represent the justice of the "last man," a merely habitual and unthinking endorsement of the conditions that foster comfortable, collective existence. Such conditions may have been essential in fashioning humanity, but that is no reason to adhere to them. The law of custom, of habitual justice, must be rejected. Such a rejection is akin to the rejection of custom represented by the modern state, but must not be confused with it.

"On the Pale Criminal," in the first part of *Zarathustra*, transports the reader into a courtroom. The court is elucidated as a space that re-enacts the ancient ritual of primitive sacrifice. Who, however, is the judge and who the judged in the narrative Zarathustra offers here? The "judges and sacrificers" of the law court are in session before a condemned man. They do not want to kill, however, until the "animal" has nodded, until he has lowered his head in submissive agreement with the sentence pronounced upon him. In other words, the judges need a specific kind of justification to reside in their sentencing of the criminal. It must be one that comes from the criminal himself. The judges need the criminal's participation: he needs to offer some kind of assent concerning the process in which he is immersed and whereby he is judged, albeit if only through an act of silent, submissive agreement. The pale criminal nods; as he does so his eyes speak "the great contempt." The object of the criminal's "great contempt" is the interpretation that his consciousness, as a bearing witness to who he is, offers up concerning his own identity, his understanding of himself, the moment of self-interpretation that says "I": "'My I [*Ich*] is something that shall be overcome: my I is to me the great contempt of man': that is what his eyes say." This is the criminal's moment of self-judgement, the point at which the self-awareness generated by the gaze of the court turns him against himself in disgust. Contempt marks the moment at which the pale criminal becomes more than he has been hitherto: he is a being who now suffers from himself, who stands as his own judge. In so far as the criminal at this moment judges and condemns himself he offers a glimpse of the human potential for self-overcoming: "That he judged himself, that was his highest moment; do not let the sublime return to his baseness!" Suffering and self-contempt is the sign that something more is possible for this pale, bleached-out being: that there is available to him some form of dignity.

Perhaps the only redemption from deep suffering of this kind is "a quick death," Zarathustra suggests. The judges who sentence to kill should only do so, however, in the right spirit. Let them condemn as an act of kindness, not as an expression of revenge. "'Enemy,' you shall say, but not 'villain'; 'sick' you shall say, but not 'scoundrel'; 'fool' you shall say, but not 'sinner.'" Moral censure, in short, is not the proper business of the just decision. After all, Zarathustra asks, can the "scarlet judge," resplendent in the gowns of his office, ultimately hold himself to be any better than the person over whom he sits in judgement? Few of us are innocent when it comes to indulgence in the violence of fantasy. If, says Zarathustra, the judge were to confess what he had "already done in thought" we would experience revulsion normally reserved for the criminal. It is, of course, one thing to think something and another to act it – even if the difference in question is only one of degree rather than difference in kind. The question, however, concerns the extent to which one owns up to one's deeds or thoughts. The pale criminal is *pale*, emptied of the vigour of life, because he has been destroyed in a specific way: "An image made this pale man pale. He was equal to his deed when he did it; but he could not bear its image after it was done. Now he always saw himself as the doer of one deed. Madness I call this: the exception has now become the essence for him. A chalk streak stops a hen; the stroke that he himself struck stopped his poor reason: madness *after* the deed I call this" (*Zarathustra*, I, "On the Pale Criminal"). What the judges in the law court do not know, says Zarathustra, is that there is a deeper form of madness that *precedes* the deed. They simplistically attribute the criminal's evil act to the desire to steal. In reality, he was a victim of bloodlust: "he thirsted after the joy of the knife!" The act of robbery that accompanies the criminal's killing of his victim is a cloak: it allows him to conceal from himself the true of nature of the desire for blood that spurred him on to kill. Posing the question as to what it is that underlies the pale criminal's lust for blood means, for Zarathustra, turning to the issue of the relation between the drives, the criminal, and the social world he inhabits. The clue as to the true nature of the criminal's violence resides here:

> What is this man? A heap of diseases, which, through his spirit, reach out into the world: there they want to catch their prey. What is this man? A ball of wild snakes, which rarely enjoy rest from each other: so they go forth singly and seek prey in the world. Behold this poor body! What it suffered and coveted this poor soul interpreted for itself: it interpreted it as murderous lust and greed for the bliss of the knife. Those who become sick today are overcome by that evil which is evil today: they want to hurt with that which hurts them. But there have been other ages and another evil and good. Once doubt was evil and the will to self. Then the sick became heretics and witches: as heretics and witches they suffered and wanted to inflict suffering. (Ibid.)

Here one is presented with another exemplary instance of Nietzsche's naturalistic historicism. Who is this person? He is an entwinement of "serpents," of dark and contrary drives that seek to express themselves and, in doing so, turn one after the other back on the environment that he inhabits. However, it is as refractions of this environment that these drives themselves are endowed with significance. The man's poverty-stricken body presents the vision of someone goaded into destructive action by his own suffering. This suffering, however, is now revealed to the sensitive interpreter as something conjoined with the cultural milieu of the sufferer, for it is precisely by way of this milieu that he is constituted as a sufferer. The criminal craves a meaning for his suffering and finds it in the joy of a violence directed at the world around him. The world hurts him, so he turns his pain back upon it, seeking to bring about harm to the very things that have brought harm to him. What in the criminal is deemed "evil" by society becomes for him a means of self-definition. The pale criminal's evil is paradigmatic: it states in bold terms what the evil of his times and culture amounts to – he is a *symptom* of the values that have given rise to what has become of him. In other times, with different tables of values (i.e. given a different hierarchy of good and evil) the self-hatred and hence self-interpretation of the criminal would take on a different form, or be found not in him but perhaps in those who now sit in judgement over him.[8]

In the past, when doubting and asserting oneself were deemed the greatest of evils, Zarathustra notes,[9] the person made sick within these rigid normative structures was deemed a heretic and witch and treated accordingly. Then, also, since they suffered thereby they interpreted themselves accordingly and sought solace by trying to inflict suffering in this form. The person who is deemed evil and a "witch" comes to see herself in these terms and resists domination by recourse to the only thing available, however mythical, namely witchcraft. Thus, the criminal's self-interpreted identity is always already mediated by the dominant norms of his or her time. What is deemed "evil" brings about, *through its being deemed "evil,"* the self-loathing and catastrophe on the part of the one judged and condemned as a deviant and outsider. This insight, Zarathustra holds, cannot be grasped within the formal space of the juridical court. The judge's ears must be closed to the truth of what Zarathustra says, for proclaiming the essential, ontological innocence of the criminal causes pain to so-called "good people." The virtue of these people, Zarathustra says, is however no more than the virtue of instrumental calculation. Their virtues are prescriptions that ensure longevity and ease. They are a product of the demand that the fabric of the everyday world be preserved. It would be better if they suffered like the pale criminal from a madness that would destroy them, for in their self-righteous claim to know already what good and evil is they represent nothing more or less than the smug self-contentment of the last man. Last man's justice is no justice at all. It is merely the power of habit and custom making itself felt. It is the expression of a social function that is numbered amongst the preconditions that must be at work for any collective form of social organization (for the community, which is an assemblage of the "weak") to exist.

Nietzsche uses Zarathustra to voice his rejection of the power of conformity that makes itself manifest in the form of the last man. As is often the case, Nietzsche treads a subtle line here. Custom has made us the creatures that we are. It is only because of the fashioning of our ancestors by customs and norms that a newer and more subtle justice can now emerge in us. The rejection of the power of custom, of customary justice and its habitual judgements concerning what is good and evil, must, it follows, be done in a careful manner. For one thing, Nietzsche's kind of

8 See also the discussion of the criminal in *Twilight of the Idols*, "Skirmishes of an Untimely Man," 45.

9 That is, in the era of the dominance of the morality of custom.

rejection of the rule of custom must not be confused with another contemporary rejection of it. What Zarathustra teaches must not be mistaken for the advocacy of something else. This "something else" is the modern state.

5. *The state is an idol; it dissolves traditions, peoples, and "herds." A people expresses through its values its sense of identity and power. All values, in other words, are a matter of locale. They express the relationship between a form of life (a people) and its environment. Values express a people's creative response to the demands of life. The modern state seeks to usurp this condition by making itself the sole object of esteem. Where customs and peoples are matters of locality, the state seeks to extend its sphere of influence; its goal is that of a formalistic, abstract, and tyrannical universalism. The modern state is a new Babylon. It takes the multiplicity of languages of good and evil and blends them into a chaotic parody of sense. Classificatory convenience rules supreme. Nietzsche's rejection of the state is not, however, a rejection of the state as such. The earliest state (see* Genealogy, *II, 17) was a tyranny, but a productive one. In modernity, the state represents nothing more than the desire for safety and predictability characteristic of the "last man." Modern, liberal, democratic social order represents the regularization of social forms by forces of mass consumption in answer to the demand for economic efficiency spawned by the worship of money. The modern state is bourgeois self-justification raised to a guiding principle of belief. Its absolutism smothers genuine experimentation with values in favour of a trivialized world of mass "entertainment" spurred on by the demand for fame and adulation. Values become reduced to mere accessories to be worn and taken off at a whim. The demands of the moment hold sway, as do the principles of a mass culture that, in spite of its apparently metropolitan aspect, is narrow and hegemonic. Modernity, in this way, threatens to revert to the customary and tyrannical condition that preceded it, but in a manner devoid of creative potential and unjust in attitude toward anyone drawn to the creative life.*

For Zarathustra, the modern state threatens a new idolatry (*Zarathustra*, I, "On the New Idol"). The modern state overturns the rule of tradition, of "peoples and herds," signalling the demise of such social forms and their competing modes of evaluation. Valuing is culture (*Zarathustra*, I, "On the Thousand and One Goals"). No culture has yet existed that did not first begin by holding something in esteem. Self-preservation requires that one esteems differently from one's neighbour. Thus, in so far as they are many, human cultures will esteem in varying and often incompatible ways. The incompatibility can be extreme: one people's good might be another's evil. Different peoples are therefore condemned to misunderstand one another. What a people regard as being difficult they call "commendable," and whatever seems to be both difficult and essential to them they call "good." What sets them free from the greatest need, that which is rarest and most difficult of all, they call "holy." "Whatever makes them rule and triumph and shine, to the awe and envy of their neighbors, that is to them the high, the first, the measure, the meaning of all things." Values, therefore, are expressions of power and locality. If one can divine a people's need, its geographical situation and its neighbours, one can readily grasp the "the law [*Gesetz*] of its overcomings" – in effect, the law that dictates its particular law-like condition of life. All good and evil is, it follows, a creation of human need. That it springs from need does not make it any less miraculous in its being created. The miracle, however, is a human miracle – one tied closely to the randomness of circumstance and unconscious forces rather than being a matter of conscious creation – but it is something miraculous nonetheless.

The modern state, however, wishes to usurp the identity of peoples and stand there in their stead as the self-proclaimed essence of value[10] (*Zarathustra*, I, "On the New Idol"). It wishes to claim for itself the status of a "people" even though it is this notion's antithesis.[11] Where the state appears and dominates, says Zarathustra, there can be no people. The state, it follows, represents a force that overturns the power of custom. The state stands against the morality of custom, but it does so only in so far as it seeks to substitute itself for it. Thus, according to Zarathustra, the modern state does not seek to overturn the kind of hegemony that the morality of custom epitomizes but to usurp it. This usurpation takes the form of a kind of bad parody. Whereas different communities and cultures spontaneously cultivate their own language of good and evil and develop their own world of customary observances, rights, and duties, the modern state merely takes these judgements and practices and mimics them. Such mimicry is necessary for the furtherance of the state's own, quite different universalistic ends. For this reason, the state reveals itself as a Babylonian-style chaos of value, as a simultaneous disordering and retention of value judgements in which various languages of good and evil are intermingled, muddled, and confused in the service of the administrative goals of regulation and prim orderliness. Zarathustra argues that this signals a death-wish. Where all spontaneously arising codes

10 One can consider Nietzsche's 1873 essay, "David Strauss, the confessor and the writer," the first of the *Untimely Meditations*, as an attack on the kind of state worship he condemns here. Strauss's celebration of German supremacy in the aftermath of political unification under Bismarck is, for him, the epitome of cultural philistinism.

11 "Where there is still a people, it does not understand the state and hates it as the evil eye and the sin against customs and rights" (*Thus Spoke Zarathustra*, I, "On the New Idol").

of good and evil are living languages that denote evaluative practices expressing the identity of the community that speaks and thereby observes them, the doubled and borrowed language that the state cultivates is one that has been severed from its conditions of life and is hence already dead. The state's codification of values is merely a fixed ordering of terms regulated according to their ability to serve the state's own hegemonic needs. For the modern state, values are not lived. They are merely convenient modes of classification.

One should note that the state in question here is not the state *per se.* Typically, for Nietzsche, nothing exists in and of itself: there is no state as such and never can be, even if the modern state might like to persuade us to believe otherwise. The modern state is not the same as the original state discussed by Nietzsche in the later text of *On the Genealogy of Morality.* The latter is the source of the tyrannical imposition of an unheard of slavery on our primitive promising ancestors whose consequence is the "internalization of man"[12] and the development of the productive sense of self-loathing that Nietzsche baptizes with the name "bad conscience" (*Genealogy*, II, 17).[13] The new idol is, in contrast, a tyranny of sterility, the world of the last man raised to a guiding principle. The modern state is the emerging liberal-democratic state. This is the state of mass culture, where exchange-value is paramount, the state that presides over a social order dedicated to servicing the economic machines of mass production and mass communication: "Behold the superfluous! They steal the works of the inventors and the treasures of the sages for themselves; 'education' they call their theft ... They vomit their gall and call it a newspaper .... They gather riches and become poorer with them. They want power and first the lever of power, much money – the impotent paupers!" (*Zarathustra*, I, "On the New Idol"). The description of the state offered here is of bourgeois culture writ large. This is a state that presides over a

12 As Nandita Biswas Mellamphy notes in *The Three Stigmata of Friedrich Nietzsche* (3–4), the moment of internalization marks, for Nietzsche, the "constitutive moment" at which the human being ceases to be a mere animal and becomes a political being. Politicization is thus marked by the "*complexification*" of mere animal nature into an instrumental entity endowed with a specifically moral memory. It is this moralization that constitutes the human animal as a specifically political subject.

13 Gilles Deleuze articulates the dynamic of bad conscience and *ressentiment* in terms of the notions of self and other. *Ressentiment* captures the dynamic of attributing blame to others ("it's your fault") and bad conscience the attribution of blame to oneself ("it's my fault"). These two conditions of judgement are the conditions in virtue of which responsibility emerges, and these three elements become "the fundamental categories of Christian and semitic thought, of our way of thinking and interpreting existence in general" (*Nietzsche and Philosophy*, 21).

world lacking creativity, one where education has become usurpation, a world dominated by a media and communications system that is a mere means to the outpouring of manipulative bad feeling sanctioned as public opinion, where the acquisition of money for power and the pursuit of self-indulgence and passive, uncreative pleasure is sanctified and deemed holy.

With the modern state and its world we are flung into the midst of the public realm of exchange, of buying and selling, of "poisonous flies" and "performers" (*Thus Spoke Zarathustra*, I, "On the Flies in the Market Place"). This is a realm of mass entertainment. "Performing" in this sense has nothing to do with the creativity that Zarathustra esteems. The world, Zarathustra holds, turns around the creators of new values, whereas the performer who dominates the arena of the market has only the crowd and fame for satellites. What counts most is the largest amount of noise, the most memorable affect that can be mustered. As with the modern state that presides over the market place so, in the market place, too, values are rendered meaningless: they become mere playthings, adornments to be worn for effect and cast aside. Values no longer exist in a meaningful sense because what is valued is what is new, and the new is valued for purely instrumental reasons; its newness is destined to decay and pass away before the end of the shortest day. The market place is thus a sphere packed with "solemn" looking clowns, pranksters who want the comfort of instant answers that can be given to them unconditionally and forgotten just as rapidly. The best place to be is as far away from such people as possible, since the danger to one whose sensibility does not accord with that of the crowd lies in his or her having to bear "all their poisonous injustice [*all ihr giftiges Unrecht*]."

The market place and the modern state together signal a new imposition of constraint akin to the tyranny of custom, but one formalized by way of public administrative machinery and capable of extending itself beyond the locality from which it springs. For Nietzsche this is regressive. It is like a reassertion of the primitive conditions governing the emergence of human sociality, subjectivity, and intellectuality, but formalized and devoid of the productive potential of the tyranny of the morality of custom. The person who thinks differently, the one who does not accede to the universal norm of conformity imposed by state and market, is destined to public excoriation. A being who does not live for the moment and for the glory of public celebration is an enigma to this modern world. If you are such a person, says Zarathustra, "They punish you for all your virtues. They excuse you at bottom only – your wrong choices. Because you are mild and have a sense of justice [*gerechten Sinnes*], you say: 'They are innocent in their little existence.' But their restricted souls think: 'Guilty is all great existence'" (*Zarathustra*, I, "On the New Idol"). The person who does not conform is, in such a situation, condemned to be the bad conscience of those around him and, in consequence, the object of resentment and hatred. The independent person who is resented most in this way is treated in a manner akin to the criminal: they are shunned and condemned as beings whose deeds exceed the domain of propriety. The exemplary instance of such a person is the creator.

6. The essence of human creativity is revealed by esteeming and valuing. Esteeming and valuing endow the world with sense. They are always a matter of particular times and places. Peoples, Zarathustra tells us, were the first creators, then individuals – the latter being itself the newest creation of culture. In the idea of the overman Nietzsche seeks to represent the essential plurality of valuing in individuated form. The overman represents the ideal of multiplicity, its acknowledgement and affirmation, raised to a guiding principle. The overman is not separated from the rest of humanity by a difference in kind. What differentiates him is something qualitative – he has what others lack: freedom. Freedom is, for Nietzsche, the condition of creativity. Being "free" for him, however, is not equivalent in meaning to being left alone ("freedom from"). Freedom, rather, is a matter of deeds. It denotes the condition in which what is at stake in an action is its sense. Being free means being free to create; it denotes a condition in which no higher court of appeal than one's own judgement can be found. In this condition, the self is at once the source and subject of its own authority: it becomes a being capable of subjecting itself to its own demands, codes, and laws. In this regard, the creative self Nietzsche articulates fulfils the historical condition that gave rise to it, namely, its endowment from Christianity. The self that Nietzsche seeks to cultivate is the consequence of the Christian cultivation of the "will to truth." Freedom happens when the self turns on the Christian cultural conditions in which it was shaped in fulfilment of a general "law of life," which makes all law-givers answerable to the law they themselves make. History is the history of the becoming and self-overcoming of values. As Christian authority recedes it leaves behind a lacuna of authority that makes explicit and thereby forces upon us the question of freedom as a question that relates to the value of values. Freedom, on this conception, concerns the most rigorous personal responsibility: it demands self-reflexivity and self-discipline with regard to what we value. Freedom is not, it follows, a matter of mere "choice," of consciousness. Freedom involves acting, performing deeds that are marked by their refusal to accede uncritically to the norm. The creative person lives performatively: they enact values.

Human creativity, for Nietzsche, is something that is revealed most tellingly in the domain of values. Peoples, in the first instance, are the creators of values (*Thus Spoke Zarathustra*, I, "On the Thousand and One

Goals"). If, Zarathustra tells us, one examines many times, places, and cultures one finds almost as many different conceptions of good and evil. Here is testimony to the created nature of values. The evaluations denoted by the words "good" and "evil" in each case are not discovered, nor are they gifts from the realm of the divine. They are made. The unconscious acknowledgement of this is expressed in the self-description implicit in the name by which our kind refers to itself, for "'man' ... means the esteemer" and measurer (ibid.). Esteeming, holding something to be of value, is the paradigm of the act of creation. It is what makes human existence rich, for it endows it with sense. A loss of this evaluative ability entails a loss of sense,[14] for sense is not a given. One cannot afford to underestimate the particularity of evaluating. It is a matter of peoples and eras and what pertains to them. If one is to embark on the path of the creation of values, Zarathustra argues, this path must bring one to the acknowledgement and acceptance of both a necessary, destructive precondition of creation and the historical unfolding of its articulation: "Changing values – that is changing creators. Always destroying, that is what one who is a creator must be. Creators were first peoples and later individuals; truly, the individual himself is still the youngest creation." In other words, evaluating is properly interpreted when it is taken semiotically, i.e. when it is read as a sign denoting human creativity. Creation permeates human identity – it is constitutive of it. Creation is made manifest in the original communal conditions of human social life and, by degrees and unconsciously, as the individual is fashioned by the normative powers of tradition and exchange, becomes a characteristic feature of some persons just as much as it has been of peoples and races. In turn, creative peoples and individuals are, from the standpoint of the hierarchies of value that precede them, essentially destructive. Doing, i.e. activity rather than abstract conceptualization, is essential in all this. A change from one system of values to another is a sign that one mode of evaluating, and hence one kind of creating, has usurped another. One might say that changes of value, of orders of giving praise and condemning, are signs of shifts in the distribution of power from one set of interests to another, of colonial redistributions of power. Evaluation is hence an exemplary case of colonization. In this regard, the idea of the overman presents the unique instance of a colonization without parallel, one that, should it be accepted, can serve to bind together the normative variety of evaluative practices and

14 Hence the madman's diagnosis in section 125 of *The Gay Science* of the death of God as a crisis of sense. With the loss of faith in the absolute measure of esteeming claimed by the God of Christian faith comes the threat of a vertiginous, absolute senselessness.

self-understandings that have hitherto characterized humankind by uniting them in one goal. Through the overman, the essentially inhuman power of "praising and censuring" (inhuman because it is a kind of monstrosity, something which flows through humanity as its animating force since it is the condition of the feeling of sense that is a requirement of human life[15]) is brought under the yoke of an all-encompassing idea simultaneously capable of unifying the multiplicity that has flowed from it and of affirming this multiplicity *as multiplicity*.[16]

The herd, the realm of the good and the just, hates the solitary, even though the individual as creator is likewise a being that has sprung from the herd (*Zarathustra*, I, "On the Way of the Creator"). Creators are not different in kind from the masses. The creative person suffers from solitude no less than everyone else.[17] The path of creative freedom, of being "a wheel that rolls itself" is, however, the only path to creation and what

15 The third essay of the *Genealogy* offers Nietzsche's most sustained treatment of this issue. Nietzsche's argument there is that sense is the distinctive and essential need of the human animal. We need sense, above all, to cope with the suffering that is part of the human lot. To be human is to be a creature that has broken with nature. But the cost of this is an antipathy to our own constitutedness. We are beings of drives and of cultural norms, and we have a resulting propensity to experience our drives and hence our embodiment in an alienated condition since, on occasion, the domain of embodiment comes into grinding conflict with the power of social structures. Our social nature, therefore, creates in us the propensity to suffer from *ourselves*. Sense, the belief in a reason that governs existence and thereby explains and justifies human suffering, is in this way the condition of humankind's redemption from itself. The ascetic priest, a universal presence in human history, is a figure who preys on this redemptive need by infecting it with the concept of guilt. That priests appear to be present in all human societies in all ages testifies to the power of the human need for sense in the face of the suffering peculiar to it alone. Nietzsche's maxim, stated at the essay's beginning and end, sums up its significance for him: we are the kind of animal that "would rather will nothingness than not will at all." Sense is thereby conjoined with the conception of will to power. An earlier discussion of this is offered in section 1 of *The Gay Science* in relation to the "great economy" of human existence.

16 It is worth recalling here the following passage, cited earlier: "'This is *my* way; where is yours?' – thus I answered those who asked me 'the way.' For *the* way – that does not exist" (*Zarathustra*, III, "On the Spirit of Gravity," 2). The overman epitomizes this conception: it offers a vision of the fulfilment of human potential, but does so in terms that refuse to claim that the source of the power of this vision resides in an authority derived from a universal norm. There is no single "way" to the overman in the sense of there being a "method" which leads inevitably to its attainment. The overman is not, in short, to be confused with a soufflé. A soufflé is made by recourse to a recipe. So long as one combines the ingredients and follows the steps of the recipe one gets one's soufflé. No single combination of ingredients and actions always leads to the overman, since what most epitomizes it is particularity - the dice throw of the unexpected (see Deleuze, *Nietzsche and Philosophy*, 25).

17 "And when you say 'I no longer have a common conscience with you,' it will be a lament and an agony."

characterizes the person who chooses such a path is not what they can endure but how they endure it. They are *qualitatively* different. Their distinctiveness lies in the fact that they are beings capable of endurance and hardness. To be such a person one must show one has both the "right [*Recht*]" and the strength that is the sign of this right: one must be "such a one as is *permitted*" the ability to escape the "yoke" of convention. In short, creativity requires freedom. Thus, freedom, evaluation, and creativity are related, and they are related by Zarathustra in terms of law: "There are some who threw away their last value when they threw away their servitude. Free *from* what [*Frei wovon?*]? As if that mattered to Zarathustra! But your eyes should tell me brightly: free *for* what [*frei wozu*]? Can you give yourself your own evil and your own good and hang your own will over yourself as a law? Can you be your own judge and avenger of your law? Terrible it is to be alone with the judge and avenger of one's own law" (ibid.). "Free," Zarathustra holds, is a word whose significance is symptomatic. To think of freedom as *being free from something*, as an escape into a state characterized by the absence of compulsion, means to take it to signify a passive, purely negative condition. The person who conceives of their liberty in this way risks nihilism, for their supposed "liberation" is in reality nothing more than a casting off of what they value. With this one also casts off what it is about oneself that makes one who one is. For Nietzsche, this notion of freedom as liberation from compulsion is thus an empty illusion, a form of self-negation that erases the very thing it purports to elevate. Having an ideal of freedom that in effect valorizes escape, the throwing off of something that is experienced as no more than a binding limitation, is not freedom at all; it is privation, the self reduced to senselessness, since its supposed emancipation renders it incapable of valuing.

Freedom, for Nietzsche, is encountered only in and as a question of action. To be free, Zarathustra contends, requires a subject who both *acts* in such a way that its actions are the embodied expression of its values and *is* in such a way that this acting and hence these values are an issue for it.[18] One's actions are thereby rendered a self-reflexive declaration of identity. Being free means asking about the sense of one's doing and consequently about the sense of one's valuing. To ask of oneself "free for what?" involves an invocation of purpose, it generates the kind of willing characteristic of freedom, the will to make values: "Willing liberates: that is the true teaching of will and liberty ... Willing no more and esteeming

18 See in connection John Richardson's discussion of freedom in *Nietzsche's New Darwinism*, 95ff.

no more and creating no more – oh, that this great weariness might always remain far from me!" (*Zarathustra*, II, "Upon the Blessed Isles") The question of freedom is in this way rendered evaluative and creative. The self liberated from the tyranny of custom and tradition encounters itself first and foremost as a free being in whom the "for what" is at stake with regard to itself. At the same time, the liberated self experiences this question in a context where any higher court of appeal is now lacking. There is for the liberated person no superior source of authority that extends beyond them, no power that does not require their active assent. In such a condition, the self becomes not only the source of its own authority but also the object of that authority; it is, likewise, witness and judge of that authority.

To be all these is to stand as both the origin of law and the subject of the law one has made. In this regard, the self refracts the condition of history that surrounds and constitutes it. This is the history that Nietzsche's thought seeks to overcome, namely the history of Christianity. Christianity may be something Nietzsche attacks, seemingly without respite in his later writings, but it is also something to be esteemed no less than it is to be denigrated, for Christianity is decisive in its shaping and sharpening of the modern soul. Indeed, such is Christianity's decisiveness in this regard that it cannot be overcome by mere refutation. One cannot simply reason oneself out of it.[19] What matters about Christianity is its greatness, a greatness signified by the fact that Christianity, like all grandly formative things, ultimately overcomes itself: "All great things bring about their own demise through an act of self-sublimation [*Selbstaufhebung*]: that is the law of life [*das Gesetz des Lebens*], the law of *necessary* "self-overcoming" in the essence of life [*das Gesetz der nothwendigen "Selbstüberwindung" im Wesen des Lebens*], – the lawgiver [*Gesetzgeber*] himself is always ultimately exposed to the cry "*patere legem, quam ipse tulisti*" ["submit to the law you

19 Consider in this context the point made by Nietzsche in sections 20 and 21 of the second essay of the *Genealogy* on the Christian "moralization" of the concepts of guilt and duty. Although, Nietzsche notes in section 21, he has just spoken at the end of section 20 as if a decline in religious belief would initiate a decline in feelings of guilt and duty, he suddenly denies this possibility: "I actually [just] spoke as though this moralization did not exist" and therefore as if the concepts of guilt and duty would cease to have meaning once the "basic premise" of "belief in our 'creditor,' in God" is erased. On the contrary, the process of moralization brings with it a sense of eternal indebtedness that the loss of religious belief does nothing to negate, for moralization conjoins the concepts of guilt and duty with the notion of individual sin. The self-hatred that springs from this, Nietzsche argues, cannot be easily wiped out by the mere loss of faith, for this sense of self-loathing has been culturally embedded and takes its place amongst the conditions constitutive of self-understanding.

yourself have made"]" (*Genealogy*, III, 27). Christian dogma was destroyed and, in its wake, Christian morality will also be destroyed, but this is not the case with regard to the legacy of Christianity, which abides. The great achievement of Christianity has been to create a human being that desires the truth and at the same time is forced to ask what this desire, this "will to truth," means. This is the moment in which freedom happens. From the compulsion inaugurated by the strict training in Christian ideals comes Christianity's own self-overcoming, as it succumbs to the very desire for truth that it sought to instil.[20] This, according to Nietzsche, is the law of life – the law that trumps all other laws: it is the organic condition that fashions all culture as it unfolds historically.[21] It is in obedience to this law of life that, as the authority of Christianity recedes, it leaves behind it a lacuna in the shape of the absence of a higher court of arbitration on the basis of which it is possible to deduce legitimate values. This loss of authority forces upon us the question of freedom as a question of creativity in relation to values. To ask "what is one free to do?" means "what is it that one should deem worthy?" To ask about this is to begin a self-reflexive enquiry into the matter of creating values, tending them, observing them, and by doing so making one answerable to oneself as judge and jury. Genuine freedom, in other words, entails the greatest form of responsibility, for it demands of a person that they both create values and judge not merely the world about them but also themselves according to the norms that these values solidify into. In the same way that Nietzsche in *Daybreak* envisages the criminal arriving at a state where they are judge and executive with regard to their own punishment, so the richest form of selfhood is possible only if one meets the requirement of the cultivation of a rigorous self-discipline.

This is the most severe form of freedom one can envisage, for it is at the same time the greatest, perhaps most tyrannical, form of compulsion.

20 In the words of Wolfgang Müller-Lauter, "the will to truth, in which truthfulness develops, is rooted in the moral understanding of the world" which is itself a cloak marking very different drives that seek domination (*Friedrich Nietzsche*, 60). Truth cannot, it follows, be separated from power.

21 Zarathustra makes Nietzsche's commitment to this "law" clear enough: "Verily, I say unto you: good and evil that are not transitory do not exist. Driven on by themselves, they must overcome themselves again and again. With your values and words of good and evil you do violence when you value; and this is your hidden love and the splendor and trembling and overflowing of your soul. But a more violent force and a new overcoming grow out of your values and break egg and eggshell. And whoever must be a creator in good and evil, verily, he must first be an annihilator and break values. Thus the highest evil belongs to the highest goodness: but this is creative" (*Thus Spoke Zarathustra*, II, "On Self-Overcoming").

As the text of *Zarathustra* tells us, real freedom seizes the self. Freedom is not a matter of conscious "choice." It erupts as a compulsion and imperative, as a necessity and an "ought" that cannot be elided without paying the price of self-harm in a manner that echoes the compulsion that is a condition of the self-understanding of the "sovereign individual" discussed in section 2 of the second essay of the *Genealogy*.[22] Nietzsche often praises the notion of solitude. Implicit in this conception is the freedom of such solitude. One is alone in the sense that one is able to turn to no higher authority than oneself when it comes to the question of judging oneself, and with that comes great responsibility – for how many of us are sufficiently free to manage such a thing, free enough to be severe with regard to ourselves first and foremost? This is why freedom is a rare (if not the rarest) of human endowments: few of us are capable of it because few are inclined to be their own sternest judge.[23] It is for this reason that Nietzsche regards the greater part of history to be comprised of mere events rather than genuine deeds. Genuine freedom does not involve acting in conformity with morality, as a thinker like Kant would argue; it involves acting creatively, making values rather than simply acceding to them. The fifth part of *Beyond Good and Evil*, "On the Natural History of Morality," bears witness to this contention. Morality, Nietzsche argues, has a "natural history," and morality can be attributed

22 The being that Nietzsche calls the "sovereign individual" in the *Genealogy*, II, 2–3, is depicted as the outcome and justification of the contingent and violent pre-historical conditions that gave rise to humankind. The sovereign individual is the outcome of the development under the tyranny of the morality of custom that gave rise to a humanity able to make promises and keep to its word. When detached from the habitual and traditional conditions that characterize its origins, this ability reveals for the first time a human being capable of autonomy with regard to the norms that characterize the community. Nietzsche calls the sovereign individual a "supra-ethical" creature whose ability to keep his or her word (i.e. "the *right to make a promise*") has led it to feel itself to be the "completion" of humankind "in general" and hence its justification. In comparison to the person driven by their impulses, the sovereign individual is a free being, a "master of the *free* will." Freedom, in other words, is no mere matter of being endowed with a "free will" of some kind; it also entails being constrained by the normative commitments one has made oneself. "The person who is free is 'the being who can promise,' said Nietzsche, with penetrating insight; and I would add: 'and the being who must keep his promise.' Through the promise I make I make myself – equivocal thought I am – unequivocal for others and for myself" (Moltmann, "Freedom in Community," in *God for a Secular Society*, 157). On the interpretation offered here Moltmann's addition to Nietzsche's view is also already Nietzsche's.

23 One might note here that the event of "the 'death of God'" pertains to this conception of freedom. The possible consequences of the fact that the Christian God has ceased to be believable are, Nietzsche notes in section 343 of *The Gay Science*, more or less invisible to the majority of people. The event's significance is manifest only to "the few" who are capable of both noting it and dwelling on its implications, by which he means those who are free.

such a history because it is a realm not of freedom but of a compulsion no less tyrannical than any other in nature – but a compulsion that has the long term consequence of making freedom possible. Culture, in other words, emerges from nature as a piece of it. Culture is hence nature turned against itself and it is this doubled relationship, this turning over and around of the realm of the drives to create a sense of inside and out (of culture and nature, community and stranger) that generates the conditions that give rise to an animal capable of transcending the nature out of which it was formed.

7. *Section 186 of* Beyond Good and Evil *explores the sense of responsibility and freedom that Nietzsche advocates. Freedom is not a matter of mere "choice," or "letting go" as opposed to being subject to compulsion. All moralities impose conditions of long-term servitude on humankind. This is not, as one might think, contrary to nature. What is "natural," for Nietzsche, is always a matter of something having been imposed, learned, imbibed, and rendered second nature. This is the precondition of freedom. Creative activity, such as that of the writer or composer, is always the product of discipline. Creative expression comes only because the creator has absorbed the discipline necessary for their craft to the point where it becomes a necessary part of them. Freedom thus springs from compulsion. Section 262 of* Beyond Good and Evil *explores this further in relation to the "aristocratic polis." Such social structures initially develop a morality that promotes some propensities and hinders others as a result of their need to survive. When life gets easier and survival is no longer threatened, the morality of the polis begins to slip, for it is no longer necessary. At such moments, one sees a sudden eruption of experiments in living as the old morality falls away but still leaves behind the disciplined type of person it has forged. Shorn of the constraints of morality individuals dare to live dangerously – they become creative. Here is the possibility of beings capable of legislating their own lives. This form of self-legislation is, for Nietzsche, the paradigm for genuine philosophical thought and* Beyond Good and Evil *seeks to rethink philosophy in the light of this paradigm. Where philosophy has hitherto been rationalistic dogma, Nietzsche proffers a "philosopher of the future" who is characterized by the ability to command and give laws.*

Nietzsche's demand for "a typology of morality" in part 5 of *Beyond Good and Evil*, "On the Natural History of Morality" (section 186) is an invitation to study the conditions from which the sense of philosophical responsibility and freedom he extols emerges. These conditions begin with morality. In contrast to "letting go," morality always appears to be "a piece of tyranny against 'nature,' likewise against 'reason': but that can be no objection to it unless one is in possession of some other morality which decrees that any kind of tyranny and unreason is impermissible"

(*Beyond Good and Evil*, 188). What characterizes every morality, above all, is the "essential and invaluable element" that each is an example of a long-lived and hence enduring "compulsion." This condition of servitude, however, is not to be too readily denigrated, for it is the precondition of

> all there is or has been on earth of freedom, subtlety, boldness, dance and masterly certainty, whether in thinking itself, or in ruling, or in speaking and persuasion, in the arts as in morals, has evolved only by virtue of the "tyranny of such arbitrary laws"; and, in all seriousness, there is no small probability that precisely this is "nature" and "natural" – and *not* that *laisser aller* [letting go]! Every artist knows how far from the feeling of letting himself go his "natural" condition is, the free ordering, placing, disposing, forming in the moment of "inspiration" – and how strictly and subtly he then obeys a thousandfold laws which precisely on account of their severity and definiteness mock all formulation in concepts (even the firmest concept is by comparison something fluctuating, manifold, ambiguous). The essential thing in "heaven and upon earth" seems, to say it again, to be a protracted *obedience* in *one* direction: from out of that there always emerges and has always emerged in the long run something for the sake of which it is worthwhile to live on earth, for example, virtue, art, music, dance, reason, spirituality – something transfiguring, refined, mad and divine. (Ibid.)

Freedom, in other words, springs from compulsion. It requires a located and fashioned selfhood that has been given form by the imposition of a multitude of laws which in the free person attain such a level of severity of articulation, richness, and complexity that they defy definition. Section 262 of *Beyond Good and Evil* develops the point as Nietzsche invites us to think of "an aristocratic community," such as the ancient Greek city-state, "as a voluntary or involuntary contrivance for the purpose of *breeding*." Breeding concerns the cultivation of a structure of institutions, practices, and norms that bind people together in a social body. Any city-state consists of a specific range of normative conditions under which certain types of human are cultivated, i.e. in which they are taught to value a certain attitude toward life and thereby cultivate propensities that are deemed to harmonize with and promote this attitude. What is cultivated in the first instance in the aristocratic *polis* is a limited type of person. The individual is limited because the survival of the community is the ruling power that governs its social order. Such communities are usually founded in conditions under which they must either survive or perish, which is why "every aristocratic morality … counts intolerance itself among the virtues under the name 'justice.'" One day, though, the fearful conditions pass and life gets easier. In consequence, by degrees the old morality loses its authority; it no longer seems necessary since it has ceased to be "a condition of existence," and therefore the limits imposed by it vanish. In the aftermath of this,

> Variation, whether as deviation (into the higher, rarer, more refined) or as degeneration and monstrosity, is suddenly on the scene in the greatest splendour and abundance; the individual dares to be individual and stand out. At these turning-points of history there appear side by side and often entangled and entwined together a glorious, manifold, jungle-like growth and up-stirring, a kind of *tropical* tempo in competition and growing, and a tremendous perishing and self-destruction, thanks to the savage egoisms which, turning on one another and as it were exploding, wrestle together for "sun and light" and no longer know how to draw any limitation, any restraint, any forbearance from the morality which stored up such enormous energy, which bent the bow in such a threatening manner – now it is "spent," now it is becoming "outlived." (*Beyond Good and Evil*, 262)

As this passage makes plain, disciplinary structures are, for Nietzsche, constraints which have the effect of channelling, fashioning, and storing up energies and propensities. With the demise of the compulsion associated with the disciplinary structure powers are unleashed and life takes on the additional dimension of experiment, of living beyond the norms that hitherto dominated. In this way, the discipline of morality cultivates, through the constraints of its institutions, an animal inclined to overcome itself. It is here, at such times of creative crisis that the moment arises when a being endowed with the potential to legislate its own existence may appear.

This notion of self-legislation is the key to Nietzsche's conception of freedom and likewise his aspiration for philosophy. Indeed, Nietzsche seeks nothing less than to rethink what philosophy is in the light of the notions of nature, freedom, and responsibility outlined above. Philosophy needs rethinking because in order to give voice to his notion of freedom Nietzsche must take us beyond the confines of what philosophical thought is traditionally considered to be. Philosophy, Nietzsche often implies, is generally misunderstood; but the greatest irony is that philosophy is most grossly misunderstood by those who feel themselves closest to it, by philosophers themselves. Where philosophy has hitherto taken itself to exemplify the highest self-consciousness and rationality, Nietzsche finds a series of unconscious ruses. Once decoded these ruses are revealed as unwitting confessions that give testimony to the drives that have made each great thinker philosophize in the way he does (*Beyond Good and Evil*, 6). Philosophy, it turns out, has all too often been mere dogmatism, not the free engagement of reflective rationality but unthinking unfreedom and adherence to convention; and this lack of freedom abides so long as the necessary and constitutive role of the drives and feelings in thought is suppressed. Dogmatism, the worship of a chimerical reason conceived of as pure thought, must be swept away and replaced by a new kind of thinking and a new species of thinker worthy of it (40–4). The notion of will to power represents one attempt at this new kind of thought in its drawing of power relations to the centre of our understanding of history, identity, and culture.[24] Here is the epitome of Nietzsche's post-metaphysical naturalism. Here, likewise, is revealed the complexity that his naturalism aspires to. Nietzsche's image of himself as a wearer of masks in section 40 of *Beyond Good and Evil* places this in context. The wearer of masks is an embodiment of contrary views on life, a site of power struggles, a person who is the battle-ground of a wealth of oppositions. Such oppositions and internal conflicts are what make human beings rich in potential and thereby make possible the kind of "free spirit" that in turn invites us to envisage the new sort of

24 The notion of will to power has been interpreted in many ways. Heidegger, for instance, interprets it as a metaphysical notion that itself erupts as a consequence of Nietzsche's critique of metaphysics. The will to power reveals that thought is constituted by power relations, and hence that the metaphysician's desire for the absolute is in reality grounded in concrete struggles. However, Heidegger argues, as soon as Nietzsche posits will to power as a universal condition of life he too capitulates to the metaphysical urge. Nietzsche is thus envisaged as a thinker who sees beyond metaphysics but remains inexorably trapped within it. For Heidegger, Nietzsche's thought about justice springs from this universalist conception of will to power. Interestingly, although Heidegger considers justice to be an important element in Nietzsche's early writings, he argues that it ultimately occupies a marginal place within Nietzsche's metaphysics (see *Nietzsche*, Volume III, "Truth as Justice" and "Justice"). Stanley Rosen has offered an excellent engagement with this aspect of Heidegger's relation to Nietzsche in *The Question of Being: A Reversal of Heidegger*, 234–45. Rosen's intention in this book is to offer a sympathetic interpretation of Platonism as a philosophy of practice and thereby defend it against Heidegger's argument that Nietzsche, as the last metaphysician of the West, is the last gasp of a metaphysics that is guided inexorably toward nihilism. Rosen questions Heidegger's attribution of justice to a place within Nietzsche's cosmology and metaphysics. As I have argued, will to power can also be read as a normative rather than metaphysical notion (see "Nietzsche, Normativity and Will to Power"). Suffice it to say that my discussions in that paper and this book take will to power to be a development of the naturalistic philosophy of practices Nietzsche initiates in *Human, All Too Human*.

philosopher, the "philosopher of the future," a being whose most prominent and hence defining attributes are those of commanding and law-giving. It is these attributes that mark them out as persons who are free.

8. Philosophers of the future will be sceptics. Their central concerns will be freedom and creativity. Suffering for them cannot be an objection to something; indeed, it is sought out by such "free spirits" as a spur to their own development. In this they exemplify and even celebrate Nietzsche's belief that all human advancement springs from being challenged by the world we inhabit. Thought, for example, emerged as a response to threatening nature as an attempt to master it. The philosopher of the future is the summation of this response, not its negation. Such persons will be creative esteemers, beings who face life armed with intellectuality. The philosopher of the future is also a person of the utmost accountability. They, like the overman, stand as testimony to the possibility of a justification for the chaos and suffering that characterizes human existence. Philosophers of this kind are held by Nietzsche to be colonizers of their experiences rather than their victims. Passion, intellect, an inclination to risk-taking, and the propensity to suffer are part and parcel of this conception of philosophical life. These virtues taken together Nietzsche baptizes as "Dionysian." Dionysian thought is the thought of temptation, for Dionysus is the god who is subversive of the authority of tradition. This subversiveness is naturalistic: it affirms a transcendence that spurns metaphysics; it embraces the body in all its plurality and potential. The Dionysian is creativity – a view confirmed by Nietzsche's discussion of it in relation to art in The Gay Science *(367). Through Dionysian creativity, the possibilities of the body are realized and transfigured. Goethe is a figure who exemplifies the kind of disciplined self-creation Nietzsche has in mind – the discipline of a rejuvenated "Dionysian pessimism." Dionysian thought transcends the sterile, formalistic concerns of the epistemologist and turns to the task of value creation. Here, rules are not followed but made. Nietzsche here envisages a kind of thought that establishes the terrain of new norms for living capable of shaping the future of humanity. The notion of will to truth is significant in this context. The creative law-giver is a consequence of the will to truth, enacting a critique of it within its horizon. The creative, law-giving thinker Nietzsche envisages thus acts self-reflexively within the domain of possibility delineated by the will to truth. Honesty (truthfulness) is the greatest virtue of the future philosopher.*

Philosophers of the future, Nietzsche tells us, are not to be confused with those who espouse "modern ideas" (*Beyond Good and Evil*, 44). They will stand against the norms that typify Nietzsche's own times – and presumably against their own. They are neither democrats nor liberals, nor are they supporters of universal equality. They spurn the comfort of the physicists' faith in a nature composed of immutable laws (ibid., 22). Their primary interest is freedom. The free-spirited philosopher of the future poses and seeks to address the defining question that, as we have seen, Zarathustra poses concerning freedom: "free for what?" This envisioning of a being driven by an interest in potentiality for freedom compels Nietzsche to characterize such philosophers as "*attempters*" (ibid., 41). The philosopher of the future will be someone in whom an attitude of creative experimentalism is paramount. A person of this kind must regard their beliefs as a matter of hard won *right*, and their right to believe pertains in each thinker's case to him or her alone, for what they cleave to is the consequence of the most rigorous individual self-discipline. This self-discipline means embracing a philosophy that rejects any universal conception of the good (ibid., 43) and this rejection is what Nietzsche sees as the defining characteristic of future philosophers, for with it they reject the spirit of modernity and the ethos of the "last man."

Those who are often mistaken for "free spirits," Nietzsche notes, abide by the ideals of the "last man": they consider suffering to be an objection to something and desire the eradication of pain from life. The future philosopher advocates no such thing (*Beyond Good and Evil*, section 44). In so far as suffering and danger have always been what has made humanity develop into something more admirable than it was hitherto they are not to be dismissed as an outrage to life but rather affirmed as something that is constitutive of its wonder. We are beings who need to be forced into growth, as plants are when light is denied them. In other words, culture and the highest cultural achievements possible spring from the provocation to strive: humans need to be challenged into engaging with their environment with a view to mastering it, and it is this which both provokes culture and allows humankind to become more than it is. The most interesting culture for Nietzsche would be a culture that fosters this provocation to development and growth.[25] One might rephrase this view in less disconcerting terms by saying that what makes us human is the fact that we need not be mere playthings of nature. We may always stand as potential victims of the ravages of nature, but in so far as we have always faced it armed with concepts and rituals and thus with the hope of somehow subjugating or pacifying it we stand in a relation to nature that no other kind of animal does. The philosophers of the future represent the ideal of this aspect of humanity condensed into a thought image comprised of single individuals who are each of them both of a kind and one of a kind. Their image conjures the vision of different attempts at creative

25 Needless to say, for Nietzsche the nearest approach of any cultural milieu to such a condition is that found in Ancient Greece, with the Renaissance running a close second.

evaluation, each of which exemplifies a humanity endowed with intellect and facing life by welcoming all that existence might throw at it. For this reason the future philosopher is presented as a being "of the most complete accountability," as someone who "has the conscience for the overall development of mankind" (*Beyond Good and Evil*, 61).

The philosopher of the future thereby exemplifies a sense of responsibility toward existence in all its plurality, contradictoriness, glorious excess, pain, and joy. The future philosopher's sense of responsibility is ethical: it springs from the refusal to blame or curse anything that may be encountered in life. The philosophers of the future could never wish to un-invent anything, could never want any event to be undone. In this regard, they represent an extravagant demand: Nietzsche thinks that it should be possible to attempt nothing less than a total accounting of the conditions that have given rise to humanity that, through such philosophers, justifies these conditions.[26] To be responsible in this sense means accepting and embracing all that has and may happen to one and thereby to make of everything that life offers an essential part of oneself. The philosopher, rethought in this way, cannot be a person who denies. Rather, this person must be a colonizer of their experiences. Beings of this kind are capable of transforming the world around them, redeeming culture from its compromised nature by fashioning from it a sense of purpose that invests life with meaning.

The philosopher of the future will be passionate, a risk taker, a celebrator of the intellect, yet capable also of suffering in great measure.[27] Above all, they will be capable of affirming their own existence, they will, in short, be what Nietzsche, returning to terminology reminiscent of *The Birth of Tragedy*, will in his mature writings call *Dionysian beings*. Dionysus, the figure celebrated in *The Birth of Tragedy* as the component essential to the tragic conception of justice, that grand figure of Delphic myth who is fundamentally an equivocal "tempter god," thus returns as Nietzsche now declares himself to be Dionysus's "last disciple and initiate" (*Beyond Good and Evil*, 295). This is a god of subversive authority, for his affirmation involves the defiant denial of the kind of solemnity and pomp that characterizes the Christian God. Dionysus's power does not rest in the

26 In the context of the *Genealogy*, this justification involves the entire violent prehistory of humankind, which put in place the conditions of culture (II). Such a justification verges on theodicy.

27 "Creation – that is the great redemption from suffering, and life's becoming-light. But that the creator can be, there suffering is necessary and much transformation. Yea, much bitter dying must be in your life, you creators! Thus are you advocates and justifiers of all transitoriness" (*Thus Spoke Zarathustra*, II, "Upon the Blessed Isles").

dogmatic and doctrinal monotheism of a universal conception of willed order. Dionysus stands for the pluralistic virtues of dance, exuberance, experimentation, and temptation. This, in short, is a god for naturalism. In his self-proclaimed worship of Dionysus Nietzsche affirms transcendence yet spurns metaphysics, for his is a worship marked by its refusal to point to a "beyond" lying outside the domain of embodied existence. The Dionysian, as Nietzsche reintroduces it in the mature writings, epitomizes creativity – the defining virtue of the philosopher of the future and the exemplification of what Nietzsche terms the "revaluation of all values."[28] As with all things creative, one cannot divorce the aesthetic from it. One should note in this connection a discussion in book 5 of *The Gay Science* that draws a distinction between different kinds of works of art, attitudes of thought, and even architectural design: "All thought, poetry, painting, compositions, even buildings and sculptures, belong either to monological art or to art before witnesses" (367). Whereas art before witnesses gains its value from the role of the spectator, monological art requires the kind of "solitude" that, as we have already seen, is for Nietzsche a condition of creativity.[29] As Laurence Lampert has noted, the view of art presented here exemplifies the aesthetics of solitary existence, of a mode of life for which the universal God is no longer a living possibility.[30] Significantly, however, the god before whom monological art can be practised is Dionysus, for Dionysus is never a mere witness but a sign of inspiration and as such a participant in the act of creation. Dionysian art is needed by those who are creative, by "those who suffer from the *over-fullness of life* – they want a Dionysian art and likewise a tragic view of life, a tragic insight" (*The Gay Science*, 370).

The Dionysian person and the impoverished soul who requires art as a palliative to life are differentiated not only by the latter's demand for an art that redeems the sufferer. The person who suffers from life also embraces "logic, the conceptual understandability of existence – for logic calms and gives confidence – in short, a certain warm narrowness that keeps away fear and encloses one in optimistic horizons."

28 "And with that I again return to the place from which I set out – *The Birth of Tragedy* was my first revaluation of all values … I, the last disciple of the philosopher Dionysus." (*Twilight of the Idols*, "What I Owe to the Ancients," 5) Although I do not intend to discuss it here, it is clear that the complex and sometimes mysterious notion of a "revaluation of all values" that Nietzsche develops in his late writings is inextricably bound up with his conception of creation. Dionysus, Thiele notes, "is a judge" (*Friedrich Nietzsche and the Politics of the Soul*, 202).

29 See section 5.

30 Here, Lampert notes, is an aesthetics of a sort "impossible in religion." See *Nietzsche and Modern Times*, 396.

The creative insight of tragedy is forestalled by the rationalist's worship of the concepts that have seized hold of them. In contrast, what the creative person needs, Nietzsche argues, is the ability to identify, celebrate, and thereby transfigure the rich and dangerous possibilities of our animal nature – to step beyond the limitations of concepts even while dwelling within their terrain. The mature Nietzsche thus once again conjoins the Dionysian and the tragic, affirming tragedy's unparalleled achievement of welding expressive force to formal content (see *Twilight of the Idols*, "What I Owe to the Ancients," 5). Through this creative synthetic union one bears witness to "the will to life rejoicing in its own inexhaustibility through the *sacrifice* of its highest types." And one does so "*Not* so as to get rid of pity and terror, not so as to purify oneself of a dangerous emotion through its vehement discharge ... but, beyond pity and terror, *to realize in oneself* the eternal joy of becoming" (ibid.). The multifaceted achievement of Goethe, the figure who from *The Birth of Tragedy* onwards Nietzsche admires most and most consistently, encapsulates the possibility of creation outlined here. For Goethe, a man who, Nietzsche remarks, as an exemplar of naturalism, a "return to nature ... disciplined himself into a whole, he *created* himself" (*Twilight of the Idols*, "Skirmishes of an Untimely Man," 49), the passions, willing, and reason are not separate spheres, but a created and integrated unity. One must follow this example and be cultured and intellectual yet capable of celebrating one's embodiment and passions. Only in this way is one capable of the degree of self-control that enables one to harness and vent the passions to their fullest creative potential. Such a person will be, like Goethe, "a man of tolerance, not out of weakness, but out of strength ... a man for whom nothing is forbidden, except it be *weakness*." A person of this sort "*no longer denies* ... But such a faith is the highest of all possible faiths: I have baptized it with the name *Dionysus*" (*Twilight of the Idols*, "What I Owe to the Ancients," 5). The Dionysian-oracular element celebrated in *The Birth of Tragedy* thus returns in Nietzsche's later thought as the basis of a creative, affirmative ethic.

Elsewhere, Nietzsche alludes to this faith as "Dionysian pessimism" (*The Gay Science*, 370). Dionysian pessimism characterizes the kind of person that Nietzsche refers to as the "*real* philosopher" (*Beyond Good and Evil*, 211). Like the scholarly "worker-philosopher" with whom Nietzsche makes a comparison, real philosophers need to possess the discipline imparted by a demanding education; in a manner akin to the Platonic philosopher king, they need to climb each rung of the ladder of knowledge. However, the real philosopher passes beyond mere competence in, for example, epistemology, and turns on the fetishization of such things with contempt and scorn.[31] Human life is not something that attains its zenith in the epistemically-oriented activities of recording, classifying, and theorizing.[32] The task of the real philosopher is the task that exemplifies the Dionysian conception of creativity and freedom. The real philosopher's task answers to the demand "that he *create* values."[33] The philosophers of the future, who must be counted the prime examples of "*real philosophers*," are different from the philosophical workers because their task is not one of service. They are creators of rules rather than mere rule-followers. Real philosophers are "commanders and lawmakers": "they say, '*thus* it *shall* be!'" In other words, the genuine philosopher is a person whose words and thoughts are *deeds*. The real philosopher is characterized by the fact that he or she issues *decrees*, and it is this ability to make decrees that reveals a person capable of establishing the "Whereto?" and "What-for?" of humankind. With creative intent,[34]

31 "Philosophy reduced to 'theory of knowledge,' in fact no more than a timid epochism and doctrine of abstinence – a philosophy that never gets beyond the threshold and takes pains to *deny* itself the right to enter – that is philosophy in its last throes, an end, an agony, something inspiring pity" (*Beyond Good and Evil*, 204).

32 Such a rejection of the primacy of theory understood in this sense represents a contribution to the task of what Charles Taylor has called "Overcoming Epistemology." Taylor links this turn in Nietzsche, and its adoption by later writers such as Michel Foucault, to the notion of "self-making," i.e. to an aesthetics and ethics of self-creation (See "Overcoming Epistemology," *Philosophical Arguments*, 16). This conception of self-creation, I argue, is for Nietzsche a question of self-legislation.

33 The philosophical labourer's task, it follows, is limited. The examples Nietzsche proffers of such "philosophical workers" are perhaps surprising, given how deservedly famous they are: Kant and Hegel. Such figures, he says, have the formative task of fixing in place, and expressing in formulas that are easy to assimilate, a great stock of facts about values. They thereby prepare the ground for the real philosopher in the same way that workers on a building site establish a building's foundations, erect its walls, put on its roof, and divide it up into spaces (rooms). Like the builder, the worker-philosopher creates a space in which life can be pursued, but human life involves much more than compartmentalizing things. If that is all there was to it life would be empty. The tasks that can be pursued in existence do not find their destination in the vision of a well-established and neatly categorized world.

34 Knowledge of the kind envisaged here is essentially productive. It shapes rather than merely reflects the world. To know the world is to shape it, to fashion our understanding of it, in new ways and hence to change it. Thought, for Nietzsche, would be nothing if it could not act on its environment. To want to know, to desire truth, means therefore to desire, to render the world pliable to the shaping power of one's will. As is argued below, such shaping is not however to be confused with the mere imposition of a capricious subjective force. The will, for Nietzsche, is normative through and through; it is engaged in its world and hence constituted in terms of its possibility by the conditions of that world. Freedom, to put it another way, is never the freedom to do anything you like.

Nietzsche says, such beings grasp toward the future, "and all that is and has been becomes a means for them, an instrument, a hammer. Their 'knowing' is *creating*, their creating is a legislation, their will to truth is – *will to power*" (*Beyond Good and Evil*, 211).[35]

The invocation of the will to truth in this last passage should not be passed over. The legitimacy of creating, knowing, and law-giving as Nietzsche conceives of them depends upon the existence of the will to truth. Nietzsche, as we have seen, holds us to be animals whose conceptual abilities are pragmatically useful but subject to profound error and injustice. Conceptual thought is a kind of violence. In so far as metaphysics has cleaved to the concept of truth it has epitomized and unwittingly celebrated this violence and thereby slipped ever further into error. The anti-naturalist metaphysician seeks a stable reality in the realms of idea and substance, and clings uncritically to the concept of being. The metaphysician thereby asks too much of truth, for he or she asks it to do something for which it is not equipped. Truth talk cannot legitimately aspire to the heavens. Metaphysics is our unconditional desire for truth (our will to truth) run amok and reified as absolutism. Truth, when it becomes the object of this theoretical fetishism, is the worst of delusions. Nietzsche seeks to overturn the power of this delusion not merely in the realm of philosophy but in thought generally. The thought-image Nietzsche seeks to cultivate represents a revolution. However, in formulating his conception of the creative, Dionysian law-giver, Nietzsche neither craves nor asks us to step outside the domain of the will to truth. Like many other human traits, the desire for truth has become constitutive of our nature to such a degree that an attempt simply to negate and thereby step beyond it would achieve nothing more than a delusory and parodic re-enactment of the errors of metaphysics. What the Dionysian future philosopher represents, rather, is a critique of the will to truth that is to be enacted within its horizon. We must always, as

35 The will to truth is in reality a will to power. It is the "will to the thinkability of all beings … You want to *make* all being thinkable." The desire is that the world shall be mastered by thought and concept. The will of the wisest people is a will that seeks to set up a world to be venerated. "Your will and your valuations you have placed on the river of becoming … Now the river carries your bark further; it *has* to carry it … Not the river is your danger and the end of your good and evil, you who are wisest, but that will itself, the will to power – the unexhausted procreative will of life" (*Thus Spoke Zarathustra*, II, "On Self-Overcoming"). One should note in this context how power, legislation, and politics come together in Nietzsche's thought, the way that "Nietzsche's re-articulation of the 'political' is expressed as the organizational complexification of materiality (of bodies, knowledges, power). After all, Dionysus – Nietzsche reminds us – is a legislator" (Mellamphy, *The Three Stigmata of Friedrich Nietzsche*, 121).

Nietzsche reminds us in the opening of *Beyond Good and Evil*, live within the ambit of thought delineated by the will to truth: "The will to truth … is still going to tempt us on many a hazardous enterprise" in the same way as it has already raised many dangerous questions so far. The narrative may already seem a long one, but it is more likely that "it has only just begun?" (1). We are, in other words, only at the beginning of the journey initiated by the desire for truth. To embark upon this journey, Nietzsche argues, requires we accede to the demand that we radically question the notion of truth and our very desire for it in ever more rigorous ways, but without ever letting go of the desire itself.[36]

If the genuine philosopher is a law-giver,[37] then their law-giving is characterized as much by what it is not entitled to enact as by what is open to it, for Nietzsche refuses us the right to transcend the problematic of truth and all that goes with it in simplistic fashion. As he comments in *The Gay Science* (344), we are obliged to remain pious if we want to be rigorous about what we know and value. What is at stake with regard to the matter of truth is not something external to us but something intrinsic to human identity and self-understanding. All knowledge involves presupposition as its condition of possibility – it presupposes values, esteeming. As long as I want knowledge I have already affirmed in advance the value of my knowing and of the truths that such knowing will yield. Here an "unconditional will to truth" can be interpreted self-reflexively. The will to truth does not attain its end in the condition of wanting not to be deceived about the world of matters of fact. Rather, it can be developed and refined so as to signify the desire to affirm above all else *not* whether this or that fact is true but rather the value of the attitude of *truthfulness* itself. The desire for truth, when grasped in these terms, denotes the active desire not to allow oneself to be subject to

36 This, of course, is speaking as if we could ever let go of such a desire – something to which, perhaps, the "last man" might aspire. Plato's contention that truth is divine may, Nietzsche notes, turn out to be "our most enduring lie" (*The Gay Science*, 344). We are, in other words, trapped within the problematic of truth. Truth talk is something one cannot get away from and, so long as one cleaves to a certain modesty when engaging in such talk, there is no reason to want to do so. But, Nietzsche insists, to do so honestly means recognizing this talk as a condition of talk, not of how things are. What matters in this view is communication, the establishment of common conventions of designation, not the question as to whether such conventions and the signs associated with them can be nailed on to reality by recourse to a single principle or method.

37 In this regard my reading accords with that of Mellamphy: "the philosopher is not the executive or ruling element, but its legislator or lawgiver (its spiritual justification)." Such a person "is not a statesman that administers *nomos*; rather he gives the law to which the rest of society is bound to adhere" (*The Three Stigmata of Friedrich Nietzsche*, 97).

delusion with regard to the nature and status of one's beliefs and hence values: "'will to truth' does *not* mean 'I will not allow myself to be deceived' but – there is no alternative – 'I will not deceive, not even myself'; *and with that we stand on moral ground*" (ibid.). Prudential considerations (e.g. that one does not want to be the victim of deception because deception has bad consequences) cannot therefore fully explain the will to truth when its significance is comprehended properly. Nature, which accidentally brought about an animal desirous of truth, is now mastered by the culture that sprang from it. The affirmation of the demand for truth and an ethical commitment to be self-critical about one's values and beliefs go hand in hand. In so far as we are driven by the desire not to deceive we are obliged to be creatures of the virtues.

Our highest virtue, then, is honesty. With this observation, Nietzsche conjures an image of humanity pitted against the fundamental condition of existence, which is a plurality of simulacra, but now in a manner whose significance is transformed. We may be subject to illusion but, as Nietzsche argues from *Human, All Too Human* onwards,[38] we are capable of comprehending this possibility. Rendered explicit in this way, the will to truth is revealed as something that needs to be subject to a "critique" capable of refashioning it in a productive manner (*Genealogy*, III, 24). Nietzsche does not mean that the will to truth must be criticized relentlessly; rather, he is proffering the possibility of a critique akin to that performed by Kantian thought. This is a critique that has as its goal the exploration of the domain of the will to truth with a view to establishing its value and limits. In short, what is needed is an engagement with the question of the value of truth that takes place within its own sphere, namely, the sphere of thought and existence that the will to truth has fashioned out of us. Since we are also moderns, a critique of this kind is initiated by naturalism and the honest atheism associated with it (*Genealogy*, III, 27).

9. The philosophers of the future are reversers of "timeless" values, figures who reveal the temporal precondition of all esteeming. This demythologization of value is the precondition of creative philosophical freedom. Such freedom may seem strange given Nietzsche's emphasis upon constraint and limitation. The latter, however, is the precondition of creative possibility, for creation cannot take place without a context and a channelling of forces. Creative law-giving of the kind Nietzsche envisages is the sign of attained selfhood. The self may be the most recent of culture's inventions but, properly understood, it is for Nietzsche the one most worthy of esteem.

38 *Human, All Too Human*, 32. See the discussion at the beginning of chapter 2.

The self is the body and the body is always already a body-politic, a miniature polis or "commonwealth." Embodiment involves the co-ordination of heterogeneous elements; the body's organizational principles cannot be deduced, for it is synthetic. It is a structure in which willing makes itself manifest and does so in the form of values. This is the case for individual and community alike. In the case of the individual, however, the communal origins of valuing are transformed by self-reflexivity. Self-reflexivity is not defined by consciousness (which is a necessary but not sufficient condition of it). Consciousness originated in communal life and the need of the body (first communal, then individuated) to bear witness to its acts. The body is the self, an order of commanding and obeying governed by a "great reason" that relates together the self's acts, values, and environment. Consciousness (the "I") bears witness to this relation. Consciousness is not, as it has traditionally been taken to be, the source of agency. Personhood is not the same as the "I." The self esteems and the "I" bears witness to this, making manifest the self's esteeming habits. The "I," however, makes self-misunderstanding possible, for it gives rise to a tendency on the part of the self to think its identity in terms of consciousness only. This error is an inversion of the self's order of command – it gives rise to the illusory notion of freedom as absence of compulsion. Genuine freedom, however, is empowerment; it is revealed in the feeling of power experienced when one is one's own commander and subject. Power is the source of freedom and creativity. It is not a given but something in need of continual attainment. Freedom is a matter of deeds; it is lived as the unity of thought and action. Simply acceding to the law, to the norm, is not being free. Convention must be transcended. Such transcendence does not negate our normative nature any more than it licenses the rule of whim and caprice. It is, rather, the sublimation of convention, custom, and law.

The image of philosophy's highest potential that Nietzsche presents us with remains one wedded to a figure locked into the future. As such, his ideal of philosophy is epitomized by a conception of humanity intent on envisaging not what it is but what it can become (see *On the Genealogy of Morality*, III, 13). The project of historical philosophy initiated in *Human, All Too Human* thereby abides by pointing beyond itself. Creation requires a specific kind of relationship with temporality. The "*new philosophers*" (*Beyond Good and Evil*, 203) will be creatures who dare to overturn, "revalue and reverse 'eternal values.'" Theirs, in other words, will be a task that involves a form of creating and legislating that reaches both forward to the question of what can be and back into the past in such a way that the significance of what has been is transformed. The "eternal" must be dragged back down to earth and history; the absolute must be revealed as concealed contingency. Only then will the kind of freedom Nietzsche aspires to be possible. From some standpoints this creation will seem to be destructive since it will involve undermining what has hitherto been taken for granted about the realm of values. Likewise, this freedom will seem to some like lack of freedom, since it is a freedom that is not afraid of the constraints that are necessary to its possibility.

Philosophy, properly understood, expresses this freedom. It is about *invention*, about the creation of values, about commanding. In so far as the genuine philosopher is a law-giving animal, he or she is a being that has attained creative selfhood. The self, as already noted, emerges as the most recent invention of culture, as a consequence of the power of norms to fashion the body (*Thus Spoke Zarathustra*, I, "On the Thousand and One Goals"). The body, Nietzsche argues, is the self, and the self is a sublimated community or, as he puts it, a "commonwealth." This commonwealth is a co-ordinated assemblage consisting of diverse elements. The unity of these elements does not depend upon any *a priori* principles, it cannot be deduced; rather, it springs from a synthetic ordering which occurs in the same manner as a political community assembles, co-ordinates, and distributes the diversity of elements (bodies, things, time, and the like) that make it what it is. "[O]ur body is but a social construction of many souls" that operates in the same manner as "every well built and happy political community" (*Beyond Good and Evil*, 19). In such a community the element that commands, "the ruling class," associates itself with what is successful about that community. This is how the self wills, for it is the case that with "all willing it is absolutely a question of commanding and obeying." In the individuated self as in any political community or culture, the condition of creation is the source of value. Just as a community affirms itself in the act of valuing and adhering to values (which means by observing norms and thereby generating communal identity) so the individual does, too. In the community, however, the act of valuing is unconscious. The community's normatively fashioned members simply act without a thought on the basis of what is valued (the norm that dictates the nature of the good). In the individual that is fashioned out of these norms this condition is open to being transformed (indeed, transfigured) by self-reflexivity.[39]

As is already clear from the discussion above,[40] selfhood and individuality are not, however, essentially characterized by way of consciousness. Self-reflexivity involves consciousness (the "I") but consciousness, for Nietzsche, is not to be confused with the source of self-reflexivity.

39 Although this does not mean that this must necessarily happen. The emergence of the individuated self is not a guaranteed consequence of normative orders. It is a contingent possibility. One of Nietzsche's later concerns centres on creating the conditions whereby the possibility of such an outcome is enhanced.

40 See section 2.

Consciousness is a necessary but not sufficient condition of self-reflexivity. The self is embodiment, an amalgam of drives co-ordinated into instincts, fashioned through the observance of customs and traditions into a being of self-reflexive possibilities. Consciousness thus originates in shared communal conditions. The "I" emerges as a witness and interpreter in service of the body, first communal and then individual; it is an expression of the body's productive interpretive abilities. The body – which for Nietzsche is the self – is, like the community it emerges from, an order of command, a hierarchy organized around the demands of the "great reason"[41] that co-ordinates its dealings with its environment.[42] The "I" is the aspect of the self that bears witness to the self's doings and comes about because, in our origins, we are communal creatures who are forced to deal with others like us. The "I" is a kind of feedback mechanism that assists these dealings. It is a product of normativity, but amongst philosophers the "I" and consciousness are the most misunderstood things. To misunderstand consciousness is to take it as the source of agency, that is, as a kind of commander and law-giver in relation to the self. For Nietzsche, however, such sovereignty does not come from the "I." Consciousness is not sovereign but subject. Its true role is to bear witness to the self's esteeming habits and their relation to the events that befall it as it journeys through life, to press this relation into form by re-presenting to the self what it esteems. The "I" thus speaks the language of the self's engagement with its environment, the language of values.

The "I" is in this regard akin to the voice. The voice is part of the self: crudely, it springs from vocal chords resonating air in the service of expression. Yet, this mere vibration of gases invokes personality – a disembodied voice can conjure for us the rich terrain of a whole person, even if this person never gets to be seen, or is a delusion or fantasy.[43] Likewise, the "I" is a kind of vibration of the self, a peculiar resonating brought about by a co-ordination of forces (social and embodied) that are superior to it; but it is not proper to consider it on its own to be a "who," a person. The "I" conjures the person, but is not equivalent to him or her. The "I" is conjured in a manner that tends to the self's concealment and self-misinterpretation, for the "I's" role as re-presenter gives rise to a confusion of order concerning the relation between voice and utterer, commanded and commander. This inversion of the order of command

41 See note 5.

42 Müller-Lauter charts the development of notions of commanding and equality in Nietzsche's thought. Thus, human identity arises from a synthesis of heterogeneous elements that culminates in the "great reason" of the body (see *Friedrich Nietzsche*, 179).

43 The same goes for the "tone" of a text – this text, for example.

creates the peculiar demand that calls for "freedom" in the sense of "free from." Freedom of this kind is characteristic of the ideal of something commanded: it sees freedom as the absence of compulsion, as the negation of command, a "peace" defined in terms of a lack of interference by the intrusive force of a greater power. The self thereby creates illusions that seduce it to envision an ideal that is counter to its genuine nature.

To be "free to," which is the freedom that Zarathustra celebrates, is to celebrate the empowerment of the embodied self in all its co-ordinated diversity. It is to find in commanding and being commanded at one and the same time the fulfilment of one's nature. Being free in this sense means not merely being able to celebrate one's own embodiment and interpretive abilities but being willing to face the ultimately dangerous condition of creativity that such interpretive abilities truly signify. Since, for Nietzsche, we are the evaluating animal – since, in other words, evaluation is our most characteristic creation – our greatest potential springs from the creative possibilities open to us with regard to the values we find ourselves empowered to create. Creation is human productivity;[44] it springs from the will as the result of the prehistoric fashioning by custom and law of our rule-following nature.[45] The consequence of this fashioning is an animal equipped with the potential to discover and unleash its own willing power. This power is the source of freedom, but freedom as it is understood here is not a mere condition that simply springs from humankind being what it is. Freedom is not a given, something we simply have because we are who we are; it must be struggled for, attained, and struggled for and attained yet again. This struggle must be continual. Freedom is not found like a thing; it is lived. Thus, the potential we have for freedom is not the same as being free. The normative fashioning that characterizes humanity's emergence as a being of law-like propensities means being an observer of the law, but simply observing the law does not make us free. In the same way that normativity is a necessary

44 Eugen Fink notes the aesthetic element inherent in this conception: "Man's essence resides in the 'productive man,' in the man who creates. With this expression, Nietzsche does not refer to the 'worker' in industrial society nor to the producers of our modern technological world, but rather to the artists, the thinkers and poets, the lawgivers and heroic founders of states. Nietzsche's image of man as a 'predator,' which was formulated in defiance of Christianity and all philanthropic 'humanism,' soon becomes an aesthetically defined naturalness" ("Nietzsche's New Experience of the World," in *Nietzsche's New Seas*, 205). To repeat the point made above, in so far as creation, as Nietzsche conceives it, turns on the notion of the artistic, we are returned in his later writings to the domain of the oracular outlined in *The Birth of Tragedy*.

45 See *Genealogy*, II, 2ff.

condition of social relations and the conflicts, struggles, and stalemates that gives rise to "justice talk,"[46] so the discipline of observing the customary, the law as it is handed down to us, is a condition of possible freedom. Creation means going beyond what is conventional, reinterpreting the stipulations of law as it now stands and thereby overcoming it.

As has been noted, however, such creation for Nietzsche does not involve a transcendence of the conditions that constitute our normative nature. Being creative and free means becoming the source of the legitimacy of one's judgements. This does not mean that one must become a petty tyrant, prey to subjective whim. The law-giving Nietzsche advocates is not to be confused with wilful imposition of power. To think thus would be to misunderstand not only what creation is, but the nature of power and command and freedom itself. The "nature of the living" is characterized by commanding and obeying (*Thus Spoke Zarathustra*, II, "On Self-Overcoming"), but neither commanding nor acceding to command mean anything when considered in isolation. That which is commanded also commands when it can, and if one commands it is because one is amenable to being commanded, too, since that which commands also obeys and is driven to do so *as a consequence of its commanding*. There is no commanding without obeying and vice versa. In the case of "the weaker," it is a matter of taking what it can from that which is more powerful and using it as a means of attaining a sense of command. In the case of the "greatest," that which commands, this also is compelled to obey and hence be subject to its own laws. To be powerful enough to create values means to risk oneself, to render oneself accountable.

Creativity thus entails responsibility. One must, as this source of law-giving, also become one's own most severe critic and judge. Like Christianity, one must subject oneself to the law one has made. The freedom of the creator is not an escape from law and constraint. It is, rather, their development and refinement through making explicit about norms, customs, and constraints what has been hitherto hidden about them, and doing so in the very domain fashioned by norm and custom. One overcomes the power of normative imposition by revealing its contingency, by showing in other words that it is a product of history and nature and that it lacks a transcendent justification. But the legacy of this history is not lost. It is not a matter of seeking to step beyond the domain of the will to truth. One must taken possession of the will to truth. The creative person thus overcomes the law by entering into and

46 See chapter 3.

transforming it, not by stepping over it or going around it. And they do so by a kind of colonization that is also an internalization: by taking what is initially experienced as external imposition and making it their own.

10. Genuine creation is the bestowing of values. In bestowing values the creator thereby takes risks. The creator's vulnerability shows that for Nietzsche the power of creation is not the simple imposition of the stronger on the weaker. New values are new competences that sublimate the values of the past and thereby overcome them and so fashion the possibility of a new justice. A new justice is a new sense of what constitutes legitimacy and right. The creator of values is a lawgiver. Their legislation is revealed in commanding, but such creative commanding is never pure force. Creation has a peculiar authority. Creative esteeming transforms the nature of hitherto taken for granted significances. It commands us because it changes us, colonizing, fashioning, and transforming the social realm of meaning and self-understanding. The creator is an experimenter who shatters the notion of a universal "law" and "justice" by subverting them with pluralistic experimentalism. Nietzsche's experimentalism holds justice to be the overcoming of revenge. Justice, for Nietzsche, refuses to judge in the universal terms characteristic of conformist conventional morality. It hopes thereby to liberate the world from the cruelty of moral condemnation, spurning the notion of a timeless "good and evil." Nietzsche does not advocate destroying ethics as such. He does not spurn the value judgements "good" and "bad." What is good is an attitude of mercy and understanding toward what is unconventional; what is bad is cruelty toward it. In this way justice is done to even the most "evil" human being, who as an instance of our kind is to be greeted as something astonishing and worthy of the humanizing respect that characterizes mercy.

It is not enough for the creator simply to take what life has given them. Genuine creation, as the opening of *Zarathustra* reminds us, involves giving. A creator is a bestower, a giver of values, someone who experiments with new ways of esteeming. Neither is it sufficient merely to give values in the same way as one might casually give someone a birthday present. In the latter case, the relation between giver and gift is limited: the thing given is soon enough forgotten, for little is at stake in the giving beyond the mere observation of a convention. The creator-giver, however, must be a living exemplar: he or she must affirm life in the living of values; he or she must give of themselves. This brings risks, for in the giving of values one places oneself at peril from the scorn of those who crave conservative conformity: "Do you, my brother, yet know the word 'contempt'? And the agony of your justice – being just to those who have contempt for you? ... You came close to them and yet passed by: that they will never forgive ... 'How will you be just [*Gerecht*] to me?' you must say. 'I choose your injustice [*Ungerechtigkeit*] as my proper lot.' Injustice and filth they throw after the lonely one … And beware of the good and the just! They like to crucify those who invent their own virtue for themselves – they hate the lonely one" (*Zarathustra*, I, "On the Way of the Creator"). As the above passage reveals, Nietzsche does not consider creative power to be merely a matter of the strongest imposing something on the weak.[47] The creator as he or she is presented here does not possess overwhelming force; they are vulnerable, as susceptible to becoming a victim as Christ – they run the risk of paying for their wisdom by being crucified for it.[48] A person of this kind is also, Zarathustra adds, at the same time their own worst enemy. The creator must be a lover of himself and hence also a self-despiser – one whose self-love acts as a spur to self-transcendence, a person who wishes to create because what they are dissatisfies them, because their love for humanity means that they feel they must be more. Creation is sheer risk and vulnerability.

Through risking oneself one creates values.[49] One thereby fashions a way, a new competence, through which the ways of the past, the old values, are transfigured. The fruits of creation are not immediate, they take

47 In this regard, my reading has close affinities with comments made by Wolfgang Müller-Lauter. Müller-Lauter, quoting Heidegger, notes that "for Nietzsche there 'can be no *sheer* overpowering, no sheer empowering of the will to power, because for him all willing is a willing something.' The overman wants power 'absolutely,' that is, in unrestricted dominance. But he can achieve and exercise power only if he grasps it in its conditionalities" (*Friedrich Nietzsche*, 80). Power cannot therefore be desired as such, since it is always the power to do such-and-such, i.e. "freedom to."

48 Terry Eagleton draws a contrast between Nietzsche's conception and Aristotle's similarly conceived great-souled man in precisely these terms: "The Overman is a supremely positive being, overflowing with rude health and *joie de vivre*. Yet he differs most fundamentally from Aristotle's great-souled man in the terrible price he must pay for his eternal yea-saying. It is … the recognition that there is no truth, no essences, no identities, no grounds, no ends or inherent values in the world … The Overman is he who plucks virtue from dire necessity, converting the groundlessness of reality into an occasion for aesthetic delight and a source of unceasing self-invention … bountiful and generous-spirited, but with the fine, carefree nonchalance of the nobleman" (*Trouble with Strangers*, 178–9). As Eagleton goes on to note, in wonderfully deflating style, one rather disappointing consequence of this is that thus understood the overman comes to look more like an "old-style aristocrat" who is "less a demonic figure than a character out of Disraeli."

49 A case in point is Socrates. According to Nietzsche, Socratic moralism runs counter to the dominant social ethos of the ancient social milieu from which he springs, for contrary to the norms of his time Socrates brings the individual to the centre of moral discourse (*Daybreak*, 9). The degree to which Socratism has been triumphant is reflected by the seeming naturalness of its dictum that virtue harmonizes with self-interest. Socrates, via Plato, is in this sense legislative: his thought constitutes the dominant mode of moral discourse in the West. One need not dwell on his fate too long to consider the price he paid for his achievement.

time. And the fruits bear the stamp of a new justice: "Go into your loneliness with your love and with your creation, my brother; and only much later will justice limp after you" (*Zarathustra*, I, "On the Way of the Creator"). The formalistic "justice" of the "the good and the just" is mere conformism, narrow and alien to creativity. In contrast, Nietzsche considers justice in the broadest and richest sense to be something that follows only *after* creation. Justice and creation go together in so far as only after the creation of values is justice, in one form or another, truly possible. Such justice transcends the current world of everyday concerns and it is this antagonistic relation to the everyday that confirms its oracular nature. Justice of this kind refashions conceptions of legitimacy and right; and it does so first by being alien to them, then supplanting them and finally taking possession of their domain for itself. The meaning of justice, in other words, is not fixed in advance. Its meaning is something that must be ceaselessly explored and worked through, since it is subject to the same kind of reinterpretation that the concept of punishment is.

What kind of commanding and law-giving does Nietzsche have in mind when he discusses the task of philosophical creativity in these terms? How is such creative legislation actually possible? Clearly, as has already been argued, such creativity does not step beyond the bounds of sense, beyond the terrain of the will to truth that constitutes its possibility. Nor is it the mere imposition of arbitrary "laws" upon a weak and vulnerable body that is simply subjected to the unyielding force of a superior will. Commanding of the creative kind is never mere forcing. It is the meeting of that which wishes to command and can with that which is amenable to being commanded. The creator is capable of legislation because genuine creation is made manifest by its being legislative in its effects, by what is commanded acceding to the authority of its command. The inventor's creativity endows a peculiar authority: creative thought transforms significance, fashions the realm of possible meaning and in this way, slowly and sometimes imperceptibly and without fuss, changes things. Above all, it changes us in such a way that we can no longer simply think and do as we once thought and did. Creation is compelling. But its compulsion, however monstrous it might seem from some standpoints, is never mere violence or intimidation. Genuine invention moulds us, colonizes us, and thereby becomes constitutive of us. The creator renders us different from how we were precisely to the extent that we are amenable to such rendering. Creation fashions the social domain and the self; it transforms self-understanding and thereby doer and deed. A passage from *Thus Spoke Zarathustra*, later appended to the conclusion of *Twilight of the Idols*, is revealing in this regard:

> "Why so hard?" the kitchen-coal once said to the diamond. "After all, are we not close kin?"
> Why so soft, my brothers, I ask you, for are we not brothers?
> Why so soft, so pliant and yielding? Why is there so much denial, self-denial, in your hearts? So little destiny in your eyes?
> And if you do not want to be destinies and inexorable ones, how can you triumph with me?
> And if your hardness does not wish to flash and cut and cut through, how can you one day create with me?
> For creators are hard. And it must seem blessedness to you to impress your hand on millennia as on wax,
> Blessedness to write on the will of millennia as on bronze – harder than bronze, nobler than bronze. Only the noblest is altogether hard.
> This new tablet, oh my brothers, I place over you: *become hard!* (*Zarathustra,* III, "On Old and New Tablets," 29)

The creator is a person driven by an imperative, by an "ought" that they must embody: he or she must "*become hard.*" What this hardness amounts to is not immediately explicit. In the passage there are two elements that recall the discussion of commanding and being commanded earlier in the text (*Zarathustra,* II, "On Self-Overcoming").[50] First, there is that which is acted upon, which yields not because it cannot resist but because it is suited to being fashioned; it is willing. Second, there is that which is active, that which is drawn to what is willing to yield to it. What acts does so in a manner that appears positive, elemental, physical, decisive, as an expression of purpose: the creative urge "flashes" knife-like through material, dividing and slicing. The creative hand impresses itself upon the world and through this it reveals the latter to be as receptive and co-operative to the power of expression as wax is to the candle maker. Creation is *inscription* and such inscription is a kind of union, something demanded no less by what is inscribed upon as by what does the inscribing. It is here that Nietzsche's earlier oracular conception of justice is most fully rearticulated in historical and naturalistic terms. What is invented, in so far as it is genuine invention, is "written" on to the topographical field of history, rendering it something that bears the mysterious impress of the creator. The inventor is a transformer of the will, hence also a transformer of dominant modes of self-interpretation. The

50 This is discussed in section 9.

creator, in other words, is a person capable of endowing the human world with sense. Such endowments of sense transform our relationship with our own times and ourselves. They represent a search for "new origins" (*Zarathustra*, III, "On Old and New Tablets," 25). Origins of this kind endow sense for they liberate us from the world of tradition and the customary by revealing hitherto undisclosed realms of human possibility. The creator reveals a path to a new way of thinking, doing, and hence evaluating. This is a person able to satisfy the human desire for meaning; one who offers a sense of purpose that redeems the contingent and threatened individual by situating them within an encompassing, justificatory narrative. In the person who coins values social order finds its fulfilment because it is furthered thereby. The sphere of "human society," Zarathustra tells us, is "an experiment" without end (ibid.). The creator is the experimenter *par excellence*, the being who fulfils "the long quest," for organizing principles that characterizes the history of social order. What Nietzsche holds to be a just situation can emerge only on the basis of this experimental condition. Social order, Zarathustra adds, can hence never be a "contract." No compact or agreement exists that is not worthy of being broken. What is just contravenes the norm; it shatters the given law in its pursuit of a new articulation of ways of living.

Precisely how the law as it stands is shattered by Nietzsche's justice is revealed by the passage in the *Genealogy* that ponders the possibility of a society that has become "*so conscious of its power*" that it comes to embrace mercy (*Genealogy*, II, 10, cited above). As in his earlier writings, here, too, real justice is mercy. A philosophy of creation, one that dares to go beyond good and evil, also transcends the formalism of legalistic conceptions of justice by revealing leniency to be at its heart. The person who shows mercy is not worried about expense or equivalence; they do not calculate the value of things according to their own advantage, they do not show resentment, but rather shrug off disadvantage with a forgiveness that refuses even to make the wrongdoer feel like a wrongdoer. If you are attacked by an enemy, Zarathustra says, do not pay back his evil by being kind and good to him or her, for that fills the enemy with shame and enmity. It is better to show the wrongdoer that they have done you a favour, that you are capable of gaining from their act, *that the evil deed has good consequences for you* – indeed, even the lesser and more immediate response of cursing is better than "blessing" in such cases (*Zarathustra*, I, "On the Adder's Bite"). If there has to be punishment then it must not be done on the basis of the cold calculation of revenge, but out of recognition of the wrongdoer's being more than simply a sinner and villain. Judgement is better when it shows respect for the miscreant, which means accepting him or her for what they are and refusing the dubious pleasure of finding reasons to condemn them. Only the one who wants to judge deserves judgement: "I do not like your cold justice; and out of the eyes of your judges there always looks the executioner and his cold steel. Tell me, where is that justice which is love with open eyes? Would that you might invent for me the love that bears not only all punishment but also all guilt! Would that you might invent for me the justice that acquits everyone, except him that judges!" (ibid.). Justice here refuses to judge in casually universalistic fashion. It goes beyond the mere application of the rule in search of the creation of new rules that acknowledge the ultimate innocence of all, for no one is guilty for being who they have become. Such justice would thus rather liberate all miscreants rather than license the vengeful desire to hold others to account.

6

Revaluation and Beyond

1. The 1886 preface to Human, All Too Human *characterizes the "revaluation of values" in terms of the pursuit of freedom. Freedom demands one be the strongest critic of one's own "virtues." It requires one grasp that a degree of injustice is a necessary ingredient even of what one esteems most. Justice, Nietzsche holds, needs to be rethought in light of the recognition that life is characterized most essentially by its multiplicity. There is a multiplicity of possible ways of living, each of which expresses a partial and restricted perspective on the whole. This restriction, which rules over every form of life, reveals why each is necessarily unjust to some degree. The more threatened (or, in Nietzsche's terms, "weak" and "meagre") a form of life (i.e. a culture or community) is, the more inclined it will be to regard itself as providing the yardstick of truth and reality. All life occurs only in virtue of limitations. These combine with humanity's communally generated capacity for self-reflexivity to create in every culture a tendency to view its dominant perspective as universal and absolute. The "weaker" a culture, the more threatened and absolutist it will be inclined to become as recourse to self-defence. The greatest injustice is therefore perpetrated against existence by what is most limited, turned in on itself and lacking in possibility. The very difference necessary to life thereby gives rise to conditions antagonistic to it. Such antagonism is exemplified for Nietzsche by priestly values. This standpoint allows Nietzsche to identify the object of his final and most vehement polemic: the Christian church. The church, according to Nietzsche, is a dictatorship of anti-experimentalism that seeks to impose its own values and eliminate the essential difference and ensuing conflict that is a condition of life. Nietzsche's late texts seek to celebrate and thereby do justice to the multiplicity that, for him, characterizes the economy of life. This celebration entails going beyond "morality" (the rule of convention and the norm) in pursuit of a vision of humanity capable of revelling in its own self-surpassing finitude. In doing justice to life in this way Nietzsche proclaims himself as an ethical thinker. Freedom is the precondition of this ethical life, which is a form of thinking beyond the confines of the norm that allows the creative possibilities of pluralism to be affirmed through the insight achieved by attaining power over one's own values. Revaluation is the precondition of attaining such power.*

Eight years after the publication of *Human, All Too Human,* Nietzsche takes a backward glance and ruminates on the beginnings of his naturalistic turn. In the preface added to the 1886 second edition of the text he argues that *Human, All Too Human* is most essentially characterized by two things. First, there is the free spirit and his or her pursuit of liberty of thought. Second, the work itself is a kind of scarred testimony to the costs of pursuing such liberty. In its striving for intellectual freedom, Nietzsche tells us, *Human, All Too Human* bears witness to the necessity of trauma. It reveals that someone who wants to be free must be prepared to pay a painful price for his or her empowerment. The pursuit of freedom obliges a person to turn against what he or she cherishes. One must become a despiser and hater of what have hitherto been one's "virtues."[1] Only in this way can values be rendered pliable to the demand of the "higher goal" of elucidating "the problem of the *order of rank*" (*Human All Too Human,* Preface, 6). This demand concerns what Nietzsche comes to elucidate in the *Genealogy* and elsewhere as the task of performing a "revaluation of values."[2]

In this transformed relationship to what we esteem, our virtues take on a new meaning. As one achieves lordship over one's "For and Against," what one endorses and what one resists, values cease to be mere inclinations; they come to serve rather than enslave. The freedom of mastery, in other words, involves creating a counter-thought that contradicts the power of prevailing norms to act only as unquestioningly obeyed directives. The acquisition of this lordship of thought requires learning one thing above all else. One must come to appreciate that the ability to have any command over one's values has its source in the cultivation of an understanding of the perspectival element essential in *all* evaluation. It is necessary to understand, in other words, that all values are tentative and partial expressions of ways of living, that there is no grand moral path to reality and truth. For this reason, "the displacement, the distortion and merely apparent teleology of horizons and whatever else pertains to perspectivism," including a self-reflexive awareness of the "intellectual penalty" that one must pay for being able to think at all, present themselves most forcibly only to the liberated

1 One should recall here the "great contempt" discussed in *Zarathustra* (I, "Zarathustra's Prologue," 3). See chapter 5 for a discussion of this.

2 See, for example, the discussion Nietzsche offers in the last section of the first essay of the *Genealogy*. See also the discussion below.

person. The person who seeks freedom is obliged constantly to recall that humanity is an unjust animal, that a quantum of "*necessary* injustice [*nothwendige Ungerechtigkeit*]" is inescapable. From whatever standpoint one may approach it, this element of injustice is "irremovable from life," since "life itself" is "conditioned by the perspectival and its injustice."[3] This does not force us to the conclusion that one must therefore simply shrug one's shoulders and give up on the pursuit of justice or abandon oneself to an indulgent subjectivism.[4] This insight is a beginning, not an end. The point is that justice is not to be taken as a given, as something inherent in the order of things and already achieved. It must be pursued and, given the above limitation, pursued in a new way. What is needed is the cultivation of the ethic of mercy and creation discussed in the previous chapter.

Life is a plurality and plenitude of experiments in living. Such experiments, however, occur in each and every case as something small, particular, and aggressively restrictive. Life, in other words, always already and only happens in virtue of necessarily imposed limitations. This narrow condition, combined with the originally communally generated capacity for self-reflexivity and self-criticism, constitutes the constant threat of injustice that plagues human existence, since it gives rise to a misunderstanding. Each culture and the values it embodies is a limited and partial expression of the rich range of possibilities that constitutes life; but every evaluative tendency is at the same time powerfully inclined to take itself and its standards of value to be universal and absolute.[5] To this point Nietzsche adds the further observation that the more "meagre" the form of life, the more inclined it is to conceive of itself and its hierarchy of values in totalizing terms.[6] Absolutism, in other words, is often a kind

3 "*das Leben selbst als bedingt durch das Perspektivische und seine Ungerechtigkeit.*"

4 The subject is, in any case, a socially constituted entity, for Nietzsche; so any possible abandonment to an autonomous "inner world" of the self, Cartesian style, is a non-starter.

5 Witness the tendencies cultures have to consider themselves as representing a kind of realization of what precedes them, or has having a world-historical role in the order of things. The British Empire (with its conception of "civilization" – a view epitomized by J.S. Mill's discussion of other cultures in their "nonage" standing in need of the guiding hand of imperial rule) offers one example; some contemporary views expressed in the United States concerning the nation's world-historical role in the promotion of freedom proffer another.

6 This point relates to the discussion of the aristocratic *polis* Nietzsche offers in *Beyond Good and Evil*, 262. So long as the conditions of life in the community are harsh, Nietzsche notes, its morality is correspondingly so. As conditions cease to be so threatening, so the power of morality diminishes. In other words, the feeling of a community's power is expressed in terms of its tendency to resist what is different from it, its "universalizing" inclination to see the world exclusively in terms of itself.

of defence mechanism, a symptom characteristic of impoverished modes of existence that feel endangered by the world: the greater the absolutism, the greater the impoverishment. The most grievous injustice, Nietzsche asserts, occurs where a form of life that is of the "smallest, most contracted and most meagre" kind takes itself to be "the goal and measure of things" (*Human, All Too Human*, Preface, 6) and as a consequence turns an evil eye on everything alien to it. Injustice is thus characterized as the constant threat of violence towards difference. Yet, this unjust tendency is at the same time a product of this very difference, of the multiplicity of potential forms that characterizes the living world. As the preface Nietzsche adds to *Daybreak* in 1886 reminds us, with this thought we are returned to the domain of the "last man" and the priestly values of the "good and the just" – notions castigated in *Thus Spoke Zarathustra* (see *Daybreak*, Preface, 3). One can see Nietzsche in this way identifying what will become the target of the most unrestrained polemic of his late writings, beginning with the first and third essays of the *Genealogy* and continuing through *Twilight of the Idols* and *The Antichrist*. This target is the Christian church and the priestly asceticism associated with it.

Nietzsche characterizes the church as an institution that seeks to seize hold of and exercise the right to dictate a universal justice for all, purportedly in the name of an ideal, pain-free existence dedicated to the pursuit of comfort and contentment (the "last man" ideal of a heavenly after-life). With it comes the threat of a universalizing tyranny in which the least experimental forms of life (those that are most "meagre" and hence threatened, which for Nietzsche means those inclined to be most conventional) are empowered to dictate the norm. From the last man's standpoint, it should be recalled, pain itself is regarded as injustice, as is plurality and the anti-consensual tension and conflict plurality necessarily induces. From this threatened perspective, tension and conflict take on the guise of something appalling that needs to be eliminated. However, as we have just noted, such apparent "injustice" is in Nietzsche's view an essential condition of life, one that must be simultaneously negotiated, guarded against, and yet also celebrated. Indeed, the meaning of this condition must be completely and relentlessly grasped and integrated into our understanding of our own humanity and hence our place in the world.[7] Nietzsche's late writings are above all characterized by their attempt to press this insight into formulas. The late texts consistently seek to facilitate a naturalistic appreciation of the multiplicity and experimentalism that characterizes the condition of

7 See *The Gay Science*, 110, discussed in some detail above (chapter 2, section 6).

life in general despite the narrow and restrictive limitations that necessarily characterize life in particular.[8] In doing so, Nietzsche seeks to pass beyond morality (that is, beyond the rule of convention, of the norm) to the vision of a humanity that joyfully questions its own limitations, a humanity that lives dangerously in the acknowledgement of its own finitude.[9] From the standpoint of convention this is a humanity that looks dangerously "immoral." In Nietzsche's conception, however, such a stance is supremely ethical in its naturalistic affirmation of the risky and uncertain plurality of possibilities that human life must face and embrace. Revaluation, in other words, involves the recasting of our ethical propensities rather than their abandonment.[10] As he puts it in the *Genealogy* (I, 17), "[W]hat I *want* ... is written on the spine of my last book, *Beyond Good and Evil* ... at least this does not mean 'Beyond Good and Bad.'"[11]

The risky nature of plurality serves as a reminder of why liberty is necessary but costly. In order to grasp fully the nature of values and become ethical rather than merely "moral" one must be free; that is, one must risk standing beyond the domain of normative compulsion that constitutes the realm of average, everyday life, the world of mere thoughtless

8 Bearing this notion of multiplicity in mind, Richard Rorty's characterization of Nietzsche as a thinker driven, like Kant, by "a desire for purity" rings true in an at best rather limited sense (see "Human Rights," *Truth and Progress: Philosophical Papers, Volume 3*, 182). It may be the case that Nietzsche to some degree valorizes "self-conscious self-sufficiency" – although, as I have argued, self-consciousness is the mere witness of such sufficiency rather than its living reality – but self-sufficiency is for Nietzsche something validated by its being in service to the distinctly "impure" and contradictory multiplicity that is made manifest in the many different forms of life that are possible.

9 See *The Gay Science*, 283.

10 Robert C. Solomon argues that "Nietzsche is not an 'immoralist' – as he occasionally likes to bill himself. He is instead the defender of a richer kind of morality, a broader, more varied perspective (or, rather, an indefinitely large number of perspectives) in which the gifts and talents of each individual count foremost" ("Nietzsche *ad hominem*," 203). While this view is clearly one I share, I would perhaps be more wary of attributing to Nietzsche the positive attitude that is implied here. Nietzsche's interest in the great individual presupposes no egalitarian condition on the basis of which a person's talents and gifts are to be valued. There is likewise no desert or otherwise involved in the realization of such talents, either. As we have seen Zarathustra say, the chances are one will suffer for one's gifts and sacrifice oneself to them to the extent of embracing misery. Nietzsche may have abandoned his early adherence to Schopenhauer, but he remains a "Dionysian pessimist" (see chapter 5, section 8).

11 As Thiele points out, "Nietzsche's object in asserting the unaccountability of man is not to deny all values, but to create new ones" (*Friedrich Nietzsche and the Politics of the Soul*, 84). For Thiele, what Nietzsche demands in place of other-worldly "moral accountability" is "earthly responsibility."

doing according to the dictates of habits and conventions. Freedom, in this regard, is necessarily creative, since by throwing up new possibilities of doing it exceeds the thoughtless repetition of value judgements that characterizes the norm. This is also why freedom, for Nietzsche, means living dangerously. In creation, one affirms the threatening manner in which "power and right [*Recht*] and extensiveness of perspective rise into the heights together" (*Human All Too Human*, Preface, 6). Power, a sense of right, and the plurality that comes from affirming one's ability to see the world from more than one perspective entwine in an all-embracing breadth of creative insight capable of endowing life with meaning. At the same time, the awareness of perspective obliges one to refuse the temptation to believe that this meaning encapsulates the totality of possible experiments in living and the multiplicity of senses they can engender. To be ethical, therefore, means to affirm plurality. Such an affirmation, however, does not for Nietzsche involve the uncritical embracing of anything and everything – it cleaves to its "good and bad" even as it refuses the absolutism of good and evil. Being free involves confronting the "chaos and labyrinth of existence" contained in oneself as well as the world (*The Gay Science*, 322), but one only does so in so far as one has cultivated the ability to discriminate and have power over one's values – what Nietzsche in *The Gay Science* calls "'giving style' to one's character" (290). The pursuit of such power, which lies at the heart of Nietzsche's creative ethic, demands *revaluation.*

2. *In the* Genealogy *Nietzsche poses the question of revaluation in increasingly physiological terms. Estimating the value of values entails asking what they are good for – what aspects of life do different systems of values promote, and what aspects do they hinder? To answer such a question means to engage in revaluation. Revaluation, in turn, requires the freedom given by having relative independence from one's own values. The philosopher's task, Nietzsche argues, is to decide on values from the standpoint of this freedom. This entails overcoming the Christian church and its pious absolutism. The notion of revaluation does not denote something entirely new: slave morality, Nietzsche notes, is an example of a revaluation of values. His own, however, claims to be unique in its relentless drive to overturn Christian moral precepts. In* Twilight of the Idols *the physiological approach outlined in the Genealogy is further developed as "symptomatology." Nietzsche's attacks on Socratic rationalism illustrate well his approach. Socrates exemplifies the kind of "weakness" outlined in the 1886 preface to* Human, All Too Human. *Values, for Nietzsche, now become signs to be interpreted: they tell us more about the esteemer than what is esteemed. Cultivating an attitude of justice toward life means one must resist the temptation to judge and condemn it, as Socrates did. This condemnatory attitude reveals Socratic thought to be a violation of reality, as does its*

tendency to equate diverse and heterogeneous elements with one another (the Socratic dialectical equation of reason, justice, and virtue). In its violence to multiplicity and heterogeneity Socratism is a close relative of Christianity. Both seek to master life by way of equating reality with the rule of the concept. Both are absolutist in spirit. Nietzsche's psychology, in contrast, embraces a naturalistic immoralism that seeks to do justice to that thing most spurned by Socratic and Christian metaphysics: the body. Revaluation, in the light of this, is conceived as resting on the contention that a person's values are the expression of a greater organizing power, the spontaneity of which receives its expression and confirmation in the "happiness" of a being who has learnt to be at ease with his or her own embodiment. Where Christianity attacks the body, revaluation demands the body be respected as the source of values. Revaluation thus cultivates respect for the passions. This forms the basis of Nietzsche's ethic of mercy. In The Antichrist, *however, this ethic is sundered by the demands of polemic.*

The *Genealogy* offers a forceful enough introduction to the notion of revaluation. The text's first essay concludes with a "Note" calling for the writing of "a series of academic prize-essays" as a means of promoting "the study of *the history of morality*" (17). For the practising academic reader, reading this passage can stimulate memories of being an undergraduate student, for we are set an essay question to ponder: "*What signposts does linguistics, especially the study of etymology, give to the evolution of moral concepts?*" It is not only linguistic scholars who should be set to work looking for clues concerning the historical development of morality in this historical way; "physiologists and doctors" should likewise be invited to contribute. This is because "every table of values, every 'thou shalt' known to history, needs first and foremost a *physiological* elucidation and interpretation, rather than a psychological one; and all of them await critical study from medical science " (ibid.). One should note here a subtle but significant shift in emphasis in Nietzsche's naturalism as it enters its last phase. Morals need to be interpreted in an increasingly historical-physiological manner rather than a historical-psychological one. Thus, the *Genealogy* develops a more overt articulation of the notion of the body as a physiological construction constituted by domains of cultural practices.[12] This shift in emphasis allows Nietzsche to pose in a more pointed way the central question associated with the notion of revaluation: we must ask "what is this or that table of values and 'morals' *worth?*" (ibid.) This is a question that, in accordance with the view

12 These are exemplified by the practices associated with punishment (see *Genealogy*, II, and chapter 4).

expressed in the 1886 preface to *Human, All Too Human,* needs to be posed from a variety of perspectives, with especial stress on the issue "'value for *what?*'" In other words, some values (and one must remember here that for Nietzsche this means something essentially *practical*: values are *ways of living* not abstract ideas) may promote one thing while hindering something else. For example, he notes, what may be of greatest value "with regard to the longest possible life-span of a race ... would not have anything like the same value if it was a question of developing a stronger type" of person. This point is clarified: what is good for many people (the majority) and what is good for some others (the minority) is not one and the same thing. The important thing to notice here is that values are always values *for* something in particular, and can never be estimated from a universal and timeless perspective. Values are, in other words, *instrumental*: they simultaneously serve and cultivate one particular psycho-physiology or another. The task of revaluation must be undertaken with this in mind. It is for this reason that revaluation requires the liberated perspective of someone who is free, that is a person no longer mastered by their esteeming beliefs but endowed with the power of lordship over them. Philosophy is thereby given its future creative task. Each of the scholarly disciplines, Nietzsche holds, "must, from now on, prepare the way for the future work of the philosopher: this work being understood to mean that the philosopher has to solve the *problem of values* and that he has to decide on the *hierarchy of values*" (ibid.). To legislate concerning this hierarchy requires daring first to overturn, "reassess and reverse 'eternal values'" (*Beyond Good and Evil,* 203). To teach a revaluation of values, in other words, is to teach the overcoming of the Christian church and its avowedly pious universalism by way of "a critique of moral values" (*Genealogy,* Preface, 6). Conventional esteeming habits, not least those of the "good and the just," must be placed in question.

In one sense, the concept of revaluation does not denote something unique to Nietzsche's thought. Revaluation is not historically original – it has its precedents and predecessors. The slave morality that Nietzsche outlines most fully in the first essay of the *Genealogy* represents one kind of revaluation, namely that of noble values, and also a kind of gruesome culmination of the power struggles of the ancient world, which led to the condition of lamentation called modernity.[13] Christianity, Nietzsche

13 The Christian revaluation, Walter Kaufmann notes, is held by Nietzsche to be the most radical overturning of ancient values possible: "He claims that the Christians turned the embodiment of classical morality into the prototype of evil" (Kaufmann, "How Nietzsche Revolutionized Ethics," in *From Shakespeare to Existentialism,* 214).

holds, inherits this revaluation, for its values are expressions of priest and slave *ressentiment* dressed up in theological garb (*Genealogy*, I, 8).[14] Christian values stand as the reversal "of all Aryan values, the victory of Chandala values, the evangel preached to the poor and lowly, the collective rebellion of everything downtrodden, wretched, ill-constituted" (*Twilight of the Idols*, "The 'Improvers' of Mankind," 4). It is against such a revaluation that Nietzsche's own is aimed. In his last book, he toys with the idea that revaluation as he characterizes it – that is, as rebellion against Christian revaluation – occurs exclusively within the sphere of his own thought (see *Ecce Homo*, "Why I Am So Wise," 1). In the *Genealogy*, this rebellion is presented as a tantalizing possibility, one that will be initiated in the grand style by Nietzsche himself in a work he is currently preparing: "The Will to Power. Attempt at a Revaluation of all Values" (*Genealogy*, II, 27). By 1888 Nietzsche holds the revaluation to have been brought to some kind of fruition not in *The Will to Power* (a book never written) but in *The Antichrist* (see *Antichrist*, 62).

Twilight of the Idols, the work Nietzsche writes immediately before turning to *The Antichrist*, talks of the notion of revaluation as posing so tremendous and ominous a question mark that "it casts a shadow over him who sets it up" (*Twilight*, Forward). Revaluation, in other words, haunts him, for it poses the most distressing of questions concerning not only what is re-valued but he or she who re-values. In *Twilight*, following the suggested approach of the *Genealogy*, physiology is brought to the fore. What matters above all is the body and the various sign-languages of esteeming associated with it. It is in this context that Nietzsche's most virulent attack on Socratic rationalism is fashioned. Socrates, the traditional paradigm of the philosopher, is a "problem": his universalism reveals him to be the exemplar of the meagre kind of life alluded to in the 1886 preface to *Human, All Too Human.* Such meagreness Nietzsche now baptizes as "*décadence*." The formalism of Socratic rationalism displays the decadent tendency to evaluate existence generally rather than deal with life in its particularity (*Twilight*, "The Problem of Socrates," 2). The problem with Socrates is that he concludes that life is good for nothing.[15] Nietzsche's

14 The creators of Christianity re-valued and thereby overcame the dominant values of their times (see *Beyond Good and* Evil, 46; *On the Genealogy of Morality*, I, 7).

15 Nietzsche has in mind Socrates's dying comment in Plato's *Phaedo* 118, that he owes the god Asclepius the sacrifice of a rooster – the traditional way of expressing thanks for overcoming an illness. This comment, Nietzsche says, is "absurd and dreadful" for those sensitive to its genuine meaning (*The Gay Science*, 340). It means life is an illness and death is its cure. The wise persons of all ages, Nietzsche concludes, have accepted this ugly presupposition (see *Twilight*, "The Problem of Socrates," 1).

deployment of a physiological reading of Socratic reason serves as a means of resisting such a dour conclusion and initiates a key strategy of revaluation. Our values do not say *anything objective* about what is valued. They are signs that betray the nature of the one who values, unwitting testimony as to whom one really is: "Judgements, value-judgements about life, for or against, can in the end never be true: they have value only as symptoms, they can be considered only as symptoms, – in themselves such judgements are stupidities" (ibid.). Because we have the tendency to evaluate the world in our own image the toughest thing to grasp is the inherent plurality of existence and the ensuing and very subtle fact that, as a consequence of this plurality, "*the value of life cannot be estimated*" (ibid.). So long as we live we are part of life, and as such can never pose as impartial "judges"[16] concerning its value or otherwise. Doing justice to life, Nietzsche argues following the argument concerning freedom presented in the 1886 preface to *Human, All Too Human*, means grasping the great finesse of this thought and spurning the "most bizarre" of Socratic temptations which seeks to set reason, virtue, and happiness in a dialectical relation of equality with one another (*Twilight*, "The Problem of Socrates," 4). This kind of equalization epitomizes the conceptual naivety that is at work in philosophy generally.[17] Philosophy's temptation to find things rigidly akin to one another is a naïve violence against reality since things are simply not equal (they are heterogeneous: reason is not the same as virtue, virtue is not the same as life, etc.) (ibid.). Socratism is revealing only in its unwitting betrayal of its true nature as decadent thought, exemplified by a priest-like hatred of the senses and the body. In this, Socratism is a close relative of Christian morality – and the latter is a revolt against life (*Twilight*, "Morality as Anti-Nature," 5).

Physiology as Nietzsche conceives it in *Twilight* seeks to do justice to the body and its history and constitutes a re-endorsement of the embodied conception of life and the self advocated in *Thus Spoke Zarathustra*. This naturalistic "immoralism" rebels against "reason" as traditionally conceived, and in so doing takes an initial step toward revaluation: "*first* example of my 'revaluation of all values': a well-constituted human being, a 'happy' one, *must* perform certain actions and instinctively shrinks from other actions, he transports the order of which he is the physiological representative into his relationships with other human beings and with things. In a formula: his virtue is the *consequence* of his happiness"

16 "*Richter*"

17 See *Twilight*, "'Reason' in Philosophy," 1, in which Nietzsche castigates all philosophers for being conceptual fetishists who unthinkingly subject lived existence to the tyranny of a formalistically conceived and narrowing dogmatism.

(*Twilight*, "The Four Great Errors," 2). In this passage we see yet another endorsement of the freedom-cultivating pluralistic attitude sketched out in the 1886 preface to *Human, All Too Human.* A person's virtues ought not to command them, but should rather be an expression of a greater organizing force. Such "happiness" as one may have is the source of one's virtues.[18] We must not, in consequence, expect happiness to emanate from the world around us. We must make it – it must be our achievement, our creation, as our virtues must likewise be. The problem with the Christian church, as *The Antichrist* sets out to show, is that it comprehends properly neither happiness nor virtue, since it refuses to acknowledge the body as anything other than an impediment to the immortal soul's salvation. Here we arrive at the essence of what Nietzsche means in *Twilight* when he calls theological morality anti-natural. Church morality is a form of "anti-nature" since it attacks the body, the realm of the passions and drives that makes us who we are, in all its aspects. In turn, "to attack the passions at their roots means to attack life at its roots: the practice of the Church is [therefore] *hostile to life*" (*Twilight*, "Morality as Anti-Nature," 1). We have seen that out of his naturalistic analysis of power relations Nietzsche develops an ethic of mercy resistant to what he considers to be the revenging and punishing morality of the church and the "good and the just." Such an ethics spurns morality as traditionally conceived (i.e. as a universalism that endorses commonly accepted notions of individual responsibility and guilt) in favour of a pluralistic view that endorses the essential innocence of humankind. *The Antichrist* represents the development of this ethics as polemic; it is an ethic of mercy given teeth.

3. The Antichrist *is a text that stakes a claim to stand outside the institutions that characterize the history of the West. It is an attempt to bring to fruition Nietzsche's naturalism and moral critique and, as such, stands as his most complete articulation of a revaluation of values. In pursuing the path of revaluation* The Antichrist *is compelled into claiming an authority that marks a departure from the approach Nietzsche adopts earlier in* Beyond Good and Evil *and the* Genealogy. *This departure compromises the ethic of mercy he has hitherto so painstakingly formulated.* The Antichrist *invokes a "Hyperborean" standpoint beyond the realm of the everyday that is both oracular and naturalistic. The Hyperborean being hails from a land of myth, a world untainted by Christian ecclesiastical influence. Hyperborean happiness, as Nietzsche articulates it, is akin*

18 What is Nietzsche's happiness? It is, he says in *The Gay Science*, "Joke, Cunning and Revenge," 2, the embarking on adventure, "sailing with every wind."

to the legislative act he attributes to the creation of values. The Hyperborean condition thus invokes the freedom of the creative will celebrated by Zarathustra. At the same time, it also invokes the naturalistic problem of values as Nietzsche conceives it: the problem of what kind of humanity shall be "willed" and "bred" that is capable of answering to the demands of "life." The conception of humanity envisaged here is akin to that of the overman presented in Thus Spoke Zarathustra *and is a counter to the "corrupt" being that the church has advocated and cultivated as the paradigmatic example of the good person. Nietzsche levels the charge of corruption in terms, he says, free of moral taint. Corruption, as he envisages it, means the predilection to choose what is harmful to one. It is this predilection that contravenes the demands of "life." In making this last claim,* The Antichrist *slips into a mode of judgement that invokes the authority of the courtroom. The Christian advocacy of pity runs counter to the "law" of life. The text thereby claims the status to be witness, judge, and physician of culture at one and the same time. In this claim to judge in a manner that invokes the authority of "life,"* The Antichrist *steps beyond the ethic of mercy that Nietzsche has formulated. The text invokes a perspective that is priestly in spirit – the words of a worshipper whose worship empowers him with the authority necessary for judgement. In this way, the oracular combines with the naturalistic in a manner that is problematic.*

In its unrestrained attack on the Christian church and its traditions, *The Antichrist* stakes a claim to being an anti-institutional utterance *par excellence*, a critical voice that emanates from somewhere beyond the realm of church and sanctified authority. The text also represents something more than a blasphemous work of counter-theology. It represents a final attempt to bring to fruition Nietzsche's critical and naturalistic immoralism. As such *The Antichrist* stands as Nietzsche's single most sustained attempt at a revaluation of values. That Nietzsche considers this to be the case is shown by the comment he makes in the forward to *Twilight of the Idols*. The forward, dated 30 September 1888, is written on the day on which the first attempt at "the *Revaluation of all Values* [i.e. *The Antichrist*]" was brought to fruition.[19] As a work of revaluation, *The Antichrist* can be interpreted as attempting a post-moral assessment of the order of rank among values in line with the project outlined at the end of the first essay of the *Genealogy*. It is thereby compelled to make authoritative claims concerning not only the meaning of moral discourse but also the relative worth of different systems of value, as it must do in order to offer an assessment of the value of values. However, *The Antichrist* does this in a manner that takes it beyond the rhetoric of

19 *The Antichrist* was begun on 3 September 1888 and finished on 30 September.

unmasking that characterizes much of *Beyond Good and Evil* and the *Genealogy*, and this in turn propels Nietzsche beyond the ethic of mercy that is embraced in his writings up to and including *Twilight of the Idols*.

As *Twilight* informs us, in whatever manner one might speak of values one necessarily speaks from *somewhere*.[20] Nietzsche's chosen ground, the place from where a first stab at revaluation will be attempted, is, he notes at the outset of *The Antichrist*, "Hyperborean." The Hyperborean standpoint is oracular and naturalistic in equal measure. Hyperboreans dwell in a mythical land of plenty that lies beyond the north winds, somewhere that has escaped the millennia-long "labyrinth" of Christian metaphysics (*Antichrist*, 1). Hyperboreans live beyond the norms of modern life. As such, they are characterized by an ability to embrace a perspective untrammelled by traditional constraints. As is so often the case with Nietzsche, intimations of distance endow the Hyperborean with the peculiar and uncanny authority associated with the defying of convention. "Happiness," the text implies early on, is the sign and seal of this oracular authority. There is a kind of "happiness" that is genuine, one opposed to the lazy ideal of resigned contentment characteristic of the "last man." Happiness is encapsulated by a dictum: it merely requires "a Yes, a No, a straight line, a *goal*" (ibid.).[21] With this we are offered a "formula" that operates like an aphoristic encapsulation of Nietzsche's conception of the creativity of the law-giving act. Law-giving, like happiness, involves a "Yes," i.e. an affirmation of something as good. In so far as such affirmation "heightens the feeling of power" (*Antichrist*, 2) it also compels us to condemn what runs counter to this feeling as bad, to say "No" to it. With these judgements comes directness, a "straight line" that corresponds to the uprightness of a moulded and stamped character. From this directness flows a sense of purpose, a "goal." Understood in this way, happiness is a sign that the "feeling of power *grows*," and this in turn is testimony that something resistant has been surmounted and incorporated. The happiness celebrated in *The Antichrist* is an analogue of the happiness that springs from the creative act of law-giving celebrated in part three of

20 See *Twilight of the Idols*, "Morality as Anti-Nature," 5: "A condemnation of life on the part of the living remains in the end merely a symptom of a particular kind of life … When we speak of values, we speak with the inspiration, with the way of looking at things, which is part of life: life itself forces us to posit values; life itself values through us when we posit values." Thus, all morality is a sign of forms of life – the question that pertains to every morality is *what form of life does it indicate?* This point must likewise be posed concerning any attempt at a revaluation, in so far as the latter cannot aspire to a standpoint beyond value, merely one "beyond good and evil."

21 As if to emphasize the continuity, this echoes *Twilight*, "Maxims and Arrows," 44.

Zarathustra and again at the end of *Twilight of the Idols*. Such happiness testifies to attained creative power and is a manifestation of the satisfying sensation of stamping one's creative will "*on millennia as on wax*" (*Twilight*, "The Hammer Speaks"). Happiness of this kind, in short, is a sign of the freedom associated with the coining of values. As such, it excites the most overwhelming sensation of an increase in power there is: through values humans are fashioned and what greater kind of alliance between creativity and power could there be than this? We are thus offered by way of this text a testimony and confirmation of the conjoining of "power and right" as the epitome of a sense of rightness.[22]

Through the text of *The Antichrist* speaks the voice of one who is free because he is empowered with the freedom to judge otherwise than Christian metaphysics would allow. On the basis of this Hyperborean authority, Nietzsche raises what is for him the key question. This question takes us to the heart of the naturalistic conception of the creative individual as it presents itself in his late thought: "The problem I thus pose is ... what type of man shall be *bred*, shall be *willed*, for being higher in value, worthier of life, more certain of a future" (*Antichrist*, 3).[23] The "problem" we are presented with here concerns the cultivation of a type of humanity that can be deemed worthier of life as a consequence of its being endowed with a sense of futurity. This amounts to a question of justification presented on a grand scale. In effect, *The Antichrist* is seeking to elucidate the value-conditions in virtue of which a form of human existence could be attained capable of justifying all that has preceded it.[24] Such a form of justification is naturalistic in that the fashioning of a "higher" humanity more assured of its own future is deemed sufficient to justify humanity, rather than the will of a God. Such justification is envisaged, moreover, as being achieved by living up to a standard of measure dictated by life itself rather than by the divine. Revaluation, as it is performed in *The Antichrist*, therefore, invokes a naturalistic authority with regard to assessing and affirming those values that are equal to and can therefore answer the demands of life.

22 This again echoes the ideas celebrated in the 1886 preface to *Human, All Too Human* discussed above in section 1.

23 In this passage, *The Antichrist* picks up on the ideas outlined in section 6 of the preface to the *Genealogy*.

24 One should perhaps note here the connection between this discussion and the notion of the "sovereign individual" presented in the second essay of the *Genealogy* (2–3). This kind of individual, exemplified by a degree of autonomy that contrasts starkly with those incapable of keeping their word, is presented rhetorically as a justification of the misery resulting from the normative compulsion and torture that precedes them.

Nietzsche is in no doubt that some examples of the future-oriented humanity he imagines, each of which might also be called "a sort of overman" (*Antichrist*, 4), have existed on earth. The problem is that each has only ever done so "as a fortunate accident, as an exception, never as something *willed*" (*Antichrist*, 3). Up to now, what has been "willed, bred, and *attained*" by the Christian church is the counter-image of this kind of human being. The achievement of the church has been nothing less than the fashioning of a "corrupt" humanity. Nietzsche is unambiguous when it comes to the charge he seeks to level here. He does not wish to prosecute the church under an indictment of *moral* depravity. The prosecution in question is to be brought in a sense that is "let me emphasize this once more - *moraline-free*," i.e. free of any tincture of moral indictment (*Antichrist*, 6). What Nietzsche deems as "corrupt" concerns a loss of the "instincts" and a consequent predilection to choose what is bad for oneself, what is "disadvantageous." In a manner that recalls *Twilight*'s discussion of "anti-nature," Christian morality is accused of being a departure from what is natural, of being a perversion of the natural inclinations of "life." Nietzsche's rhetoric thereby takes on a judgmental aspect in *The Antichrist* in a manner that is not found in the texts that precede it, including *Twilight of the Idols*. "Life" has become a word of authority, for what Nietzsche now invokes in order to condemn the Christian church is nothing less than "*life itself*": "Life itself is to my mind the instinct for growth, for durability, for an accumulation of forces, for *power*: where the will to power is lacking there is decadence." The hitherto purportedly "highest," Christian values lack this will. It is this absence of a will empowered by life that makes them decadent and "*nihilistic*" (ibid.).[25]

Nietzsche thereby mounts an attack on Christianity that replicates the sphere of the courtroom. What does not fulfil the demands laid down by "life itself" is fit only to be indicted, on a charge of decadence, to stand trial in the court of life. The teachings of the church are those of the religion of pity. Pity and life, Nietzsche asserts, do not mix, not least because "Pity makes suffering contagious" and in so doing it "crosses the law of development, which is the law of *selection*. It preserves what is ripe for destruction ... From the standpoint of the instinct of life, a remedy certainly seems necessary" (*Antichrist*, 7). In attacking Christian pity, Nietzsche is thus attacking what he conceives to be inimical to life, what is "anti-natural." In making this criticism, however, *The Antichrist* stakes a claim to a standpoint coterminous with that of "life itself." The authority Nietzsche invokes in order to criticize Christianity springs from his

25 For some thought-provoking discussion of this matter see Bull, *Anti-Nietzsche*, 44ff.

homage to the drives and the body, to the domain of what is "natural." Thus empowered, he lays claim to the status of a cultural diagnostician and in this way sets himself up as the oracular mouthpiece through which life itself pronounces judgement. Life now "speaks" in the guise of a self-styled physician of culture who in speaking becomes endowed with authority and identity in equal measure: "To be physicians *here*, to be inexorable *here*, to wield the scalpel *here* – that is *our* part, that is *our* love of man, that is how *we* are philosophers, we *Hyperboreans*" (ibid.). It is here that the revaluation as Nietzsche conceives it in *The Antichrist* oversteps the bounds of the ethic of mercy he has hitherto endorsed. To speak like a physician means to speak as one who claims to know not merely who is sick but how to cure them. It means to claim authority to judge universally in virtue of possessing knowledge gleaned from the standpoint of life concerning what is sick and what is not. In the very act of revaluation the text recoils into metaphysics as Nietzsche here invokes a kind of legitimacy reminiscent of the priest – the authority of one who has borne witness to the demands of "life." However post-metaphysical the reasons for engaging in such talk might be, the one who ultimately worships "life itself," even in opposition to the Christian God, remains a kind of priest to the extent that he or she seeks to judge and thereby condemn in the name of what is universally "true." "True," Nietzsche makes perfectly clear, here denotes that which is beneficial to "life": to *speak truly* is to make a judgement – to speak in a manner that is affirmative of life (*Antichrist*, 9). Some values are affirmative, some are not – some values are "true" and some not. In thus endorsing this conception of the "true" Nietzsche assumes the mantle of empowered Dionysian worshipper and oracle. The reader who allows *The Antichrist* authority on this basis would have to accept the role of a passive initiate into the text's wisdom concerning what it means to worship life.

4. The problematic nature of the combination of oracular and naturalistic elements in The Antichrist *is revealed when the text curses Christianity. The unreserved nature of issuing a curse undermines Nietzsche's previous desire to avoid the language of condemnation. Nietzsche's naturalism, as hitherto articulated, does not license such vehemence. Indeed, the condemnatory tone in* The Antichrist *also runs counter to his own insight elsewhere (e.g.* Genealogy, *I, 7; II, 11, 13) into the positive value of what is here so unreservedly attacked. On the basis of the latter insight, Christianity does not need to be damned but merely overcome in a spirit of generosity and even gratitude. In this regard, Nietzsche's writings prior to* The Antichrist *paradoxically take one step beyond this text in their invocation not of "life" but of "law" as a means of overcoming morality by extending its domain toward critical self-reflection and embracing the insight that what lives has an essential innocence at its core. To grasp this innocence as it is celebrated in* Twilight of the Idols *or* Assorted Opinions and Maxims *is to embark on the path of seeking to overcome accepted ideas of the relation between judge and judged – to accept humanity in its plurality, dangerous though that plurality might at times seem. It is to think of the miscreant in a manner that refuses to attribute the kind of illusory guilt that condemns and curses unreservedly. This is a way of thinking to be found in Nietzsche's conception of the creator as law-giver. Such legislating gives values in a manner that does not seek to force, but rather undermines the rule of the norm through creativity. It is here that the political invitation posed by Nietzsche's texts makes itself manifest. This conception of legislation marks a return to the Nietzsche of* The Birth of Tragedy *and thereby provokes reflection on the enchantment of myth. Nietzsche's thought pays testimony to the way in which naturalism is a liberation from the nihilistic realm of metaphysics that at the same time brings with it its own threat of nihilism. Nietzsche's answer to this threat is to institute a naturalized oracular vision in the form of the creative law-giver and overman. This answer pays testimony to the necessity and danger of myth as it is articulated in the context of a modernity haunted by what Horkheimer and Adorno call the "dialectic of enlightenment." Nietzsche's thought is at the same time an incursion into this dialectic and its re-articulation in self-critical, problematic form.*

On the basis of this presupposition of authority *The Antichrist* concludes with a final judgement of its own, with a revaluation of Christian values:

> I pronounce my judgment. I *condemn* Christianity. I bring against the Christian Church the most dreadful of all indictments[26] that a prosecutor[27] has ever uttered. It is for me the highest of all conceivable corruptions ... it has made every value into an un-value, every truth into a lie, every integrity into a vileness of soul ... draining all blood, all love, all hope for life ... This eternal indictment of Christianity I will write on all walls, wherever there are walls ... I call Christianity the one great curse, the one great innermost corruption, the one great instinct of revenge ... I call it the one immortal blemish of mankind. And one calculates the time from the *dies nefastus* [unlucky day] with which this calamity began – from the *first* day of Christianity! *Why not rather from its last? From today?* Revaluation of all values! (*The Antichrist*, 62)

26 *Anklagen.*
27 *Ankläger.*

The Antichrist thereby ends in a tone of condemnation. It is a tone reflected by the subtitle Nietzsche finally added to the work: "Curse on Christianity." This subtitle, like the concluding condemnation, replicates the very thing Nietzsche accuses Christianity of being culpable for. It is a curse. In revaluing Nietzsche judges and in judging he is driven into a way of speaking that he otherwise elsewhere consistently spurns, however ironic and judgemental he can often be. To appreciate the full extent to which this is the case, one must consider what a curse is and what it means to issue one. The person who *really* curses does not do so lightly, casually, or in a manner that pertains to limits. A curse is unreserved. It pertains to a kind of absoluteness that claims universality. I might, in contrast, express my low opinion of someone, but such an opinion is limited in so far as it is mine. The possible universality of a judgement that another is somehow of lesser worth is like Kant's conception of beauty:[28] it elicits agreement from others; its logic (however dubious and violent) is consensual. Judgements of opinion can always be modified by degrees. A curse, however, stands as it is or falls and ceases to be what it is. A curse thereby aspires to immortality in two senses. First, there is the status of immortal awfulness bestowed on the thing cursed. Second, there is the immortality (that is, the "truth") of the curse itself that identifies this terribleness and, in doing so, paradoxically preserves what has been identified as terrible even as it rejects it. A curse therefore cannot even die a little when the thing cursed dies, for its judgement is without reserve. Curses colonize. As Nietzsche issues his curse the judgement engulfs the sense of mercy he has so lovingly cultivated: the refusal to accuse, find guilty, and condemn is itself refused. The hallmarks of Nietzsche's immoralism, however much he may protest to the contrary at the beginning of the book, are compromised. A curse is never free of moral venom.

At most, the kind of naturalism Nietzsche elucidates up until *The Antichrist* legitimizes him to consider Christianity as something unfortunate due to the extent to which it is driven to judge and hold accountable in a manner that denigrates the body and stifles the creative experimentalism of value creation. But, as the first and third essays of the *Genealogy* tell us, one must also be grateful even for the priestly type, for it has been instrumental in cultivating intellectuality and has helped preserve our kind from despair and destruction (*Genealogy*, I, 7; III, 11). Indeed, the ascetic priest is, in this last regard, considered in the *Genealogy*

28 I am thinking, of course, of the famous discussion in Kant's *Critique of Judgement*.

to be life affirming: "this apparent enemy of life, this *negative man*, – he actually belongs to the really great forces in life which *conserve and create the positive*" (*Genealogy*, III, 13). As a consequence of the painful socialization of the drives humanity suffers from itself, and the ascetic priest offers a way of making this suffering bearable by offering an explanation for suffering. There is, on this basis, no need to curse Christianity. One needs merely to spurn it, and to do so generously and appreciatively rather than unconditionally – such a position allows one the luxury of retaining those elements that might be considered worthy in what one denies. In this regard, the spirit of Nietzsche's writings prior to *The Antichrist* actually takes one beyond the revaluation proposed by it.

With this, we are returned to the retraction of belief in the integrity of morality that characterizes the majority of Nietzsche's mature writings beginning with *Daybreak*. In this book, Nietzsche says in the 1886 preface, "faith in morality is withdrawn – but why? *Out of morality!*" (*Daybreak*, Preface, 4) Here, it is not "life" but "law" that demands the cultivation of a sceptical attitude concerning our moral beliefs. Nietzsche and the fellow thinkers he imagines and hopes for may be immoralists, "But there is no doubt, there still speaks a 'thou shalt' to us too, we too still obey a strict law that has been set over us – and this is the last ethic, that which to us too still makes itself audible, that [ethic according] to which we too know how to live; here, if in anything at all, we are still men of conscience: namely, that we do not return again to what we regard as outlived and rotten, to something 'unworthy of belief,' be it called God, virtue, truth, justice, brotherly love" (ibid.). Such an attitude does not demand a break with morality in the name of "life," as *The Antichrist* does in its search for a culmination in revaluation, but envisages instead an ethics that is at once a continuation of morality and its overcoming, one that represents an extension of "the German integrity and piety of millennia" in its openness and refusal to judge precipitately. Being just, on this conception, is a matter of specificity, of sensitivity to the particularity of every human situation. The possibility of genuine justice thus begins with the affirmation of an essential innocence as being characteristic of all of us. "Our teaching," Nietzsche says in *Twilight of the Idols*, is that no one can be held accountable for being who they are (*Twilight*, "The Four Great Errors," 8). We are not the products of a design or will, be it that of our own making or another's. Our lot is to find ourselves, to discover our identity, in the midst of an essential and constitutive contingency. To be is to be necessary, to be part of the whole, but since there is nothing that can stand apart from the whole there is no ultimate standpoint from which to judge others. We are therefore strictly speaking immune from any tribunal of judgement that would claim the right to be able to correct us, to straighten out our being and make it conform to a pre-given norm of rightness. To be just means to liberate from condemnation, to refuse to hold accountable in moral terms: "that alone is the great liberation; with this alone is the innocence of becoming restored."[29] With this comes a way to judgement that begins with the affirmation of mercy as its guiding principle; mercy is the first gesture, the initial step with which one embarks in search of a rule. Nietzsche's view as it is expressed in his late writings thus fulfils a sentiment found in the earlier text of *Assorted Opinions and Maxims*: "'Nature is too beautiful for you poor little mortal' – this way of feeling is not rare, yet a few times, by way of an intimate look at everything human, its abundance, strength, delicateness, inter-woven complexity, it feels to me, as if I must say, in all humility: 'humanity also is too beautiful for the men who observe it!' – and indeed not only the moral person, but each and every one" (342). Here is a sense of the justice that embraces a love of humanity that inverts the traditionally sanctioned power relation separating judge and judged. To contemplate humankind with fairness one must first refuse to assume the right to censure it on moral grounds. What is remarkable about humanity must be recognized and acknowledged with regard to all of its plurality of forms – even the so-called "evil" human being must be acknowledged as representing something astonishing, something that demands they be done justice through the act of acknowledgement, through recognition that they are more than merely "evil." Faced with humankind one must love it all and so seek to do justice to it. One must remain in the condition of humility that accompanies being astonished by what humankind is and what it might be. This is *amor fati*, love of fate, which is Nietzsche's formula for greatness (*Ecce Homo*, "Why I Am So Clever," 10). Such an attitude does not mean we should endorse everything about what we are and welcome a free-for-all in which every mode of life is equally valued. Nietzsche does not seek to overturn all differentiation in ethical judgement. As we have already noted, he is happy to remain with the discursive domain of "good and bad" (*Genealogy*, I, 17).

29 "What does 'innocence' mean?" asks Deleuze. It is, he answers, "the truth of multiplicity" (*Nietzsche and Philosophy*, 22). It is linked, Deleuze continues, to the thought of Heraclitus and via this to the problem of justice: "Heraclitus is the tragic thinker. The problem of justice runs through his entire work. Heraclitus is the one for whom life is radically innocent and just. He understands existence on the basis of an *instinct of play*. He makes existence an *aesthetic phenomenon* rather than a moral or religious one" (ibid., 23). The affirmation of pluralism that drives Nietzsche's conception of justice has its roots in the tragic, oracular conception that provides the motivation for *The Birth of Tragedy* and is retained in the mature thought in the form of "Dionysian pessimism." See, in connection, the discussions in chapters 5 and 6.

Thinking in terms of good and bad rather than good and evil, however, means knowing the difference between when pragmatic justifications are at stake and when ethical issues really count. It means accepting that when a society punishes it does so as a condition of its existence not because it has an unquestionable moral right to do so, that revenge is never the best course of action, and that mercy is always the better option if one can afford it. So long as one is tempted to think otherwise and to find guilty, one is a potential victim of mythology: "Just bear in mind the notorious witch-trials: at that time, the most perspicacious and humane judges did not doubt that they were dealing with guilt; the 'witches' *themselves did not doubt it,* – and for all that guilt was lacking" (*Genealogy*, III, 16). All judgement, in other words, is framed within webs of cultural beliefs permeated by the primitive tendency to find easy reasons for the justification of punishing. There is, however, no natural (i.e. pre-given and absolute) justice. Justice, as mercy and creation, must find its way, it cannot be given it.

The dubious attempt in *The Antichrist* aside, one should not expect too much by way of ostentatious showiness from Nietzsche's justice. "Great events," Zarathustra notes, tend to be quiet, largely invisible things (*Zarathustra*, II, "On Great Events"). They are altogether more subtle than the storming of palace gates or the pulling down of a measly tyrant's statue or cursing, acts which often *look* impressive enough but generally change little and still less often change them for the good. "The greatest events – they are not our loudest, but on the contrary our stillest hours. Not around the inventor of new noise: around the inventor of new values the world turns itself; *noiselessly* it turns itself" (ibid.). As I have argued, creativity is legislative because it is transformative: the creator is the person who takes us in thought to a place from which we can never return unchanged, who shows us a familiar landscape in a new and unforgettable light, who challenges irrevocably how we think of ourselves and thereby creates the possibility of new ways of valuing and new experiments of living. On this view, the invention of values trumps all other forms of agency for change. The creation of values, in short, is the ultimate political act – and this political act is cataclysmic precisely to the extent that it is at the time of its coming to dominance something unseen, unheard, unremarked. Here is an invitation to a new politics of subtlety. This is a politics that seeks subtly to undermine the norm through the creative pursuit of refashioning values. It seeks thereby a new justice that is never merely a revolution that changes rulers, but rather one that registers itself as a change in us.

In its affirmation of this conception of legislation, Nietzsche's thought completes its own specific kind of revolution. This revolution returns us to the thought of myth that occupies his first book, *The Birth of Tragedy*. There, artistic creation (genuine metaphysics) makes possible the reinvigoration of a sense of myth that, in turn, can be put to service in fashioning a rejuvenated culture capable of overcoming the stale emptiness of Alexandrian modernity. Nietzsche's embracing of naturalistic historical philosophy in *Human, All Too Human* sunders myth. Yet, even as he seeks to expose the presuppositions of the primitive illogic at work in the heart of metaphysics and modern culture alike, Nietzsche does not escape from myth's enchantment.[30] His articulation of an ethics founded in the individual creation of values indeed testifies to the fact that he is driven to acknowledge the impossibility of liberation from myth. Naturalism initiates the possibility of an overcoming of metaphysics. In the *Genealogy* this possibility is given perhaps its most powerful expression with an account of human identity, values, and intellectuality that has no need of first principles, divine origins, or metaphysics, proffering instead a full-blown philosophy of power. At the same time, naturalism threatens a suspension of authority that brings about the nihilistic loss of faith in all values.[31] The thought of the overman and the creative ethic that Nietzsche subsequently formulates, an ethic that celebrates power as mercy and affirms creation as giving and suffering, counters nihilism. It does so, however, only by reinstating an analogue of the oracular power of insight that *The Birth* celebrates as metaphysics. The creator of values (that is, the real philosopher) is a commander, but the power of such commanding needs must be invisible to the commanded in order to be what it is. In this sense, philosophical thought must make its bid to take us over. It must achieve its end by colonizing us before we are aware of

30 Nietzsche's thought is characterized in an essential way by a constant recognition of this. One needs here to recall a passage cited earlier from *Daybreak*: "We still draw the conclusions of judgments we consider false, of teachings in which we no longer believe – our feelings make us do it" (*Daybreak*, 99). As creatures of the passions we are driven by habits of judgement from which we cannot escape. Myth, in this regard, is inescapable. "The greater the enigma, the more mystery, the better, or so says the spiritually healthy man" (Thiele, *Friedrich Nietzsche and the Politics of the Soul*, 90). The central question is what one makes of myth in the light of the acknowledgement of its inescapability and, indeed, its positive value. It is this point that allows for some important insight into the vexed question of Nietzsche's relation to the Enlightenment. Reason cannot answer our most demanding need: the need for the endowment of some kind of sense to life. This is the point of Nietzsche's discussion in the third essay of the *Genealogy*. The human animal is the suffering animal and this suffering does not spring from the mere fact that what lives must endure pain but from the need to invest pain with significance. Modern reason (science and critical scholarly understanding) cannot posit values and hence cannot provide the kind of sense capable of fulfilling this demand.

31 See chapter 2, section 3.

the event. We are changed by the creator's transformative power, moulded in his or her image as willing accomplices. In this way, Nietzsche carves out a naturalism that, in seeking to go beyond good and evil but not to transcend good and bad, must of necessity return us to the realm of myth. At it most excessive, this return erupts in the polemic of *The Antichrist* and its attempt to invoke the oracular power of the realm of "life itself" in condemnation of the church. Nietzsche's first attempt at revaluation founders on the limits sketched out so perceptibly by his own thought. Authority cannot be deduced. Even the liberal "agreement" of a social compact is coercion; value-neutrality is an illusion. This is because the relation between commanded and commander cannot be analysed from a standpoint exterior to it. There are no disinterested parties, since we are always already commanded and commanding beings.

We are, Nietzsche emphasizes, driven by the will to truth. This means that we are commanded by an imperative that we must follow simply in virtue of being who we are. With this conjoining of knowing and valuing, a question is posed. Does naturalism signal the end of metaphysics, or is it merely another articulation of its logic? If metaphysics is ethics at its worst, as much of Nietzsche's thought often implies, then in pursuing its own ethics his thinking does not seek to stand simplistically "outside" of metaphysics any more than it endorses the naivety of a purportedly pure or enlightened "reason" supposed to occupy a position immune from the incursions of myth. Nietzsche's naturalism can, in this regard, be seen as the most striking manifestation of the struggle that characterizes what Adorno and Horkheimer characterized as the dialectic of enlightenment.[32] In this dialectic, reason, seeking to escape from myth, inexorably recapitulates the very logic it overtly scorns. Enlightenment, which was born out of the spirit of liberation from tyranny, recoils into a repression no less mythical and no less obdurate for its being performed in the name of science. Nietzsche's incursion into this dialectic is thinking at its most surprising and creative. As historical philosophy, naturalism seeks to overcome the domain of traditional metaphysics in the liberating spirit of enlightenment; but as resurgence of myth it makes manifest the impossibility of such liberation attaining completeness, unless it is in the guise of illusion and falsehood or the excess that characterizes *The Antichrist*'s regression into an essentialist metaphysics.

32 See Adorno and Horkheimer, *Dialectic of Enlightenment.*

Conclusion

WHAT CAN BE LEARNT FROM NIETZSCHE concerning our dominant conceptions of justice and law? Even a relatively cursory glance reveals Nietzsche as highly critical of commonly accepted notions of justice, and of the political movements associated with them. On the one hand, he has little time for socialism and its egalitarian articulation of justice, which is arguably one of the most powerful and in many ways most constructive political forces of the nineteenth and twentieth centuries.[1] He is equally critical, and perhaps more perceptive,[2] in his discussions of the more general political transformations associated with the culture of burgeoning nineteenth century capitalism – not least the rise of mass representative democracy.[3] What is common to both the rise of capitalist power and socialist reaction, however, is the dominant social milieu within which they develop: that of liberal modernity.[4] This is a milieu in which the increasing power of industrial capital occurs within a synthesis of powerful and contradictory tendencies. Liberal modernity is a world

1 Consider in this context the Labour Party's creation of the National Health Service in the United Kingdom, one of the most powerful and positive forces of radical change in twentieth-century British history.

2 It must be said that many of Nietzsche's critical remarks concerning socialism depend more on assertion than argument. They exhibit, in short, a bourgeois suspicion of the political radicalism, connected with the working classes fashioned by the forces of Industrial Revolution, that is not untypical of other nineteenth century thinkers – not least utilitarian liberal J.S. Mill, with whom Nietzsche clearly (and often with good cause) feels himself to have little or nothing in common.

3 I have offered some consideration of Nietzsche's attitude to modernity and capital in *Nietzsche's Economy* (see chapters 1–2). For the most unrestrained, polemical treatment of Nietzsche in relation to socialism see Lukács, *The Destruction of Reason*.

4 I am tempted here to recall a comment once made to me by a long-time socialist friend and colleague at Cardiff University, Barry Wilkins: "Marxists are the truest liberals."

dominated by vehicles of mass communication concentrated in the hands of powerful individuals (for example the daily papers Nietzsche is, on occasion, so dismissive of), yet also a world in which political resistance is provoked; it is a world of industrialization and shifting power relations, a scenario in which egalitarian democratic attitudes and politically representative institutions develop against the backdrop of powerful conservative forces. As noted in the introduction, a good deal of interesting critical work has been devoted to considering the ways in which Nietzsche's thought can contribute to debates about the nature of modern liberal-democratic social orders. Nevertheless, in many ways Nietzsche stands *outside* the terrain that characterizes such discussion. This is not because Nietzsche's writings are "apolitical," as some have mistakenly argued.[5] It is rather because Nietzsche's thoughts on the nature of law and justice point *beyond* the very tradition of liberal-democratic debate, and thus beyond the terms in which much discussion of the politics of his thought remains mired.[6] Nietzsche's thought provokes doubt in the progressive potential of the model of enlightened, liberal reason associated with Kant.[7] It questions the degree to which a rationally directed model of social order necessarily results in political emancipation. These things are well enough recognized. But Nietzsche also questions the worth and very possibility of such emancipation and invites us to rethink emancipation in creative terms that challenge the legitimacy of moral certainties. Nietzschean pluralism is not liberal pluralism. It neither seeks nor requires reasoned consensus as the basis of authority, but cultivates dissent and struggle as virtues. It does not endorse a conception of tolerance intended only to serve as a negative condition of political life that enables the private citizen to pursue their own ends. As opposed to liberal tolerance, Nietzsche endorses a conflict-producing pluralism wherein constant experiment threatens the incorporation and colonization of the stronger by the weaker. Nietzchean thought does not lead us to embrace the ideal of a world characterized by the harmonious co-operation of all in a common pursuit of freedom. It seeks to cultivate an understanding of the need for many freedoms, of diverse expressions of empowerment which are likely to be disruptive and disturbing to the

5 See the introduction for some discussion of these.

6 In this regard, my own approach is close to that of Christa Davis Acampora and Don Dombowsky.

7 Kant's formulation of Enlightenment presents probably the most powerful articulation of the case for a politically progressive agenda of enlightened rationality. See "An Answer to the Question: What is Enlightenment?," in *Perpetual Peace and Other Essays on Politics, History, and Morals.*

status quo. All this requires the development of a sense of the value of mercy, of a rethinking of the terms of our moral and political language. We must, for example, desist from criminalizing the criminal, for in this way we affirm our own power *as mercy* – and in this affirmation power reveals itself as the potential for generosity and the strength for forgiveness.[8] Understood thus, power becomes a virtue. It is for this reason that Habermas rightly echoes Horkheimer and Adorno's well-known characterization of Nietzsche as "one of the 'black thinkers' of the bourgeoisie."[9] Nietzsche's thought, in other words, is disturbing. It disrupts received notions of what is politically desirable and because of this cannot be easily recuperated to satisfy the goals of contemporary political discourse. In simple terms, the central tenets of Nietzsche's philosophy not only involve criticism of the liberal political culture of modernity and all that is associated with it, but also present a fundamental challenge to liberal modernity's central presuppositions concerning the nature of individuality, value, and social progress: all things that liberalism associates with the pursuit and fulfilment of human freedom.

We have already seen in chapter 5 that Nietzsche considers freedom to be possible in so far as it is understood as a creative rebellion against dominant mores in pursuit of the fashioning of values. This concept of freedom, Nietzsche tells us in *Twilight of the Idols*, must be contrasted to the illusory one celebrated by the liberal tradition. Genuine freedom emerges from struggle, and struggle is indeed something that is manifest in the battles that have been fought to secure liberal political structures. One should not, however, mistake the one for the other: "Liberal institutions cease to be liberal as soon as they are attained … they level mountain and valley and call that morality; they make men small, cowardly and hedonistic – every time it is the herd animal that triumphs with them. Liberalism: in plain words, herd-imbrutement" (*Twilight*, "Skirmishes of an Untimely Man," 38). In other words an achieved liberal political culture is a culture in which the most regressive, brutal human propensities for conformity to oppressive norms are encouraged. But the struggle to secure a liberal political culture is another matter altogether. In the liberal's battle against the norm, which occurs as a necessary characteristic of such struggle, freedom is truly promoted. One should not, however, mistake what is striven after (the goal, i.e. liberal ideals and institutions) for the *source* of the freedom that is thereby promoted. The connection

8 For this reason, one might add, Nietzsche is never as far away from the Christian tradition as he often would have us believe.

9 See Habermas, *The Philosophical Discourse of Modernity*, 106. See, also, Adorno and Horkheimer, *Dialectic of Enlightenment*, 117.

between liberal values, liberal justice, and freedom is, in other words, contingent; freedom is fostered by liberalism and endures at its hands only so long as the norms the liberal seeks to overcome in his or her battle against conservatism endure. Once liberalism becomes the norm, struggle ceases and the liberal conformity that ensues becomes coercion pure and simple. The power to create values, which Nietzsche holds to be the sign of authentic freedom, is thus initially and accidentally cultivated by liberal forces but is ultimately sacrificed to the administrative structures that a victorious liberal ethos evolves in order to maintain itself. Liberalism triumphant, in short, is oppression. For Nietzsche, liberalism, however "civilized" and bourgeois or modern it may appear to be, threatens reversion to the brute injustice typical of the most primitive communal orders dominated by the morality of custom. Liberalism thus has a tendency to majoritarianism no less than other dominant social forms hitherto.[10] As we have seen in chapter 4, contemporary liberal culture, according to Nietzsche's interpretation, reflects this primitive element: it still seeks to punish and make guilty, and is driven by a tendency to bogus moralistic justification in its demonization of the so-called "criminal."

Nietzsche's ideas lead, however, to criticisms of liberal thought that dig deeper than the above points, for they take us to the heart of the presuppositions at work within its conceptions of freedom and justice. From John Locke or J.S. Mill to such notable recent figures as Friedrich Hayek or John Rawls, liberalism can be characterized by its faith in the individual conceived of as an essentially autonomous, rational entity endowed with the ability to make choices. Such a conception of the individual gives rise to an essentially negative conception of freedom. The freedom that the individual can enjoy is regarded as a given capacity that springs effortlessly from its source and hence stands in need only of defence from the threat of incursion by powers external to it. Understood thus, the individual's essence resides in their status as a morally accountable being whose just desert is measured according to the degree of effort put into the project of acquisitive self-advancement. The goods of the world are, on this view, the legitimate possessions of "the industrious and rational."[11] All freedom requires for the liberal is placing institutional limits on the degree of coercion that can be exercised over the individual either by others or by the institutional power of the sovereign

10 In this, one can detect in Nietzsche a similar anxiety to that expressed by J.S. Mill's phrase the "tyranny of the majority" (see *On Liberty*). Nietzsche, as already noted, is however no fan of Mill.

11 Locke, *Second Treatise of Government*, section 34.

state itself. The second of Locke's *Two Treatises of Government,* the work that stands at the origins of liberal thought, offers a good illustration of this. Locke, echoing aspects of the thought of Thomas Hobbes,[12] holds that the legitimate state comes into being as a result of rational individuals situated in a "state of nature" coming together and making a social pact for reasons of mutual self-interest. The state of nature is a condition devoid of the institutions of civil government but populated by individuals endowed with autonomous rational ability. Rational ability is taken primarily to be a matter of self-interest. In turn, legitimate government for Locke derives its authority from the same condition that characterizes a freely chosen contract as it would be entered into in the state of nature: it depends upon agreement. Government is held to be an extension of principles of what is deemed "natural right." Natural right presupposes basic principles of justice rooted in the concept of exchange, which provides the principle whereby a wrong suffered by the individual situated in the state of nature can be justifiably compensated. The principle of natural justice states that an eye or its equivalent can be taken in compensation for suffering the loss of an eye. Since, as Locke famously argues, the self-interested individual is hardly the best judge concerning the degree of compensation appropriate for the injustices he or she may suffer at the hands of others, a third party is required to ensure fairness in the dealings of disputants. This requirement is met by the institution of civil government. The state fulfils its proper function only so long as it defends principles of equal treatment for all based upon principles of natural right: "Where there is no longer the administration of justice, for the securing of men's rights, nor any remaining power within the community to direct the force, or provide for the necessities of the public, there certainly is no government left."[13] On the Lockean account, natural justice is held to precede civil society such that it constitutes the legitimacy of proper governance. Justice is, in this way, presupposed to be a universal, unmediated and ahistorical condition rooted in an equally timeless principle of exchange. To put it another way, the principle of "an eye for an eye" is not, for Locke, an achievement of culture forged out of social practices and the conflicts of interest that characterize them, but is rather a naturally existing condition that serves to ground the legitimacy of just political practice and the institutions most suited to it.

12 See Hobbes, *Leviathan.*

13 Locke, *Second Treatise of Government,* section 218.

Rawls's search for fundamental principles of justice in *A Theory of Justice* replicates the logic of Locke's position, albeit in modified form. Hayek's well-known articulation of the notion of liberty likewise depends upon similar presuppositions.[14] All take freedom to be a given and justice to be a matter of elaborating and managing the pluralistic worldview that ensues from this given. One can consider, in this context, Hayek's typically liberal dismissal of what he calls "inner" freedom[15] and even more emphatically "metaphorical freedom"[16] (the "freedom to do what I want") as unworthy and dangerous notions in the context of political theory. Political questions are, for him, conceived as having an essentially formal nature – and they have this because they can be elaborated on the basis of a conception of individual freedom that is essentially unproblematic. The subject is taken as being already endowed with the propensities that make liberty something that can be realized through no more than the governmental administration of conditions limiting

14 See Rawls, *A Theory of Justice.* Although Rawls does not endorse the Lockean contention that civil order springs from an actual social compact, for him a truly free and just society would take the same shape that self-interested individuals situated behind a "veil of ignorance" that rendered them unaware of their place in the social order would rationally choose to inhabit. Justice, in other words, can be derived from an autonomous principle that exists independently of the contingencies of history and society and gains its legitimacy from this insulation. This conception of rational agency likewise lies at the heart of the conception of freedom that economic liberals such as Hayek defend (see *The Constitution of Liberty*). Whatever the differences between Rawls, Locke, and Hayek, for the latter, too, what is paramount is an account of freedom insulated from the vicissitudes of social struggle and any ensuing contestations over meaning that might arise from them. Freedom is "that condition of men in which coercion of some by others is reduced as much as possible" (*The Constitution of Liberty,* 11). It has "a distinct meaning and ... describes one thing and one thing only" and this thing is "varying in degree but not in kind" (ibid., 12). We are able, in other words, to think of freedom in a manner that is immune to the incursions and revisions that might otherwise be wrought by historical forces. Freedom, on this view, has an authentic, unified, and unchanging sense. In turn, and despite his expressing reservations about making such distinctions, Hayek deems liberty to be an essentially negative concept rather than a positive one. The word "freedom," in short, is held to delineate a neutral space in which the individual, unmediated by social and historical forces, is set at liberty to roam in search of its own ends and satisfactions. The liberal state, in turn, gains its legitimacy in so far as it functions as the impartial administrator of this space. A view of this kind presupposes a subject endowed with the capacity for choice, one who is by definition "free" to engage in the pursuit of the goods associated with the accruement of personal wealth. In this regard, Hayek's characterization of what makes for a "progressive society" – his theory of liberty, in other words – is primarily economic (*The Constitution of Liberty,* 42ff).

15 Hayek, *The Constitution of Liberty,* 14.

16 Ibid., 16. When people confuse freedom with empowerment liberty, Hayek argues, becomes identified with wealth (ibid., 17).

the degree of coercion that may be exercised over the autonomous individual who has been given the capacity for the free pursuit of personal advancement by a generous nature.[17] A Nietzschean account, in contrast, turns the order of relations between liberty and justice, on the one hand, and culture and history, on the other, upside down. Nature is neither a realm of law nor does it contain principles of natural justice. Exchange itself is a cultural achievement fashioned accidentally in the communal realm of custom. In so far as we are law-like beings we are thus always already creatures who have been rendered in terms of social norms. The creation of norms is a direct outcome of concrete practices that constitute subjectivity. Neither law nor justice nor the subject they concern can be called "natural" or autonomous conditions in any sense: they are (accidentally) created ones. Their creation, Nietzsche is keen to emphasize, is indebted to primitive conditions from which it is hard to escape – it is mired in blood and violence. Such conditions are expressions of power relations. With this insight, the neutral space of the Lockean state of nature, into which liberalism plants its conception of the state and law, withers. The formalization of customs into law-like practices, and such practices into what are subsequently deemed to be just, does not emanate from naturally existing principles that determine what is fair, but is rather a consequence of power struggles between competing interests that have been wrought in the realm of culture. History, in short, is paramount in Nietzsche's elucidation of our understanding of what is just or otherwise.

Freedom, in turn, as Nietzsche conceives it, stands in stark opposition to the negative conception that characterizes the liberal's attitude. Liberty is not a neutral space of possibility for action through which a rationally endowed deliberative subject moves as a kind of autonomous causal force. One does not simply have freedom as a natural endowment of selfhood. One must cultivate and thereby attain it. In turn, such attainment expresses itself as the feeling of empowerment. Freedom, in short, is not a negative condition - not "freedom from," as liberal theory deems it – but "freedom to."[18] Freedom of this kind must be made and constantly re-made in a continual struggle with the norm. The self must, for this reason, be in continual strife, both with the dominant norms of social order and its own dominant habits of thought and judgement. One does not, on this account, gain fulfilment by amassing resources

17 One might consider here the work of Adam Smith, whose thought is a powerful influence on Hayek.

18 Freedom in this sense is concretely experienced: "to will one's liberation [from the norm] is to *feel* one's freedom" (Thiele, *Friedrich Nietzsche and the Politics of the Soul*, 94).

and wealth with a view to the efficient preservation of one's own discrete and narrow interest. To attain selfhood is to be engaged in constant over-expenditure, to be a living sacrifice in pursuit of creation – and this creation concerns, above all, the making of values. The authority of such values cannot, however, be deduced nor is success the proof of their veracity, for values are rooted in the contingencies of life.

In its exposure of the essential contingency underlying our dominant beliefs about legitimacy in terms that trace that contingency to the heart of our valuing practices, Nietzsche's thought is thus itself a kind of unsettling question mark. It is here that we must take what inspiration we can from him. Nietzsche's inestimable importance as a thinker of values resides in the exposure of this contingency. This exposure is inexorably political and social in import. His thought points to the constitutive role of practices in the world of human meaning; to the essential element of chance that human life must confront; and to the absence of ultimate authority, which obliges us to seek the positively negative virtues of experimentalism and mercy. Such virtues are positive in that they seek a standpoint beyond rancour and revenge, a standpoint that affirms the justice of plurality. They are negative in that in order to experiment, the experimenter must never be happy with what they believe and have, and in so far as the person of mercy must negate all desire for compensation in order to be merciful. These virtues often strain toward the kind of self-critical reflexivity that Horkheimer and Adorno justly praised when criticizing the instrumentalization inherent within the unreflective project of Enlightenment. Nietzsche's return to the oracular bears witness to the clouded condition that besets human reason. It illustrates the impossibility of the dream of a "pure" Enlightenment capable of emancipating itself entirely from myth. Nietzsche's recognition of the need to affirm something beyond the confines of instrumental "reason," something that reaches beyond the totalizing and yet limited ambitions of fetishized "method," points to the irreducible element in thought – to the fact that our virtues cannot be causally elucidated without remainder. In seeking to think the problem of creation as the problem of values, Nietzsche gestures to the sinister and unrecoverable condition underlying our esteeming nature – and with that, to the fact that mercy is never something that emerges out of pure light.

Bibliography

TEXTS BY FRIEDRICH NIETZSCHE
(Chronologically by Original Date of Publication)

The Birth of Tragedy. In *Basic Writings of Nietzsche,* translated by Walter Kaufmann, 15–144. New York: Modern Library, 1968.

Untimely Meditations. Translated by R.J. Hollingdale. Cambridge: Cambridge University Press, 1983.

Human, All Too Human, vols 1 and 2. Translated by R.J. Hollingdale. Cambridge: Cambridge University Press, 1986.

Daybreak: Thoughts on the Prejudices of Morality. Translated by R.J. Hollingdale. Cambridge: Cambridge University Press, 1982.

The Gay Science. Translated by Walter Kaufmann. New York: Vintage Books, 1974.

Thus Spoke Zarathustra. In *The Viking Portable Nietzsche,* selected and translated by Walter Kaufmann, 121–439. New York: Penguin, 1976.

Thus Spoke Zarathustra. Translated by R.J. Hollingdale. Harmondsworth: Penguin, 1973.

Beyond Good and Evil. In *Basic Writings of Nietzsche,* translated by Walter Kaufmann, 191–435. New York: Modern Library, 1968.

On the Genealogy of Morality. Edited by Keith Ansell Pearson. Translated by Carol Diethe. Cambridge: Cambridge University Press, 1994.

Twilight of the Idols. In *The Viking Portable Nietzsche,* translated by Walter Kaufmann, 463–563. New York: Penguin, 1976.

The Antichrist. In *The Viking Portable Nietzsche,* translated by Walter Kaufmann, 565–656. New York: Penguin, 1976.

Ecce Homo. In *Basic Writings of Nietzsche,* translated by Walter Kaufmann, 671–791. New York: Modern Library, 1968.

The Will to Power. Translated by Walter Kaufmann and R.J. Hollingdale. New York: Vintage Books, 1968.

Sämtliche Werke: Kritische Studienausgabe. Edited by Giorgio Colli and Mazzino Montinari. 15 vols. Berlin: Walter de Gruyter, 1980.

Briefwechsel: Kritische Gesamtausgabe. Edited by Giorgio Colli, Mazzino Motinari, Norbert Miller, and Annemarie Pieper. 20+ vols. Berlin: Walter de Gruyter, 1975.

SECONDARY SOURCES

Acampora, Christa Davis. "*Demos Agonistes Redux.* Reflections on the *Streit* of Political Antagonism." *Nietzsche-Studien* 32 (2003): 374–90.

Adams, Maurice. "The Ethics of Tolstoy and Nietzsche." *International Journal of Ethics* 2 (October 1900): 85–105.

Adorno, Theodor W. and Max Horkheimer. *Dialectic of Enlightenment.* Translated by John Cumming. London: Allen Lane, 1973.

Ansell-Pearson, Keith. *Nietzsche contra Rousseau: A Study of Nietzsche's Moral and Political Thought.* Cambridge: Cambridge University Press, 1991.

– *An Introduction to Nietzsche as Political Thinker.* Cambridge: Cambridge University Press, 1994.

– *Viroid Life, Perspectives on Nietzsche and the Transhuman Condition.* London: Routledge, 1997.

Anon. "Nietzsche's Obituary." *The Academy and Literature* 59 (1 September 1900): 175–6.

Anon. "The Philosophy of Power." *The Athenaeum* 4616 (April 1917): 168–72.

Anon. "Philosophy with a Hammer." *The Academy and Literature* 57 (8 July 1899): 31–2.

Anon. "Teutonismus." *The Athenaeum* 4537 (10 October 1914): 347–8.

Apel, Karl-Otto. *From a Transcendental-Semiotic Point of View.* Edited by Marianna Papastephanou. Manchester: Manchester University Press, 1998.

Appel, Frederick. *Nietzsche contra Democracy.* Ithaca: Cornell University Press, 1999.

Arnold, Mathew. *Culture and Anarchy: An Essay in Political and Social Criticism.* New Haven and London: Yale University Press, 1994.

Benhabib, Seyla. *Situating the Self: Gender, Community and Postmodernism in Contemporary Ethics.* Cambridge: Polity, 1992.

Brobjer, Thomas. "The Absence of Political Ideals in Nietzsche's Writings." *Nietzsche-Studien* 27 (1998): 387–93.

Bull, Malcolm. *Anti-Nietzsche.* London: Verso, 2011.

Cameron, Frank, and Dombowsky, Don, eds. *The Political Writings of Friedrich Nietzsche.* Basingstoke: Palgrave Macmillan, 2008.

Clark, Maudmarie. *Nietzsche on Truth and Philosophy.* Cambridge: Cambridge University Press, 1990.

Clausen, Detlev. *Theodor Adorno: One Last Genius.* Translated by Rodney Livingstone. Cambridge: Harvard University Press, 2008.

Connolly, William. *Political Theory and Modernity.* Oxford: Blackwell, 1988.

Conrad, Joseph. *Notes on Life and Letters.* London: J.M. Dent and Sons, 1949.

Conway, Daniel W. *Nietzsche and the Political.* London: Routledge, 1997.

Deleuze, Gilles. *Nietzsche and Philosophy.* Translated by Hugh Tomlinson. London: Athlone Press, 1986.

Dombowsky, Don. "A Response to Thomas H. Brobjer's 'The Absence of Political Ideals in Nietzsche's Writings.'" *Nietzsche-Studien* 30 (2001): 387–93.

Dombowsky, Don. "A Response to Alan D. Schrift's 'Nietzsche *for* Democracy.'" *Nietzsche-Studien* 31 (2002): 278–90.

Dowling, Linda. *Language and Decadence in the Victorian Fin de Siècle.* Princeton: Princeton University Press, 1986.

Eagleton, Terry. *Trouble with Strangers: A Study of Ethics.* Oxford: Wiley-Blackwell, 2009.

Fink, Eugen. "Nietzsche's New Experience of the World." In *Nietzsche's New Seas: Explorations in Philosophy, Aesthetics, and Politics,* edited by Michael Allen Gillespie and Tracy B. Strong, translated Michael Allen Gillespie, 203–19. Chicago: University of Chicago Press, 1988.

Goodrich, Peter, and Francis J.Mootz III, eds. *Nietzsche and Law.* Aldershot: Ashgate, 2008.

Goodrich, Peter, and Mariana Valverde, eds. *Nietzsche and Legal Theory.* London: Routledge, 2005.

Habermas, Jürgen. *Communication and the Evolution of Society.* Translated by T. McCarthy. Boston: Beacon Press, 1979.

Habermas, Jürgen. *The Philosophical Discourse of Modernity.* Translated by Frederick Lawrence. Cambridge: MIT Press, 1988.

Harries, Karsten. "The Philosopher at Sea." In *Nietzsche's New Seas: Explorations in Philosophy, Aesthetics, and Politics,* edited by Michael Allen Gillespie and Tracy B. Strong, translated Michael Allen Gillespie, 21–44. Chicago: University of Chicago Press, 1988.

Hatab, Lawrence J. *A Nietzschean Defense of Democracy: An Experiment in Postmodern Politics.* Chicago: Open Court, 1995.

Hayek, Friedrich. *The Constitution of Liberty.* London: Routledge & Kegan Paul, 1962.

Heidegger, Martin. *Nietzsche,* volume 3. Translated by David Farrell Krell, Joan Stambaugh, and Frank A. Capuzzi. San Francisco: Harper Collins, 1982.

Hobbes, Thomas. *Leviathan.* Edited by Richard Tuck. Cambridge: Cambridge University Press, 1996.

Jackson, Holbrook. "Review of Elizabeth Förster-Nietzsche's *The Young Nietzsche.*" *The Bookman* 42, no. 251 (August 1912): 215–16.

Kant, Immanuel. *Perpetual Peace and Other Essays on Politics, History, and Morals.* Translated by Ted Humphrey. Indianapolis: Hackett, 1983.

Kaufmann, Walter. *Nietzsche: Philosopher, Psychologist, Antichrist.* Princeton: Princeton University Press, 1974.

– *From Shakespeare to Existentialism.* Princeton: Princeton University Press, 1980.

Knoll, Manuel. "Nietzsches Begriff der Sozialen Gerechtigkeit." *Nietzsche-Studien* 38 (2009): 156–81.

Lampert, Lawrence. *Nietzsche's Teaching: An Interpretation of Thus Spoke Zarathustra.* New Haven: Yale University Press, 1986.

– *Nietzsche and Modern Times: A Study of Bacon, Descartes, and Nietzsche.* New Haven: Yale University Press, 1993.

Legros, Robert. "The Nietzschean Metaphysics of Life." In *Why We are Not Nietzscheans,* edited by Luc Ferry and Alain Renaut, translated by Robert de Loaiza. Chicago: University of Chicago Press, 1997.

Leiter, Brian. *Nietzsche on Morality.* London: Routledge, 2002.

Magnus, Bernd and Kathleen Higgins, eds. *The Cambridge Companion to Nietzsche.* Cambridge: Cambridge University Press 1996.

Locke, John. *Two Treatises of Government.* Edited by Peter Laslett. Cambridge: Cambridge University Press, 1988.

Loeb, Paul S. *The Death of Nietzsche's Zarathustra.* Cambridge: Cambridge University Press, 2010.

Lukács, Georg. *The Destruction of Reason.* Translated by Peter Palmer. London: Merlin, 1980.

Mellamphy, Nandita Biswas. *The Three Stigmata of Friedrich Nietzsche: Political Physiology in the Age of Nihilism.* Basingstoke: Palgrave Macmillan, 2011.

Milbourne, H. "The Hammer of Thor." *International Journal of Ethics* 28 (October 1917): 1–17.

Mootz III, Francis J. "After Natural Law: A Hermeneutical Response to *Law's Quandary.*" *Rutgers Journal of Law and Religion* 9, no. 2 (Spring 2008) at http://lawandreligion.com/volume-9. Last accessed 13 May, 2013.

Moltmann, Jürgen. *God for a Secular Society: The Public Relevance of Theology.* Translated by Margaret Kohl. London: SCM Press, 1999.

Müller-Lauter, Wolfgang. *Friedrich Nietzsche: His Philosophy of Contradictions and the Contradictions of His Philosophy.* Translated by David J. Parent. Urbana: University of Illinois Press, 1999.

Petersen, Jens. *Nietzsches Genialität der Gerechtigkeit.* Berlin: Walter de Gruyter, 2008.

Rawls, John. *A Theory of Justice.* Oxford: Clarendon, 1972.

Richardson, John. *Nietzsche's New Darwinism.* Oxford: Oxford University Press, 2004.

Rorty, Richard. *Truth and Progress: Philosophical Papers, Volume 3.* Cambridge: Cambridge University Press, 1998.

Rose, Gillian. *The Broken Middle.* Oxford: Blackwell, 1992.

Rosen, Stanley. *The Question of Being: A Reversal of Heidegger.* New Haven: Yale University Press, 1993.

Saunders, T. Bailey. "Nietzsche's Obituary." *The Athenaeum* 3801 (1 September 1900): 281–2.

Schacht, Richard. *Nietzsche.* London: Routledge and Kegan Paul, 1983.
Schrift, Alan D. "Nietzsche *for* Democracy?" *Nietzsche-Studien* 29 (2000): 220–33.
Sedgwick, Peter R. *Descartes to Derrida: An Introduction to European Philosophy.* Oxford: Blackwell, 2001.
– *Nietzsche's Economy: Modernity, Normativity and Futurity.* Basingstoke: Macmillan, 2007.
– "Nietzsche, Normativity and Will to Power." *Nietzsche-Studien* (2007): 201–29.
Siemens, Herman. "Nietzsche's Political Philosophy: A Review of Recent Literature." *Nietzsche-Studien* 30 (2000): 509–26.
Sophocles. *The Theban Plays.* Translated by E.F. Watling. Harmondsworth: Penguin, 1982.
Steiner, Rudolph. *Friedrich Nietzsche: Fighter for Freedom.* Translated by M.I. deRis. New Jersey: Rudolph Steiner Publications, 1960.
Strong, Tracy B. *Nietzsche and the Politics of Transfiguration.* Berkeley: University of California Press, 1988.
Taylor, Charles. *Philosophical Arguments.* Cambridge: Harvard University Press, 1995.
Thiele, Leslie Paul. *Friedrich Nietzsche and the Politics of the Soul: A Study of Heroic Individualism.* Princeton: Princeton University Press, 1990.
Thomas, Edward. "Review of Various Nietzsche Literature." *The Bookman* 36, no. 213 (June 1909): 140.
Thucydides. *History of the Peloponnesian War.* Translated by Rex Warner. London: Penguin, 1972.
Waite, Geoff. *Nietzsche's Corps/e: Aesthetics, Politics, Prophecy, or, The Spectacular Technoculture of Everyday Life.* Durham and London: Duke University Press, 1996.
Warren, Mark. *Nietzsche and Political Thought.* Cambridge: MIT Press, 1991.
Zeitlin, Irving M. *Nietzsche: A Re-Examination.* Cambridge: Polity, 1994.

Index